# Anomia

Naming is a fundamental aspect of language. Word-finding deficit, anomia, is the most common symptom of language dysfunction occurring after brain damage. Besides its practical importance, anomia gives a fascinating view on the inner workings of language in the brain. There has been significant progress in the study of anomia in recent years, including advances in neuroimaging research and in psycholinguistic modelling. Written by two internationally known researchers in the field, this book provides a broad, integrated overview of current research on anomia. Beginning with an outline of psycholinguistic research on normal word retrieval as well as the influential cognitive models of naming, the book goes on to review the major forms of anomia. Neuroanatomical aspects, clinical assessment, and therapeutic approaches are reviewed and evaluated.

*Anomia: Theoretical and Clinical Aspects* gives a thorough and up-to-date examination of the research and treatment of naming disorders in neurological patients. It covers both theory and practice and provides invaluable reading for researchers and practitioners in speech and language disorders, neuropsychology and neurology, as well for advanced undergraduate students and graduate students in the field.

**Matti Laine** is a Professor of Psychology at the Swedish-speaking university in Finland, Åbo Akademi. With a background in clinical neuropsychology, he has conducted research on both normal and deficient language processing and their neural correlates over the last two decades.

**Nadine Martin** is an Associate Professor in the Communication Sciences Department of Temple University, Philadelphia. She has a background in speech and language pathology and cognitive psychology, and her research in theoretical and clinical aspects of word retrieval and verbal short-term memory has been supported by the National Institutes of Health for the last two decades.

Brain Damage, Behaviour and Cognition:
Developments in Clinical Neuropsychology
Titles in Series

# Anomia
## Theoretical and Clinical Aspects

**Matti Laine and Nadine Martin**

**Psychology Press**
Taylor & Francis Group

HOVE AND NEW YORK

First published 2006 by Psychology Press
27 Church Road, Hove, East Sussex, BN3 2FA

Simultaneously published in the USA and Canada
by Psychology Press
270 Madison Avenue, New York, NY 10016

*Psychology Press is an imprint of the Taylor & Francis Group, an
informa business*

Copyright © 2006 Psychology Press

Typeset in Times by Garfield Morgan, Mumbles, Swansea
Printed and bound in Great Britain by TJ International Ltd, Padstow,
Cornwall
Cover design by Jim Wilkie

This publication has been produced with paper manufactured to strict
environmental standards and with pulp derived from sustainable
forests.

*British Library Cataloguing in Publication Data*
A catalogue record for this book is available from the British Library

*Library of Congress Cataloging-in-Publication Data*
Laine, Matti.
  Anomia : theoretical and clinical aspects / Matti Laine and
Nadine Martin.
    p. cm.
  Includes bibliographical references and index.
  ISBN-13: 978-0-86377-722-6
  ISBN-10: 0-86377-722-8
  1. Anomia. I. Martin, Nadine, 1952– . II. Title.
  [DNLM: 1. Anomia    WL 340.2 L186a 2006]
  RC425.6.L35 2006
  616.85'52–dc22

                                                2006001244

  ISBN 13: 978-0-86377-722-6
  ISBN 10: 0-86377-722-8

# Contents

# Series preface

From being an area primarily on the periphery of mainstream behavioural and cognitive science, neuropsychology has developed in recent years into an area of central concern for a range of disciplines. We are witnessing not only a revolution in the way in which brain–behaviour–cognition relationships are viewed, but also a widening of interest concerning developments in neuropsychology on the part of a range of workers in a variety of fields. Major advances in brain-imaging techniques and the cognitive modelling of the impairments following brain injury promise a wider understanding of the nature of the representation of cognition and behaviour in the damaged and undamaged brain.

Neuropsychology is now centrally important for those working with brain-damaged people, but the very rate of expansion in the area makes it difficult to keep up with findings from the current research. The aim of the *Brain Damage, Behaviour and Cognition* series is to publish a wide range of books that present comprehensive and up-to-date overviews of current developments in specific areas of interest.

These books will be of particular interest to those working with the brain-damaged. It is the editors' intention that undergraduates, postgraduates, clinicians, and researchers in psychology, speech pathology, and medicine will find this series a useful source of information on important current developments. The authors and editors of the books in this series are experts in their respective fields, working at the forefront of contemporary research. They have produced texts that are accessible and scholarly. We thank them for their contribution and their hard work in fulfilling the aims of the series.

CC and GH
Sydney, Australia and Birmingham, UK
Series Editors

# Acknowledgements

We are indebted to Hugh Buckingham, Antoni Rodríguez-Fornells, Karen Sage and Janet Webster for their valuable comments on the book draft; they helped to make the book better. ML is grateful to Antoni Rodríguez-Fornells for the invitation to visit to the Psychology Department at the University of Barcelona: that visit provided the much-needed opportunity to concentrate on finishing this project. A number of colleagues, either knowingly or unknowingly, have contributed to the book over the decade it took us to complete this work mainly as an intercontinental email enterprise.

We wish to dedicate the book to the memory of our teachers in aphasiology, Harold Goodglass (ML) and Eleanor Saffran (NM).

# Introduction

"We met in the Mediterranean . . . what was that island again . . . Corfu, no
. . . Gree-Crete!"

Occasional word-finding difficulties are common to us all. Gropings for
words and the accompanying frustration give us a glimpse of the more
severe and more persistent anomic experience, word retrieval deficits caused
by brain damage. They also show that word retrieval, like any cognitive
skill, is by its nature not error free but sensitive to various perturbations.
Given the size of our mental lexicons and the speed with which we retrieve
words, it is actually surprising that we do not err more often! Nevertheless,
the spectrum of word retrieval difficulties, ranging from normals' slips
and tip-of-the-tongue experiences to profound word-finding problems in
aphasia, may present a continuum rather than a dichotomy. In other words,
it is possible that these seemingly different phenomena could be understood
by unitary theoretical terms. This is one of the ideas that will be entertained
throughout the book.

"Word-finding" is a rather general term and the same is true for the label
of its pathology, anomia (or dysnomia). We retrieve words from our mental
lexicon in very different contexts. Most often this happens in conversation
where lexicon, syntax, and pragmatics interact in complicated ways. However, part and parcel of this is the act of naming, i.e., retrieval of specific
lexical items. It is this basic language act—experimentally studied, for
example, by naming of single pictured objects—that has received most
attention in the study of lexical retrieval and its disorders. Accordingly, a
considerable part of the present book is devoted to reviewing these studies
and various psycholinguistic models of word production developed on the
basis of them.

Anomia is clinically the most common symptom of language dysfunction. It is present in practically every aphasic patient, and it is an important
feature of several other forms of neurological disease like dementing illnesses. Thus a detailed analysis of anomia holds the promise of telling us
something about the language production system that is both fundamental

and clinically relevant. In recent decades, there has been significant progress in the study of anomia and its neural correlates in the form of improved physiological and functional diagnostic measures. The former have been based on improved neuroimaging techniques and the latter on greater refinement of psycholinguistic modelling. These exciting advances will be covered in this book as well.

An ultimate test of the practical use of basic research on anomia is its import to therapy. In recent years there has been an increasing research interest in anomia therapy. A number of studies have explored various approaches to anomia treatment, enabling us to take at least the first steps towards theoretically motivated anomia therapy. At the same time, one should keep in mind that this is a rapidly developing field, and state-of-the-art reviews may thus become outdated quite soon.

The book is organised as follows. We will first go through psycholinguistic research on word retrieval in normals and review some influential cognitive models on naming (Chapter 1). This is followed by a review of the major forms of anomia and their interpretation in the light of the cognitive models discussed earlier (Chapter 2). Based on lesion data and functional neuroimaging with normals and anomic patients, Chapter 3 provides an overview of our current understanding on the neural correlates of naming and its disorders. Clinical assessment of naming and the role of anomia in some common neurological conditions are dealt with in Chapter 4. This is followed by a review and evaluation of therapeutic approaches to anomia (Chapter 5). We will wrap up with some concluding remarks and suggestions for future research in Chapter 6.

# 1　Cognitive models of lexical retrieval

A cognitive model of language processing depicts a theory of the content and organisation of mental processes that mediate comprehension and production of speech and language. These models are both theoretically and clinically relevant. They provide a framework that researchers can use to formulate predictions that will test specific hypotheses about language behaviour. Data that have been used to test such predictions include speech errors produced by normal (e.g., Garrett, 1975) and aphasic speakers (Dell, Schwartz, Martin, Saffran, & Gagnon, 1997), naming reaction time data (e.g., Schriefers, Meyer, & Levelt, 1990), analyses of hesitations and pauses in speech production (Butterworth, 1975, 1979) and analyses of tip-of-the-tongue phenomena in normal speakers (Brown & McNeill, 1966; Jones & Langford, 1987). Converging evidence from these sources has spurred the ongoing development of cognitive models of language and other cognitive systems. Clinically, cognitive models of language have been most successfully applied to diagnosis of language disorders. Assessment batteries developed within the framework of such models (e.g., *Psycholinguistic Assessments of Language Processing in Aphasia—PALPA*, Kay, Lesser, & Coltheart, 1992) include measures of the many processes and representations hypothesised in cognitive models of language. Such test batteries yield detailed profiles of spared and impaired processes which enable the clinician to identify more precisely the nature of the language impairment and what aspects of language to treat.

Here, we focus on models of one component of language processing, word retrieval. We will review three families of contemporary cognitive models, functional, local connectionist, and distributed connectionist, and discuss the kinds of data that have led to their development. Functional models use an information-processing framework to model cognition. An important feature of such models is that they define representations and processes involved in word retrieval. The other two model groups embody recent computational methodologies and aim to capture dynamic aspects of word processing (e.g., its time course or the effects of lexical competition on word retrieval). Our discussion of each model will include a description of its most pertinent features, its empirical support, and its major contribution (or potential to contribute) to our understanding of word retrieval processes in general and more specifically diagnosis and treatment of impaired word retrieval processes.

## EARLY NEUROPSYCHOLOGICAL MODELS OF WORD PROCESSING

Current cognitive models of word retrieval have their origins in the neuroanatomical models of language breakdown in aphasia advanced by neurologists of the 19th century. Many forms of aphasia had been described by the early 1800s (see Goodglass, 1993, for a review), but in the 19th century, scientists began to consider the implications of aphasic syndromes for our understanding of language processing. In 1825, Jean-Baptiste Bouillaud distinguished between two types of impairment of language production, one that affected the "memory" for words and one that affected planning and execution of speech movements. Jacques Lordat made a similar distinction in 1843. Their research is especially noteworthy for its contribution to our knowledge of neurological localisation of language functions. Broca (1865) identified the third frontal convolution as the site of expressive ("articulate") language, and Wernicke (1874) linked language comprehension to the posterior two-thirds of the left superior temporal lobe. Although these investigations were intended primarily to localise neuroanatomical sites of language, they also yielded rudimentary cognitive models of language processing that would serve as a foundation for subsequent more detailed models of mental operations underlying production and comprehension of language. Wernicke's (1874) and Lichtheim's (1885) work resulted in one of the first elaborated cognitive models of the language system, the "Wernicke–Lichtheim" model as it is known today (Figure 1.1). The model identifies components of a language processor including a centre for auditory images (A), motor images (M), concept elaboration (C, or B for "Begriffszentrum" in the original model), auditory perceptual components (a) and motor encoding components (m). Different profiles of aphasia, for the first time, are described in terms of a cognitive theory and disruption (slashes with numbers) to a model of that theory. For example, a lesion at site 3 would disrupt flow of information between auditory and motor images, but not information flow to and from the concept elaboration centre. This lesion would result in good comprehension and fluent production but poor repetition, a profile that closely resembles conduction aphasia (although production is also often affected in that syndrome). Although the Wernicke–Lichtheim model provides a very cursory description of language operations compared to the detail of current models, many of its assumptions remain viable and present in those models. This model and the research carried out during this period served as a foundation for classical taxonomies of aphasia that grouped lesion locations with typical characteristics of aphasic syndromes (see Goodglass, 1993).

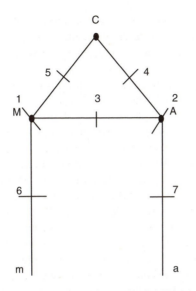

*Figure 1.1* A depiction of the Wernicke–Lichtheim model of language processing (Lichtheim's "house") and the different aphasia profiles accounted by the model. (Redrawn from Lichtheim (1885).)

## COGNITIVE MODELS OF WORD PROCESSING: THE NEXT GENERATION

The models of the 19th century were concerned with the identification of language components and their neuroanatomical correlates. This brain–behaviour approach was dominant through the 1960s and 1970s (e.g., Benson, 1979; Geschwind, 1965) but was eclipsed for a time in the 1970s and 1980s when researchers focused somewhat exclusively on the cognitive organisation of language (e.g., Dell, 1986; Ellis, 1987; Garrett, 1976; Howard & Franklin, 1988; Morton & Patterson, 1980). The language system was modelled in the form of an information processor, a blueprint of component representations, storage buffers, and pathways of the language system. The purpose of the models developed during this period was to illustrate the mental representations and processes involved in encoding and decoding language. These descriptive models are termed functional models of language but are also more casually referred to as "box and arrow" models. The boxes are the "stores" of a particular representation (e.g., semantic, phonological, morphological), and the arrows represent the processes between representations: output of one representational store and access routes to the next. These functional models have proved to be useful clinically as diagnostic frameworks, as will be discussed in Chapter 5. A detailed description of the components of the language processor enables researchers and clinicians to pinpoint the cognitive deficit underlying a language disorder.

Importantly, the functional approach to modelling provided a vocabulary to describe language and other cognitive deficits that was more closely tied to behavioural phenomena than classical clinico-anatomical characterisations of aphasic syndromes. This advance was an important one and remains so today, even as interest in behavioural–neuroanatomical correlates has been revived by advances in neuroimaging (Chapter 3). Descriptions of word-processing deficits in terms of mental behaviours are more directly translatable to methods of diagnosing and treatment of language impairments in the rehabilitation clinic, where the emphasis is on restoration of mental abilities and their corresponding behaviours. Moreover, the link between functional models and diagnosis of language deficits can be regarded as a two-way street. While a model can be used to diagnose and guide treatment of the language deficit, a systematic case study of language dissociations and associations in acquired language deficit (e.g., anomia) can be used to test and modify the structure of the cognitive models of language. This use of aphasic data to develop cognitive models of word processing will be discussed later in this chapter.

The 1980s marked the beginning of what might be viewed as a paradigm shift in cognitive modelling, but more accurately reflected a logical next step towards understanding and representing the mental processes underlying cognition. Advances in the technology of computer simulation of behavioural phenomena were soon applied to cognitive theories of language, leading to the development of "connectionist" models of language processes. It has been said that connectionist models hypothesise the processes within and between the "boxes" in functional models. This is true to some extent, but connectionist models potentially offer much more. These models are able to explore the temporal features and other properties of language processing in normal and impaired word retrieval (e.g., Dell, 1986; Dell & O'Seaghdha, 1992; Harley, 1984; Martin, Dell, Saffran, & Schwartz, 1994; Plaut, 1996; Schwartz, Saffran, Bloch, & Dell, 1994; Stemberger, 1985). Moreover, they have the potential to explore changes in language behaviour in response to a number of variables that are inherent in therapy techniques used in the clinic. For example, the effects of variations in stimuli characteristics (e.g., high vs. low imageability) on ability to repeat or read words has been examined using connectionist models (Martin, Saffran, & Dell, 1996; Plaut & Shallice, 1991). The use of connectionist models to address clinical issues is a relatively recent development and is in its early stages. And yet, in principle, these models are poised to address questions about dynamics of language processing that will advance our understanding of learning in aphasia and treatment of aphasic disorders.

We will return to a more detailed discussion of the functional and connectionist models of word processing shortly. Before doing so, however, it is important to acquaint the reader with the kinds of data that motivated and constrained development of these models. Many of the data come from investigations of how speech production can go wrong. Studies of naturally occurring speech errors in normal speakers, hesitations and pauses, tip-of-the-tongue phenomena, and reaction times under dual-task conditions all provide information about the stages and representations of the language system. These sources of information will be discussed in the next section.

## METHODS AND DATA USED TO HYPOTHESISE AND TEST MODELS OF WORD RETRIEVAL

### Evidence from speech error research

Speech errors make up a very small proportion of the total verbal output in normal speech, and yet they occur often enough that they are handled casually, competently, and often with good humour by speakers and listeners alike. That is, they are often (though not always) corrected by the speaker, recognised and untangled by the listener, and sometimes remarked upon by both speaker and listener, especially if the outcome of the error produces some particularly humorous combination of sounds or words. The study of naturally occurring speech errors has led to important insights into the mental operations underlying word production (e.g., Dell & Reich, 1981; Fromkin, 1971; Garrett, 1976; Harley, 1984; Shattuck-Hufnagel, 1979; Stemberger, 1985). Additionally, studies of speech errors generated experimentally as well as those that occur in aphasia have confirmed and augmented the information gained from studying naturally occurring errors.

Analyses of error patterns, their relationship to the intended word or sound, and the context in which they occur, indicate that occurrence of errors is constrained by the properties of the language production system. That is, their occurrences are probabilistically restricted to certain kinds of contexts, depending on the linguistic unit involved (e.g., phoneme, whole word), its semantics, and its grammatical role. This probabilistic behaviour is what makes them useful informants of the representations in the language system. Thus, although errors represent breakdowns of the normal language system, the normal operations of that system can be inferred from them. Fromkin (1971) proposed that the existence of these linguistic units in speech errors indicates their psychological reality. That is, at some point in the course of speech/language processing, these linguistic units are represented cognitively (and neurobiologically).

The logic behind speech error research as a window to the componential representations and processes that enable smooth production of speech has been questioned precisely because speech errors represent a breakdown in the language system, and therefore may not be ideal indicators of the organisation of the system (Levelt, Roelofs, & Meyer, 1999). The claim of this particular group of researchers is that reaction time studies using probes of normal word production are the ultimate test of this process because they do not depend on "infrequent derailments of the process"

(Levelt et al., 1999, p. 2). However, these probe interference studies artificially tamper with the word production system by using spoken probe words presented at different points in time during picture naming in order to provoke interference (alterations in reaction times) with different stages of production (e.g., semantic, phonological). Thus, it cannot be said that these are more ideal conditions for examining the components of the word retrieval process. Rather, the ideal approach to the study of a cognitive system such as language, which presents as a whole process but in fact has parts (sounds, words, meanings) that are isolable, is one that looks for converging evidence from multiple approaches of investigation.

Speech errors include additions, deletions, substitutions, or movement (anticipation, perseveration, exchange) of linguistic units including words, bound morphemes, syllables, phonemes, and possibly even phonetic features. Speech errors made by aphasic individuals are, for the most part, *qualitatively* similar to those observed in unimpaired speech, but differ from normal speech errors in two ways. First, as might be expected, the *quantity* of errors is often greater than in normal speech, although this factor varies with severity. Second, and importantly, the error types observed in anomic speech may *vary proportionately* depending on the stage of word retrieval that has been affected by the brain damage. That is, although both normals and people with aphasia make both semantically related and phonologically related word substitutions in naming, the relative proportions of each type might not be the same in normal and aphasic speakers. Anomic impairments might result in predominantly semantic errors (e.g., Caramazza & Hillis, 1990) or sound-related word substitutions (e.g., Blanken, 1990). The similarities and differences in normal and aphasic error patterns suggest the importance of examining naming data from both groups in order to fully understand the word retrieval system. In what follows, we summarise the most important properties of speech errors made by normal speakers that constrain models of word production.

### Phoneme-level errors

Phoneme errors respect phonotactic rules of the language in general. That is, the erroneous phoneme will be a legitimate phoneme of the language and will occur in a context that results in sound co-occurrences that are part of the language. Phoneme-level errors include substitutions, additions, deletions, and movement errors. Phoneme substitutions often share distinctive features with the target phonemes, suggesting that they are errors of selection. The substitutions can result in a word form (e.g., bat → mat) or a nonword (e.g., bat → lat). Additions (e.g., bake → brake) and deletions (brake → bake) may have a more complex origin. Some models postulate word frames that specify consonant-vowel (CV) sequences in words (e.g., cat (/kæt/) – CVC; pillow (/pɪlo/) – CVCV; track (/træk/ – CCVC) and suggest that additions and deletions represent a mismatch between the phonemes retrieved and the CVC frame retrieved (e.g., Shattuck-Hufnagel, 1979). Another possibility is that they are blends of two words.

Phoneme "movement" errors involve the displacement of a sound from its intended position to another position within the target word or another word in the utterance. These errors can be anticipatory (e.g., candle → dandle), perseverative (candle → cancle), or full exchanges (e.g., dancle). As in the case of substitution errors, phoneme movement errors sometimes form new words (e.g., chicken → kitchen) or not (chicken → chichen).

Movement errors are of interest for several reasons. Their occurrence indicates that we are planning utterances ahead. Second, the patterns in which they occur indicate the linguistic units that are accessible before or after they are intended to be produced and the temporal-structural boundaries of that accessibility.

### Morpheme and word errors

Errors in retrieval of morphemes and words are also of several forms, and their suspected origins parallel those of sound-level errors. As in the case of phoneme substitutions, when one word is erroneously substituted for another, the two words often share semantic features (e.g., elbow → knee), phonological features (e.g., ankle → apple), or both (e.g., penguin → pelican). This pattern of error suggests that there are at least two stages of word retrieval at which selection of a word's representation can break down: retrieval of the word's meaning and retrieval of the sounds of the word (Dell, 1986; Garrett, 1975, 1976; Harley, 1984). Those errors that are both semantically and phonologically related to the intended target word (known as mixed errors) could be the result of chance, but suggest the possibility of interaction between the two stages of lexical retrieval. These possibilities will be discussed below.

### Word movement errors

These errors can be anticipations, perseverations, or complete exchanges. Word exchanges typically cross phrase boundaries, and the exchanging words frequently share the same syntactic category, but are less likely to share phonological characteristics. Movement errors (both sound and word) were critical data in support of two-stage models of word retrieval. Their contribution in this regard will be discussed more fully when we describe Garrett's (1975, 1976) model of word retrieval.

### Environmental intrusions

An interesting and particularly informative type of word substitution is the environmental intrusion, also termed plan external error. The source of this error is within the speaker's span of attention, but not within the local target utterance. These errors have been eloquently described and analysed by Harley (1984, 1990). Most examples of "environmental intrusions" are unintended references to objects in the physical environment of the speaker, but they can also be intrusions from one's thoughts. Below is an example of this error type, taken from Harley, 1990, p. 48).

Intended: You haven't got a screwdriver, have you?
Error: You haven't got a computer have you?
Circumstances: The speaker addressed the question to someone sitting at a computer.

Environmental intrusions have been taken as evidence that word retrieval is being processed in parallel with other cognitive processes (Harley, 1990). Presumably these errors originate at an early stage of word retrieval when the message itself is conceived. Although there is no evidence that they tend to be semantically related to the target word, Harley (1990) has shown that, like semantic errors, "environmentals" tend to be phonologically similar to the target word. This finding constitutes support for models that postulate interactive or overlapping retrieval of semantic and phonological representations of words.

These and other observed constraints on error occurrence are assumed to arise from a system that represents these constraints, i.e., grammatical category distinctions, meaning, phonological form, segmental positions of phonemes, and so on. The development of cognitive models of language has been, in part, aided by rules that apparently govern error occurrence. By assuming that these same rules govern language generation, language researchers have developed cognitive models of language (e.g., Dell, 1986; Garrett, 1976) that in turn are tested with other sources of language data.

## Experimentally generated errors

In conjunction with studies of naturally occurring speech errors, some researchers designed experiments to induce errors in normal speakers in order to investigate specific questions about the nature of language processing. In particular, these experiments proved useful in addressing a key question about language processing and one of considerable debate: are stages of retrieving meaning and sounds of a word interactive (do they influence each other) or are they independent of each other? For example, Baars, Motley, and Mackay (1975) examined the phenomena of phoneme movement errors and the possibility that these were influenced by the word outcome of such an error. That is, will a phoneme movement error be more likely to occur among two words if the resulting outcome is two words (e.g., barn door → darn bore) rather than one or two nonwords (e.g., car door → dar coor). They used a technique known as priming to elicit phoneme movement errors. Subjects read two word pairs with initial phonemes that would prime an exchange of initial phonemes in a third pair. In one group of word pairs, the final pair would result in a new word pair if the initial phonemes were exchanged (1) and in the second group, the final pair would not result in two words if the initial phonemes were exchanged (2):

(1)  dog bone
     dash board
     barn door → "darn bore"
(2)  paint can
     push cart
     cold pack → "pold cack"

Baars et al. found that exchanges were more likely when the resulting error forms were real words (1) than when they were nonwords (2), a phenomenon that became known as the lexical bias effect.

Martin, Weisberg, and Saffran (1989) used a paradigm to generate whole word substitutions by normal speakers in order to investigate whether processes of retrieving semantic and phonological aspects of a word interact and influence each other, or whether they are independent. They borrowed a paradigm from Levelt (1983) in which speakers had to describe a series of coloured circles in various patterns connected by lines. Those experiments were intended to observe how speakers monitor their speech when they make mistakes or change directions within the patterns they were describing. Martin et al. (1989) substituted pictures of objects for the coloured circles. They varied the composition of the pictures connected by lines such that they were either semantically related or their names were phonologically related or both semantically and phonologically related. Speakers had to describe the patterns and name the pictures as part of their descriptions. In the course of these descriptions, they made numerous word substitutions.

Martin and colleagues hypothesised that more substitutions would occur among words that were both semantically and phonologically related (so-called mixed errors) than either words that were just semantically related or words that were just phonologically related. This outcome was predicted by interactive activation models of word retrieval (Dell, 1986) which assume that spreading activation between semantic and phonological levels of representation keeps the influences of these representations on word retrieval active during the entire word retrieval process, and mutually influences a word's competitive stance within the lexicon and the likelihood that it will or will not be retrieved. In contrast, this outcome would argue against independent models of word retrieval (Levelt, 1989) which state that a word's semantic representation is retrieved prior to and independently of retrieval of its phonological representation. In fact, Martin et al. (1989) found that more errors occurred among words that were both semantically and phonologically related than among those that were either just semantically or just phonologically related, thus demonstrating that the stages of semantic and phonological retrieval together influence the probability that a word will be retrieved (see also Brédart & Valentine, 1992, for a similar experiment and results).

## Study of error patterns associated with language impairment

Another source of error data that constrain models of language, and one that is of special importance in this book, are those errors produced by patients whose language-processing abilities have been disrupted by brain damage (aphasia). The errors in production and comprehension of language in this population are much more numerous than normal speech errors, and yet are equally systematic in character and occurrence (Dell et al., 1997). With the exception of the most severe cases, language breakdown in aphasia is not necessarily affecting all components of language processing. More often than not, language components (e.g., syntactic processing, word retrieval, serial ordering of sounds), are differentially affected, enabling researchers to observe how specific aspects of language processing are organised.

The relatively selective impairments and sparings of cognitive abilities in brain-damaged individuals have proved to be especially revealing of cognitive processes that underscore speech and language behaviour. They can be used to confirm observations of normal speech errors and models of word production. At the same time they can provide insights into aspects of word retrieval that are not easily examined in normal speech production. For example, category-specific naming deficits that affect retrieval of words from some semantic categories but not others are present in language-impaired individuals but not in normal speakers. This pattern reveals an important aspect of semantic organisation: representations might be clustered by virtue of their semantic category membership or underlying semantic features that give rise to apparent semantic categories. Language impairment has also provided a window to other naming-related phenomena that are not easily addressed in studies of normal language, including evidence for separate input–output phonological networks and separate oral and written output systems. Additionally, studies of impaired word retrieval have provided useful information about the internal organisation of semantics and of the phoneme assembly system.

## Other relevant language performance data

### *Monitoring, hesitations, and pausing analyses*

Researchers have long been interested in the manner in which speakers monitor and edit their errors and the potential for this behaviour to reveal cognitive operations underlying word retrieval. Editing behaviours are not random, but rather appear to be constrained in ways that suggest underlying logical operations (Levelt, 1983). Studies of hesitations and pauses in the flow of speech indicate that they vary in duration depending on the contextual predictability of a word (Goldman-Eisler, 1958, 1968). This finding suggests that these pauses reflect momentary difficulty in lexical access. In addition to pauses and hesitations in speech, speakers will actually edit their output during production if it is partially or completely incorrect. The pioneering work of Levelt (1983) concerned self-monitoring of speech errors in connected speech production that indicate mechanisms for monitoring spoken words as well as internal speech. In the former case, the intruding error is completely articulated and the speaker pauses, goes back, and produces the correct word (e.g., "in the box . . . I mean the drawer, in the drawer"). In the latter case, the speaker begins to articulate the erroneous word, but cuts off the production mid-word and then attempts to produce the word or phrase once more (e.g., "over the bri . . . I mean over the fence"). This work is of great interest as it provides yet another avenue for investigating processes that are not easily observed in normal, accurate speech production.

### Tip-of-the-tongue states

Another form of "normal" word retrieval breakdown that temporarily stops the flow of speech, but more explicitly than hesitations or pauses, is a phenomenon known as the "tip-of-the-tongue" or TOT state. In this situation, a speaker knows what he/she wants to say, but cannot think of the word to express it. The TOT state is not an instance in which we search for an appropriate word to express a concept, choosing among one of several almost-appropriate words that best convey the intended message. Rather, in the TOT state, we know there is a specific word to express a concept, but can't recall its phonological form (an experience often compared to what people with anomia experience when they cannot retrieve a word). Harley (1995) characterises the TOT state as an extreme version of pauses that precede words of low predictability.

Accounts of the TOT state fall into two categories. One theory attributes them to partial activation of all the representations needed to produce a word (Brown, 1970; Burke, MacKay, Worthley, & Wade, 1991; Harley & MacAndrew, 1992). Another hypothesis (Woodworth, 1938) suggests that the elusive word is being actively blocked by another word representation competing for retrieval. Jones and Langford (1987) found that phonological competitors provoke a TOT state but semantic competitors do not, providing some support for this hypothesis. However, evidence provided by Perfect and Hanley (1992) and Meyer and Bock (1992) indicated that the presence of these competitors was not essential to the occurrence of the TOT state.

## Chronometric studies of lexical retrieval

Another important source of data used to constrain models of word production comes from a priming/dual-task paradigm that enables researchers to track the time course of semantic and phonological access during word retrieval. Levelt and colleagues (Levelt, Schriefers, Vorberg, Meyer, Pechmann, & Havinga, 1991; Schriefers et al., 1990) pioneered the use of priming in chronometric studies of lexical activation and retrieval. Using dual-task methodology that combines picture naming with either lexical decision or listening to a spoken word, they demonstrated that reaction times in a picture-naming task are affected at different points in time when words that are related to the pictured object semantically or phonologically are introduced at specific intervals. Specifically, they found that semantically related probes presented 150 milliseconds prior to the onset slowed naming but had no effect at later times. At 150 milliseconds after the picture appeared, a phonologically related probe word facilitated production (Schriefers et al., 1990). This information has been taken to reflect the time course of retrieving semantic and phonological representations of words, and has been used to determine whether activation of semantic and phonological representations of words occurs in two discrete or overlapping stages. The methodology used to examine the time course of word retrieval has not been without its critics. The findings of Levelt and colleagues have not been consistently replicated, and the effects appear somewhat dependent on the stimuli (Peterson & Savoy, 1998). Nevertheless, it is well regarded as an advancement in the tools available to investigate word retrieval processes. We will discuss this source of evidence in more detail when we review the model of Levelt and colleagues.

In addition to the behavioural methods of investigation used to study language processes and the time course of retrieving semantic and phonological representations, it is important to note recent efforts to validate this time course by neurophysiological methods, i.e., by electroencephalography (EEG) and by magnetoencephalography (MEG). The relevant MEG studies are discussed further in Chapter 3, but the reader is also referred to the review by Jansma, Rodríguez-Fornells, Moeller, and Muente (2004).

In the next section, we will discuss the ways in which theorists used these various sources of data to develop models of word processing. As we review each model, it should become evident that converging evidence has been an advantage for scientists who study word production. Cognitive models of word production are by and large more detailed and are founded on more solid empirical grounds than models of other cognitive phenomena. Moreover, models of word production have served as frameworks to develop descriptive schema for other cognitive phenomena such as action errors (Schwartz, Montgomery, Fitzpatrick-DeSalme, Ochipa, Coslett, & Mayer, 1995).

# CURRENT MODELS OF WORD RETRIEVAL

In the past 25–30 years the evolution of word retrieval models has been both rapid and dramatic. Consequently, the enterprise has accumulated a bit of history. As we have discussed so far, models of word processing have become increasingly sophisticated in their detail of mental structures and processes involved in comprehending or generating a single word. Current models can be classified as one of three types: functional (box-and-arrow), local connectionist, and distributed connectionist models. The first group uses an information-processing framework to characterise structures and functions involved in lexical retrieval, as discussed earlier. We will focus first on three functional models, those of Fromkin (1971), Garrett (1975, 1976), and Levelt (1983, 1989). These three models, as well as other similar models developed during this same period (e.g., Butterworth, 1982, 1989; Morton, 1970; Morton & Patterson, 1980), share an important assumption about word retrieval: semantic and phonological representations of a word are retrieved independently of each other. Also, they postulate at least three stages of word retrieval that correspond to the kinds of impairment that are observed in aphasia (see Chapter 2). These include retrieval of a word's meaning, retrieval of a corresponding word form, and retrieval and assembly of the phonemes that comprise that word. Morton's (1970) and Morton and Patterson's (1980) logogen model has influenced our thinking about language processes as much as Fromkin's, Garrett's, and Levelt's models. We will return to the logogen model in subsequent chapters because it was particularly influential in aphasiology and still serves as a framework for diagnosis and treatment of language impairments.

Following the review of functional models, we will discuss a localist connectionist model, that of Dell (1986; Dell & O'Seaghdha, 1992) that has been influential in understanding aphasic naming disturbances. This and other contemporary localist connectionist models (e.g., Harley, 1984; Harley & MacAndrew, 1992; Stemberger, 1985; Rapp & Goldrick, 2000) share the assumption of functional models that word production involves several stages including retrieval of semantic and phonological representations of a word. Additionally, many of the localist connectionist models assume that there is interaction among some or all of the stages of word retrieval, an assumption that is not shared by many of the functional models (e.g., Butterworth, 1982, 1989; Levelt, 1983). With the introduction of localist connectionist models the focus of research shifted from the information in the boxes to the information carried by the arrows between the boxes.

The third group of models that we will review are the distributed connectionist models of word processing. Some of these models have been applied directly to problems of word retrieval (e.g., Plaut & Shallice, 1993a—optic aphasia), while others have addressed issues in word reading that also apply in principle to other word-processing tasks (e.g., Plaut &

Shallice, 1993b) or treatment (Plaut, 1996). Although the application of these models to aphasic language has been limited, they have made some notable contributions and show promise for future application in this domain.

An important contribution of local and distributed connectionist models is their use of computer simulations to test a theory's predictions about dynamic aspects of word retrieval processes (e.g., activation and decay processes responsible for access to or retrieval of semantic and phonological representations of words). This development expanded the use of cognitive models of language from descriptions of a theory to a tool that generated detailed predictions of that theory, which in turn could be examined in normal and impaired speakers.

In Chapter 5 of this book we will discuss the application of these models to the study of recovery and treatment of anomia, focusing especially on studies based on functional models of word processing (e.g., Morton & Patterson, 1980) and interactive activation models (e.g., Dell & O'Seaghdha, 1992).

## Functional (and modular) models of lexical retrieval: Models of Fromkin (1971), Garrett (1975, 1976), and Levelt (1989)

In 1971, Victoria Fromkin published a comprehensive analysis of a corpus of naturally occurring speech errors in normals. These errors revealed internal regularities and constraints on their occurrence that suggested the psychological reality of a number of linguistic representations (e.g., phonemes, morphemes, syntactic rules or structures). On the basis of these data, Fromkin developed a detailed model describing stages involved in producing a single word. This model and other similar models (e.g., Garrett, 1975) hypothesised that the meaning (semantic) and form (phonological) representations of a word are retrieved independently. This idea received support from work by Garrett (1975, 1976) who analysed a large corpus of word and morpheme movement errors in sentence production. He identified properties that distinguished two kinds of whole word or partial word movement errors. One type of exchange called a stranding error (1 below) occurs within a phrase (sound or morpheme shifts that leave a portion of the word "stranded").

(1)   I thought the truck was parked. → I thought the park was trucked
(Garrett, 1980).

Sound and morpheme shifts frequently involve words within phrases that are likely to be from different syntactic categories. The two words from which the exchanging sounds originate also tend to share phonological characteristics (e.g., syllable position, vowels). This type of error is attributed to a second stage of sentence processing, the positional level.

*Table 1.1* The five stages of language production in
         Garrett's model

| Process | Representation |
| --- | --- |
| Stage 1: Inferential | Message level |
| Stage 2: Logical and syntactic | Functional level |
| Stage 3: Syntactic and phonological | Positional level |
| Stage 4: Regular phonological | Phonetic level |
| Stage 5: Motor coding | Articulatory |

The second type of exchange is the movement error that spans phrases (3 and 4 below) including whole word exchanges, anticipations, perseverations.

(2)   This seat has a spring in it → This spring has a seat in it
                                                      (Garrett, 1980).

(3)   They forgot it and left it behind → They left it and forgot it behind
                                                      (Garrett, 1975).

In contrast to the within-phrase movement errors, across-phrase movement errors tend to share the same syntactic category and are less likely to be phonologically related. These types of relationships are more typical of an earlier "functional" stage of processing that is concerned with semantic/syntactic roles of words in an utterance.

On the basis of these data, Garrett proposed a model of five stages of language production, each of which generated a representation of an utterance being produced, two of which were concerned directly with word retrieval (Table 1.1). The message-level representation is a conceptual representation of the intended communication. This is followed by the functional level which entails development of the predicate argument structure and identification of words to be retrieved. At this stage, multi-phrasal planning occurs; semantically specified word representations are assigned thematic roles according to the message level of representation. The third stage results in the positional-level representation. Here, phonological forms of content words are retrieved and ordered within a phonologically specified syntactic frame that has been generated on the basis of the functional representation of the utterance. The positional level is a single-phrase planning stage at which phonological representations of words are inserted into a syntactic frame that is generated according to the functional-level representation (Garrett, 1975). The word's representation at the functional level has been termed the "lemma" and at the phonological level, the "lexeme" (Kempen & Huijbers, 1983; Levelt, 1989).

Additional evidence for two stages in word retrieval comes from the observation of word substitution errors that are either semantically or phonologically related to the target word (Fromkin, 1971). The existence of such errors confirms that retrieval of a word's semantic representation and its phonological representation are dissociable operations. Whether or not these two stages overlap is open to question. The existence of mixed errors (word substitutions that are both semantically and phonologically related to the target word) suggests some "communication" between the two stages that affects the probability of what words are activated as potential substitution errors. Garrett's (1982) analysis of his error corpus showed that the probability of mixed errors was no greater than that of semantically or phonologically related word errors, suggesting that the mixed errors arise only by chance. This finding supports the independence assumption. Other analyses such as the studies of Baars et al. (1975) and Martin et al. (1989) discussed earlier and Dell and Reich (1981) discussed later in this chapter indicate the opposite conclusion.

Fromkin's and Garrett's model influenced studies of word retrieval impairment associated with aphasia, particularly in the United States in the 1970s and early 1980s (e.g., Pate, Saffran, & Martin, 1987; Saffran, Schwartz, & Marin, 1980; Schwartz, 1987). The identification of two distinctive stages of word retrieval fitted neatly with the findings of different types of anomia that appeared to disrupt retrieval of semantic and/or phonological information about a word. At about the same time, other word production models such as those of Butterworth (1982, 1989), and Morton and Patterson (1980) were having a similar influence on aphasiologists in the United Kingdom. Morton and Patterson's model of single word processing, based on Morton's (1970) logogen theory, has been especially influential in aphasiology. Far more than a simple model of word production, this model encompasses all aspects of single word processing. Although primarily a descriptive functional model, it was a precursor to connectionist models that focus on processing aspects of word production because it describes a process by which word representations are activated to a threshold before they are retrieved for production or recognised. While other stage models of the time merely describe retrieval as a process of selection and passing on through various stages of representation, Morton and Patterson's model recognised the need to describe this process in more dynamic terms. Nonetheless, this model differs in important ways from connectionist models that were to follow, in that it assumes that the structures and functions underlying word retrieval are independent of each other and can be selectively impaired.

Morton and Patterson's model played an important role in cognitive neuropsychological research during the 1980s and 90s, serving as a framework within which many researchers formed hypotheses about the expected behaviour patterns underlying anomic disorders and other acquired word-processing impairments (e.g., dyslexias, conduction aphasia). We will discuss the role of Morton and Patterson's model in clinical diagnosis and treatment of anomia in Chapters 4 and 5.

Another important functional model of word processing developed during this period which remains highly influential is that of Levelt (1983, 1989, 1992; Levelt et al., 1999). This model has been computationally instantiated since the early 1990s, but differs from many of the computational models of language in that it is modular and assumes independent stages of semantic and phonological word retrieval. This model also differs from most of its contemporary models of word production (e.g., Fromkin's and Garrett's models) in that the data supporting this model came from experimentally induced naming errors (Levelt, 1983) and reaction time data from naming interference paradigms that enabled the tracking of semantic and phonological retrieval in word production (Levelt et al., 1991; Schriefers et al., 1990). As in the Fromkin and Garrett models, Levelt proposed that lexical retrieval occurs in two independent stages: retrieval of the semantic/syntactic representation and retrieval of the phonological form. Although two stages of retrieval are common to most, if not all, theories of lexical retrieval, the assumption that they are independent is not shared by all models. The claim that each stage of word retrieval occurs independently of the other has been articulated most clearly in Levelt's theory.

Levelt and his colleagues (e.g., Levelt, 1989, 1992; Levelt et al., 1999) have developed a theory of lexical access in speech production that incorporates this discrete two-stage assumption in a larger scheme. The model details links between conceptual representations and lemmas in the first stage of retrieval, as well as the phonological encoding operations on the lexeme, the product of the second stage of retrieval. A lemma is an abstract lexical representation of a word that is linked to the concept denoted by the word and also to its phonological form (the lexeme). Additionally, it is assumed to contain all the syntactic properties of a word. Currently, their theory is, in part, computationally instantiated in a model known as WEAVER (Word Encoding by Activation and VERification; Roelofs, 1992; Levelt et al., 1999). The stages of this model are depicted in Figure 1.2 and the functions of each stage are described below. The Figure illustrates each process involved in retrieval of a word (in standard typescript) and the output of that process (in italics).

### Conceptual preparation of the lexical concepts

Here, the act of converting a message (intended communication) into a spoken word is begun. All of the meaning information (sensory, logical, emotional, etc.) of a particular lexical concept is gathered and linked with the appropriate lexical concept or concepts. A message may require a single word to be understood by the listener, or multiple words. This stage of the theory has been modelled by Roelofs (1992) with a conceptual network of

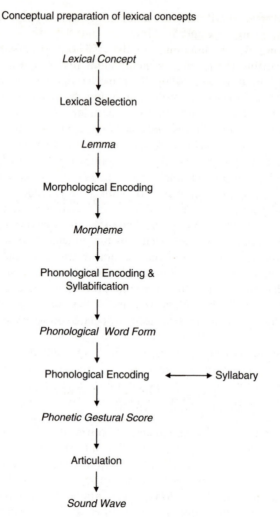

Conceptual preparation of lexical concepts

↓

*Lexical Concept*

↓

Lexical Selection

↓

*Lemma*

↓

Morphological Encoding

↓

*Morpheme*

↓

Phonological Encoding &
Syllabification

↓

*Phonological  Word Form*

↓

Phonological Encoding  ←——→  Syllabary

↓

*Phonetic Gestural Score*

↓

Articulation

↓

*Sound Wave*

*Figure 1.2* A discrete-stage model of word retrieval proposed by Levelt et al.
(1999).

concept nodes that include all the meaning elements of a lexical concept
and which is sensitive to auditory or visual input.

### *Lexical selection*

In Levelt's model (1989) and its more recent version (Levelt et al., 1999)
words are formulated in two stages. The first stage is selection of a lemma
(word node) that is retrieved from the mental lexicon on the basis of input
from the lexical concept that was most active at the conceptual preparation

stage. Selection of the lemma is based on conceptual-semantic and grammatical factors, an assumption similar to Garrett's model of functional-level encoding of semantic and syntactic aspects of words. A critical assumption in this theory is that *one and only one lemma* is retrieved and passed on to the next stage, phonological encoding. An exception to this occurs by chance and is the model's account of a blend error; when two lemmas with similar grammatical structure (e.g., similar semantics and grammatical class) are selected simultaneously, both are passed on to the phonological encoding stage, and the result is a blend error (e.g., lecture/session → lection).

### *Morphological encoding, phonological encoding and syllabification*

In the current version of Levelt's model (Levelt et al., 1999) accessing a word's form involves activation of three representations of a word: its morphological form, its metrical shape, and its phonological content. The morphological information is retrieved first (e.g., verb + past tense marker) and then the metrical and segmental properties are specified. Syllabification occurs later and is dependent in part on the phonological environment of the word. The representation that results from these stages is passed on to phonetic encoding mechanisms which yield a phonetic representation that guides articulation of the word.

### Challenges to the assumption of modularity and independent stages of semantic and phonological retrieval

The model of Levelt and colleagues shares much with other structural independent stage models such as those of Garrett and Fromkin. It is more detailed in certain respects (e.g., it proposes mechanisms of syllabification) and it is computationally instantiated. The assumption shared by these models, that word retrieval occurs over several *independent* stages, was seriously challenged by evidence from the very data (speech errors) that inspired their development. In particular, two phenomena observed in speech error data that were discussed earlier in this chapter challenged the independent stage assumption: lexical bias of sound errors and a mixed error bias in word substitutions. Recall that lexical bias of sound errors (Baars et al., 1975) refers to the tendency for phoneme errors to result in word outcomes (e.g., barn door → darn bore) rather than nonword outcomes (York Library → lork yibrary), and mixed error bias (Martin et al., 1989) of word substitutions refers to the greater likelihood of a word substitution if the intruding word is both semantically and phonologically related to the target word (e.g., penguin → pelican is more likely than penguin → owl or penguin → pencil). Butterworth (1982, 1989) offered an account of lexical bias and mixed errors in a model of word production that shares much in common with Garrett's, Fromkin's, and Levelt's models.

Word retrieval is assumed to occur in two independent stages—retrieval of a word's meaning and its form. To account for lexical bias and mixed error effects in his model, Butterworth proposed a post-lexical editing mechanism that filtered output. By assuming that the editor used lexical criteria for letting output pass on to production stages of speech, it would be logical that such an editor would fail more often when phonological errors resulted by chance in a real word form. A similar conclusion can be drawn for the mixed error effect if one assumes that this editor is sensitive to meaning and form of the output. The logic is similar: if the lexical retrieval system chooses an incorrect word, and that word form is both meaning- and sound-related to the intended word, the post-lexical editor is more likely to *not* recognise the error than if the word error is only meaning-related or only sound-related or not related at all to the intended word.

Although Butterworth's model preserved the independence of the semantic and phonological retrieval stages, the addition of a post-selection editor to a word production mechanism necessitated that all the information in the lexical production system be replicated in that editor, a solution that violated the law of parsimony. It would be more parsimonious to assume a mechanism built into the lexical processor, a "built-in editor". This is exactly what the interactive spreading activation models (e.g., Dell & O'Seaghdha, 1992; Eikmeyer, Schade, Kupietz, & Laubenstein, 1999; Harley, 1984) provide—an internal mechanism that supports activation of the most appropriate candidate for word retrieval, but also one that occasionally slips because similarities among words sometimes lead to a competitor word being selected as opposed to the intended word.

For some time, the debate of interactivity vs. independent levels of representation was carried out mostly in the research domain of normal language processing. Investigations of aphasia were framed primarily within the functional, box-and-arrow-style models. Eventually, however, the limits of these models' explanatory power became apparent, and in the late 1980s research efforts began to explore connectionist models of normal language processing as a means of explaining the complexities of aphasic impairment. Saffran, Schwartz, Dell, and colleagues began a series of studies demonstrating the usefulness of the interactive activation model of word retrieval in accounting for word processing in both normal and impaired systems. This model and studies are discussed below.

## Interactive activation models (localist connectionist models) of word retrieval: Dell (1986; Dell & O'Seaghdha, 1992; Foygel & Dell, 2000); Rapp and Goldrick (2000)

In 1986, Gary Dell published a highly influential paper reporting a computer-instantiated model of word retrieval as part of a theory of sentence production. It shared the assumption of the functional independent stage models that word retrieval occurs in two stages. However, his model

LEVEL OF
REPRESENTATION

Conceptual

Semantic features

Lexical

Phonological

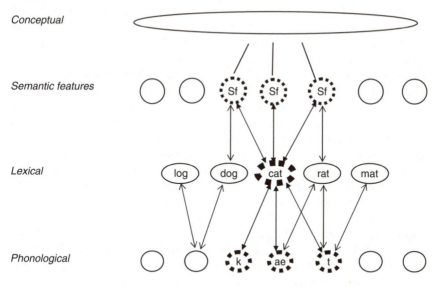

*Figure 1.3* An interactive spreading activation model of single word production. The figure shows the levels of word representations involved in word production and the bi-directional connections between them.

differed from these models in an important way: it postulated that the two retrieval stages were not independent, but in fact were highly interactive. The empirical support for this model is much the same as that for the independent two-stage models: speech error data with corroborating evidence coming from other breakdowns in language production (e.g., TOT states, pauses, hesitations). What Dell captured in his model of word retrieval was a means of accounting for lexical bias and mixed error effects in speech errors without postulating an extra, post-lexical mechanism.

The interaction of semantic and phonological influences on word retrieval arises from two mechanisms of the model: (1) access to semantic and phonological representations of a word, which occurs via spreading activation that feeds forward and back between stages of representation, and (2) the overlap in time of the two stages of word retrieval. Thus, retrieval of a word node (something like a lemma) is influenced by the strength of activated semantic and phonological representations. Figure 1.3 shows a version of Dell's production model that addresses exclusively the word retrieval process (following Dell & O'Seaghdha, 1992), as opposed to word retrieval and sentence production in Dell's earlier model (Dell, 1986).

In this model, there are three levels of representation: semantic, lexical, and phonological. Conceptual representations that support lexical-semantic representations are assumed in this model, but not detailed. In word production, feedforward activation spreads from primed semantic feature nodes to lexical nodes and from there to corresponding phonological nodes. This spreading activation is a two-way process, meaning that at each stage of activation there is feedback activation spreading to the preceding level of representation. The phonological segments activated by lexical nodes return a proportion of that activation to all words with which they are connected. Over time, the feedforward–feedback processes serve to reinforce activation of a targeted array of phonological nodes which corresponds to an existing morpheme or word. This built-in "editor" prevents nonword utterances from being generated and is the interactive model's alternative to the separate editor proposed by Butterworth (1989) and others to account for lexical bias and mixed error phenomena. At the same time, it is this feedback mechanism that leads to other types of errors by activating word and morpheme units that compete with the targeted lexical node.

The debate on interactivity vs. independence of semantic and phonological representations during word retrieval continues to flourish. Rapp and Goldrick (2000) argue on the basis of data from aphasic individuals that interactivity is only present between lexical and phonological stages. Levelt and his colleagues have conducted numerous studies looking at the time course of semantic and phonological activation during word retrieval in normal speakers and claim that their data support an independent stage model. Furthermore, they argue that although speech errors suggest semantic-lexical-phonological interaction (e.g., lexical bias, mixed errors), they are the outcome of multiple operations and may not accurately reflect the normal online operations of word retrieval. It is important, however, that a model of cognition be able to account for both normal and impaired operations. In this regard, the interactive activation models have been very successful, especially in the area of word retrieval. Below, we illustrate the application of the interactive activation models to a theory of word processing and also to diagnosis of word retrieval impairments.

## The IA model's account of aphasic impairment: Some illustrations

Schwartz et al. (1994) reported one of the first studies that used the interactive activation model to account for aphasic speech errors. They evaluated the error patterns of FL, an individual with jargon aphasia, comparing his rates and distribution of errors to those of normal speakers (from the London–Lund corpus of speech errors, Garnham, Shillcock, Brown, Mill, & Cutler, 1982). Their investigation revealed similar relative proportions of open- and closed-class errors in the two corpora but that FL produced a much higher rate of unrelated word substitutions (e.g., gone → caught). Schwartz and colleagues noted that this and other aspects of FL's error pattern could not be accounted for by discrete two-stage models (e.g., Garrett, 1982). FL produced few formal paraphasias (sound-related word errors, e.g., food → fuse) but many phonologically related nonword errors (e.g., speak → /spisbid/). Schwartz et al. (1994) used an interactive spreading activation theory of word retrieval (Dell, 1986; Dell & O'Seaghdha, 1992) to account for the error patterns of FL. As noted earlier, this model has three stages of representation: semantic, lexical, and phonological. Activation spreads across (but not within) levels of representation, in a series of feedforward–feedback activation cycles (see Figure 1.3). The spread of activation is regulated by two parameters, connection strength (the rate of activation spread) and decay rate (the rate of activation decline towards resting level). Additional parameters include noise and the number of time steps before a word is retrieved. Spreading activation primes the intended word and related word representations. At the moment that retrieval occurs, the most activated word representation (usually the intended utterance) is retrieved over other activated representations. Post-activation inhibition then "turns off" the representation of the retrieved word. This word retrieval stage is then followed by a second stage in which the phonemes of the selected word are encoded.

Schwartz et al. (1994) postulated that FL's error pattern was due to a weakening of connection strength in the word activation process. Normally, phonologically related word errors occur when spreading activation primes phonological nodes and feeds back to the lexical network. This feedback refreshes activation of the targeted lexical node ("cat" in Figure 1.3) but also primes phonologically related word nodes ("mat" in Figure 1.3). These primed competitors are not normally retrieved, but if the target node's activation is reduced it is more likely that one will be retrieved in error. When connection strength is reduced, feedback activation between phonological and lexical levels would also be weak and less likely to activate phonologically related lexical competitors. In this situation, nonword phonological errors, which occur at the post-lexical phonological encoding stage, would predominate. Perseverations would also increase when connection strength is weakened (see also Martin & Dell, 2004). This is because residual activation of words retrieved in prior utterances would make them stronger competitors when activation of the current target word is weak.

Dell's (1986; Dell & O'Seaghdha, 1992) IA model was used by Martin et al. (1994) to explain the naming and repetition error patterns of NC, a young man who suffered from an acute aphasia secondary to a cerebral aneurysm. His production, although fluent, contained numerous semantic errors and phonological word and nonword errors. Additionally, although auditory comprehension was severely impaired, reading comprehension was only mildly affected. There were two noteworthy features of NC's error pattern. First, he produced semantic errors in single word repetition (a pattern known as "deep dysphasia"). Second, in speech production he produced a relatively high rate of formal paraphasias (sound-related whole word substitutions). NC's naming error pattern not only deviated from the error pattern of unimpaired speakers, but had rarely been reported in the aphasia literature (e.g., Blanken, 1990; Howard & Franklin, 1988). Moreover, NC's naming error pattern was quite different from that of FL, who produced very few formal paraphasias and many nonword phonological errors. Martin et al. proposed that NC's error pattern resulted from impairment to the second of the two spreading activation parameters in the Dell model, decay rate. Specifically, they hypothesised that activated nodes decayed too rapidly and that this impairment affected all nodes in the semantic-lexical-phonological network. How could this result in a high rate of formal paraphasias?

We noted earlier that formal paraphasias occur at the lexical level when connection strength is strong enough to feed back activation from phonological nodes to that level during lexical activation. Figure 1.4 illustrates the time course of feedforward–feedback processes in word retrieval production.

Figure 1.4 shows that as feedforward–feedback activation cycles are initiated, the target node (*cat*) and semantically related competitors, *dog* and *rat*, are the first nodes to be activated. Spreading activation reaches the phonologically related lexical nodes, e.g., *can*, later and only by feedback activation from primed phonological nodes. When a representation is "primed" its activation level increases, but then immediately that activation begins to decay at a certain rate until the next cycle of activation occurs and "re-primes" it once more. This cyclical "activation-decay-refreshment" process keeps activation levels in check until word retrieval occurs.

Typically, the word that the speaker intends to say receives the most activation because it is the target. At the same time, competing representations are receiving certain dosages of activation throughout the priming cycles of feedforward and feedback activation. Which of these would be the next most highly activated, i.e., the closest competitor with the target (and thereby, potentially the most likely of word errors)? In naming, the semantically related lexical nodes (*dog, rat*) would be more active than phonologically related words because they are primed earlier and have more time to accumulate activation over the time course of lexical selection. Additionally, activation levels of those semantically related competitors that are also phonologically related (*rat*) to the target word are raised further because they receive additional feedback activation from phonological levels of representation. As Figure 1.4 shows, other lexical neighbours with phonological relationships with the target or with one of the semantic competitors are also primed by feedback activation from phonological representations, but the activation levels of these neighbours are relatively small. This raises the question of how the least active of competitors, phonologically related word nodes, could be selected in error at unusually high rates, as in the case of NC. Martin et al.'s (1994) hypothesis that NC's word retrieval impairment was due to a too rapid decay of activation can explain this puzzle. When all connections in the network are subjected to an increase in the rate of activation decay, the activation advantage of

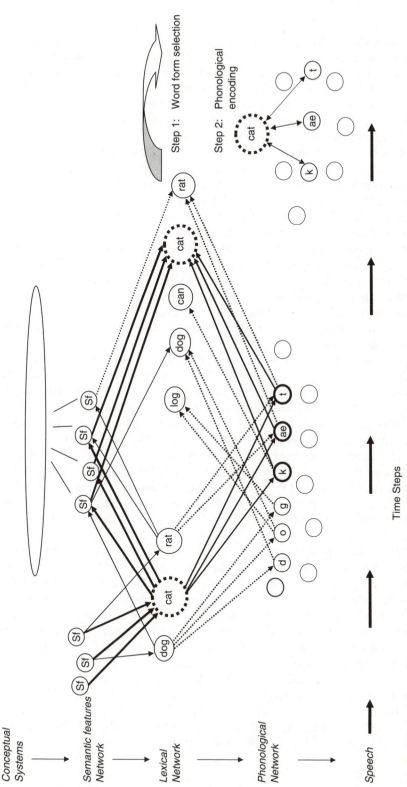

*Figure 1.4* An interactive activation model of word retrieval as it occurs in the task of word production (as in picture naming). The figure is based on Martin et al.'s (1994) model of word repetition. Here, it shows the path of spreading activation over a series of time steps preceding selection of a word form from the lexical network (Step 1) and phonological encoding (Step 2).

semantically related competitors actually turns into a disadvantage, because these earlier primed representations (target and semantic competitors) are subjected to more of the cumulative effects of the increased rate of decay compared to those representations primed later (phonologically related word nodes). Thus, as decay rate is increased beyond the "normal" setting, the probability increases that these late-activated competitors (phonologically related words) will be selected in error.

Figure 1.5 illustrates the time course of feedforward–feedback processes in lexical access when the task is to *repeat* a single word. In this task, a decay rate lesion would lead to an increased rate of *semantic* errors, because in repetition it is the target word (*cat*) and phonologically related word nodes (*cab, rat*) that are primed first, and semantically related competitors are primed later by feedback from semantic levels of representation. The same principles underlying the shift in probabilities of formal and semantic errors in naming apply in repetition, only the shift is reversed. When decay rate is increased, nodes primed early on (the target *cat* and phonological competitors, *can, rat*) lose more activation over the course of word retrieval than semantically related nodes that are primed later, with a net effect that shifts probabilities to favour semantic errors (see Martin & Saffran, 1992, for further discussion).

Martin et al. (1994) tested their hypothesis that too rapid decay of activated nodes was responsible for NC's semantic errors in repetition and formal paraphasias in naming. Importantly, they demonstrated that a single lesion to Dell and O'Seaghdha's (1992) model (a global increase in decay rate) could account for NC's patterns of naming and repetition. The studies of Schwartz et al. (1994) and Martin et al. (1994) validated the idea of a "processing" impairment and confirmed that error patterns could vary based on the *type* of processing impairment. Whereas Schwartz et al. (1994) showed that weakened connection strength could account for FL's phonological nonword errors and perseverations, abnormally fast decay rate could explain NC's high rate of formal paraphasias in naming and semantic errors in repetition.

These findings were extended to a multiple case study in 1997. Dell, Schwartz, Martin, Saffran, and Gagnon attempted to fit the IA model to the naming performance of 21 aphasic subjects. Dell and colleagues set out to test what they termed the "continuity" hypothesis, which holds that aphasic error patterns lie on a continuum between a "normal" error pattern and a random pattern. Starting with Dell's model of naming, they proposed that aphasic impairment could be captured in the model by altering two parameters: connection weight, which modulates the strength of activation spread, and decay rate, which controls the rate at which activated nodes decay. A further assumption was that these impairments affected the word retrieval system globally rather than selectively semantic or phonological levels of representation. Dell et al. (1997) successfully demonstrated the model's ability to simulate the distributions of normal and aphasic error

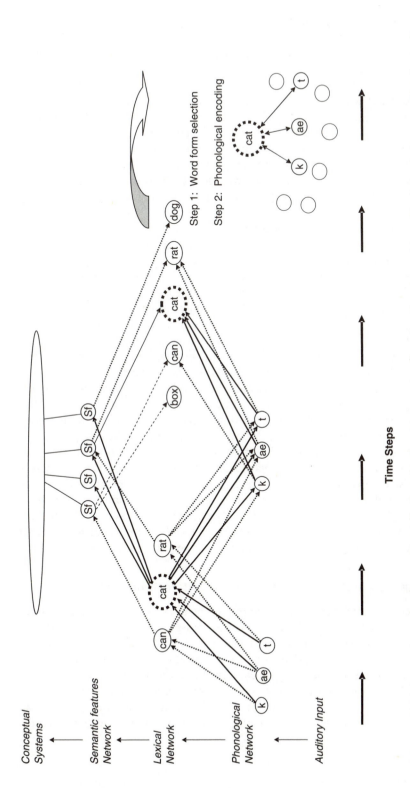

*Figure 1.5* An interactive activation model of word retrieval as it occurs in the task of word repetition. The figure is based on Martin et al.'s (1994) model of word repetition. Here it shows the path of spreading activation over a series of time steps preceding selection of a word form from the lexical network (Step 1) and phonological encoding (Step 2).

patterns by varying these two parameters globally within the semantic-lexical-phonological network.

Of course it is easy enough to create a computer model that can simulate a pattern of error. Dell et al. (1997) note that the true validity of a model is when it can be used to predict other phenomena outside the model's capacity but which depend on the functions captured by the model. They used the output of their model (the patterns of connection weight and decay rate impairment) to predict other such phenomena. First, they tested a prediction that true formal paraphasias should preserve word-class information because they presumably occur at the lexical level. In Dell's model, formal paraphasias can be true word-selection errors that occur at the lexical level or they can be phonological errors that form real words by chance. In a picture-naming task where the target words are nouns, formal paraphasias that arise at lexical level should also be nouns more often than would be expected by chance because they are true word-level errors. Additionally, these true formal paraphasias should be more common in subjects with too fast decay rate and strong connection strength. This is because strong connections are needed to support spread of feedback activation to the lexical network. Phonological errors that by chance form words should be nouns only at chance rates. Also, this pattern of error should occur more often in subjects whose naming impairment is due to weakened connection weights. To test these hypotheses, Dell et al. (1997) divided their subject group into those whose error patterns were modelled with strong connection weights and those with weak connection weights. The predicted outcomes were confirmed: formal paraphasias were nouns at rates greater than chance in the strong connection weight group and were nouns only at chance rates in the weak connection weight group.

Dell et al. (1997) also tested a prediction about another type of error that depends on strong feedback activation. This is the mixed error, which is both semantically and phonologically related to the target word. These errors should be more prevalent in subjects whose naming error pattern reflects strong connection weights. This prediction was also confirmed: subjects with strong connection weights showed a substantial mixed error effect while subjects with weak connection weights did not.

## Using computational cognitive models to test theories of language

The efforts of Dell et al. (1997) to model the data from real patients did not go unnoticed. Although the work was recognised as pioneering, it was strongly criticised by Ruml and Caramazza (2000). They raised several questions about the validity of using computational models to evaluate theories of lexical processing. They argued that the fits of Dell et al.'s model to the patient naming data were poor in absolute terms, and for this reason could not be taken as support for their theory of lexical access. Ruml and Caramazza (2000) developed a mathematical model that provided closer fits to the data. However, because the model was not based on a theory, it could not be used to formulate and test predictions about other language phenomena. Although Dell et al. (1997, 2000) emphasised that the success of a model is based on its ability to make predictions based on its fit to the data, Ruml and Caramazza (2000) claimed that the predictions made by Dell et al.'s (1997) model did not substantiate their claims about the nature of lexical access and aphasic impairment.

The somewhat lively exchange between these two research groups marked a great advance in the field of computational modelling of language data. These papers are highly recommended to readers who are interested in this aspect of communication science. Ruml and Caramazza offer important considerations when evaluating the validity of a modelling exercise, and Dell et al. (2000) provide an interesting discussion of the role that computational modelling should play in developing theories of language. Importantly, models represent theories and are used to test theories against real data. If a model cannot be fitted to data, then the assumptions of the theory are wrong or the model is not capturing an aspect of the phenomena that it is trying to model. Sometimes computational models include simplifying assumptions because they cannot instantiate computationally all aspects of a particular phenomenon. The science of developing computer models to test theories of cognition is quite new and the debate between Dell et al. (1997, 2000) and Ruml and Caramazza (2000) provides a good introduction to the limitations and potential contributions of computational models to help us understand mental processes of language. In what follows, we recount another line of research that stemmed from criticisms of Dell et al.'s modelling efforts.

### What happens when a model cannot account for all error patterns?

Dell et al.'s (1997) model was not able to account for all aphasic error patterns reported in the literature. Importantly, their model does not account for "no responses", a frequent error type in anomia. When asked to name a picture, for example, subjects often give a "no response", stating something like "I know it, but I can't say it." There is no mechanism in the computer instantiations of the IA model used by Dell et al. (1997; Foygel & Dell, 2000; Martin et al., 1994; Martin et al., 1996) that yields "no response" errors, limiting its ability to account for those aphasic speakers who produce a high percentage of "no responses" on picture-naming tasks. However, the model has recently been modified with a selection threshold parameter (Laine, Tikkala & Juhola, 1998; Roelofs, 1992) to address this problem (Dell, Lawler, Harris, & Gordon, 2004).

Another error pattern that could not be accounted for in the Dell et al. (1997) study is the occurrence of a high rate of semantic errors and few instances of any other error type except "no responses". Although this pattern of error is not common, it has been reported, for example by Rapp and Goldrick (2000). In their study, they evaluated the ability of several different word retrieval models to account for normal speech error patterns and those of three brain-damaged individuals with less typical error patterns in naming. The models they explored differed in their assumptions about interactivity. They included: (1) a cascading spreading activation model, (2) an interactive spreading activation model, (3) a partially interactive model, and (4) a model with no interactivity at all. They evaluated these models' accounts of impairments of two patients, KE and PW, which yielded an error pattern in naming characterised by semantic errors and no responses in naming. Language assessment suggested that KE had a central semantic deficit because semantic errors were present in a variety of input and output tasks that draw on semantic processes. PW's semantic errors appeared to have a post-lexical origin because he performed well on input word-processing tasks such as picture–word matching tests. Rapp and Goldrick (2000) showed that the model with interaction restricted to lexical and phonological levels could account for the two impairments. They called this the "restricted interactive activation" (RIA) model.

From this study and the studies of Dell and colleagues (Dell et al., 1997; Martin et al., 1994; Martin et al., 1996; Schwartz et al., 1994), we can see that data from individual patients can provide invaluable information on language operations. Dell et al.'s (1997) and Rapp and Goldrick's (2000) modelling efforts have focused on different aspects of word processing and potential sources of its impairment. Dell et al. (1997) introduced the notion of overall processing impairment, i.e., language impairment could result from slowed activation or too fast decay. In contrast, Rapp and Goldrick (2000) emphasised the traditional approach to aphasic impairments that focused on the locus of impairment. Foygel and Dell (2000) followed up the Rapp and Goldrick study with another version of their model that was lesioned by locus of impairment. This is discussed below.

### Exploration of local lesions in the interaction activation model

Foygel and Dell (2000) examined the ability of two versions of the interactive activation model of lexical access to account for aphasic speech error patterns in a picture-naming task: the weight-decay model (Dell et al., 1997, 2000) and the semantic-phonological model. The weight-decay model that we reviewed above predicts that patterns of speech error can be accounted for by lesions to parameters that regulate activation flow in the system: connection weight (strength of activation spread in the network) and decay rate (rate at which activation decays). Decay lesions (an increase in decay rate, but with connection strength being normal) account best for error patterns that reflect good interaction, for example, higher rates of formal paraphasias that require strong feedback to occur. Connection weight lesions (reduced connection weight, normal decay rate) accounted best for error patterns that reflected diminished interaction (e.g., phonological nonword errors). Foygel and Dell (2000) showed that the semantic-phonological model could capture these same differences in error patterns by postulating one type of processing impairment (reduced connection strength) but setting the locus of damage to either connections between semantic and lexical nodes or connections between lexical and phonological nodes, or some combination of both. They showed further that error patterns reflecting good interaction (like the decay rate lesions) were best captured in the semantic-phonological model with reduced semantic weights and normal or near normal phonological weights, and that error patterns reflecting reduced interaction were best captured with reduced phonological weights and near normal semantic weights.

Foygel and Dell's semantic-phonological model was able to account for all the data that had been modelled with the weight-decay model, thus showing that traditional classifications of aphasic impairment (in terms of semantic and phonological impairment) could be captured in the interactive activation model. And yet, the model still could not account for patients whose error patterns consisted of mostly semantic errors (such as PW, reported by Rapp & Goldrick, 2000). However, they approximated this pattern using a pure lexical-semantic lesion, which resulted in a high rate of semantic errors, but also some formal paraphasias (not present in PW's pattern).

Since this flurry of modelling studies in the late 1990s and early 2000 period, there have been a few additional studies of importance. Schwartz and Brecher (2000) used Dell et al.'s (1997) model as theoretical framework to examine recovery of naming abilities. Specifically, the interactive activation model had made some predictions about how error patterns should change in relation to severity of naming impairment and recovery. Recovery should be reflected in a reduction of phonological errors, but not semantic errors. This is the pattern that they observed. Another advance, as noted above, was the addition of a threshold component that enabled the model to capture error patterns that included no responses. Recently, Schwartz, Dell, and Martin (2004) reported a complete replication of the original studies with 97 subjects (the original study included 21 subjects) using both the global weight-decay model and the semantic-phonological model. They found that the semantic-phonological model did a better job of accounting for all of the data.

These studies using localist connectionist models mark a significant advance in linking cognitive models to issues that are critical to our under-standing of the nature of aphasic impairment and the mechanisms underly-ing recovery in and treatment of aphasia. Additional insights have been drawn from recent studies using distributed connectionist models, although in this area there have been fewer instances of direct modelling of patient performance. The localist connectionist models have been much more successful in that regard. Still, there are some important studies using distributed connectionist models that have captured various effects that are evidenced in aphasic language performance. These are discussed below.

## Distributed connectionist models of word processing

Distributed connectionist models of word processing are similar to localist connectionist models in that they are concerned with the dynamics of word processing and address questions about effects of stimuli characteristics, time course of processing, and other dynamic variables on word retrieval. They differ from localist connectionist models in two important ways: (1) their assumptions about how words are represented, especially the semantic representations of words, and (2) their ability to learn. There are several types of distributed connectionist models, including parallel distributed processors (McClelland & Rumelhart, 1988), attractor networks (Hinton & Shallice, 1991), oscillator models of serial order (Vousden, Brown, & Harley, 2001), and models that incorporate self-organising map networks (Kohonen, 2001). These models represent semantics as a set of semantic features that are organised in a space by the extent to which they overlap with each other. Words (phonological representations) are linked to their meanings (sets of semantic features that make up the concept denoted by a word). This aspect of their organisation is not unlike that of the interactive activation model except that the latter model has a layer of lexical nodes that interface between the semantic and phonological representations. Also, in the inter-active activation model, connections between semantic and phonological representations are not learned but rather are pre-set.

Distributed models of word processing have successfully demonstrated certain aspects of processing that are relevant to issues about diagnosis and treatment of language disorders. Plaut and Shallice's (1991) model of word reading included a semantic network that supported concrete and abstract words (with abstract words having fewer features). They were able to "lesion" this model in a way that reproduced the characteristic reading pattern in deep dyslexia, a reading disorder in which concrete words are read more accurately than abstract words and semantic errors are made in single word reading. Their modelling study is a fine example of early efforts to account for cognitive phenomena in computational models. A few years later, Plaut and Shallice (1993a) modelled another phenomenon observed in aphasia, whole-word perseverations. They were able to demonstrate an often observed aspect of perseverations, namely that they are more common when the language impairment affects semantics.

Plaut and colleagues have since produced a number of modelling studies that help to explain various phenomena that are observed in aphasia (e.g., access/refractory impairment in aphasia and "degraded-store" semantic impairments in semantic dementia, Gotts & Plaut, 2002). In our chapter on treatment of anomia, we will discuss one of Plaut's computational studies that addressed the issue of relearning in aphasia (Plaut, 1996). This study provided important insights into how learning and relearning takes place most efficiently and how stimuli in training can be organised to maximise relearning. The predictions that came out of this study were soon tested directly in the clinic (Kiran & Thompson, 2003) and proved to be right on the mark.

## CHAPTER SUMMARY

Our review of cognitive models of word retrieval indicates their usefulness in investigations of the nature of aphasia. Some models have been used directly to account for language behaviours of specific cases and others have been used to demonstrate how general effects observed in aphasia and other cognitive disorders can be represented in a model. The models of Fromkin, Garrett, Levelt, Dell, and Morton and Patterson have influenced our understanding of the stages of word retrieval in normal speech production. Moreover, they have had considerable influence on models of anomia, the breakdown of word retrieval after brain damage. These models and others (e.g., Caplan, 1992) were used by aphasiologists as frameworks to characterise possible sites of impairment leading to a breakdown in the word retrieval process. Word-processing models of the 1970s and 80s were cognitively oriented with, at most, only a metaphorical link to neurological structures. The goal was not to find out where a particular aspect of language processing occurred in the brain, but rather to define the psychological representations of language, and the sequence of stages and mental operations needed to translate non-linguistic concepts into spoken words. Although it is of obvious importance to identify the neural substrates of language, the value of the more strictly "cognitive or psycholinguistic" models is that their level of description is compatible with the needs of practitioners of aphasia therapy. This aspect makes these models especially relevant for diagnosis and treatment of anomia, as will be discussed further in subsequent chapters.

# 2   Major forms of anomia

As became evident in Chapter 1, all models of word production assume that this process entails several stages. Given this, one would expect that even word retrieval impairments come in different forms. In other words, brain lesions could lead to more or less specific disturbances of the processing chain employed in word production. These disturbances also serve as a testing ground for normal-language processing models: one can argue that a language processing model cannot be considered adequate unless it can account for both normal and impaired performance (Nickels, 1997). Specific word retrieval deficits are often viewed as local functional lesions that disturb one or several processing units in the underlying mental architecture of word production but, as discussed in Chapter 1, they are more recently viewed as general impairments of interactive localist or distributed systems as well.

For the purposes of the present chapter, we adopt the former, traditional approach and make a rough differentiation of three major types of impaired lexical retrieval. These three anomia types—semantic anomia, word form anomia, and disordered phoneme assembly—correspond to the main stages of word production in a standard logogen model shown in Figure 2.1, namely retrieval of meaning (semantics), retrieval of word form (phonological output lexicon), and programming the relevant phonological output (phonological output buffer). These anomia types also find their correspondences in more recent functional word processing models. For example, in the Levelt et al. (1999) model (see Figure 1.2) semantic anomia would roughly correspond to conceptual- and lemma-level deficits. The former level refers to semantics proper (i.e., lexical concepts) while the latter represents the syntactic descriptions of words. Word form anomia would be related to difficulties in accessing the lexeme that specifies morphological and phonological information of the to-be-produced target word. Disordered phoneme assembly would then correspond to impairments in the later processes of syllabification and phonetic encoding that are needed to create the "articulatory score" of the target word for motor output.

A differentiation between semantic vs. phonological causes of anomia is by no means a new idea (see e.g., Benson, 1979), but it was the cognitive

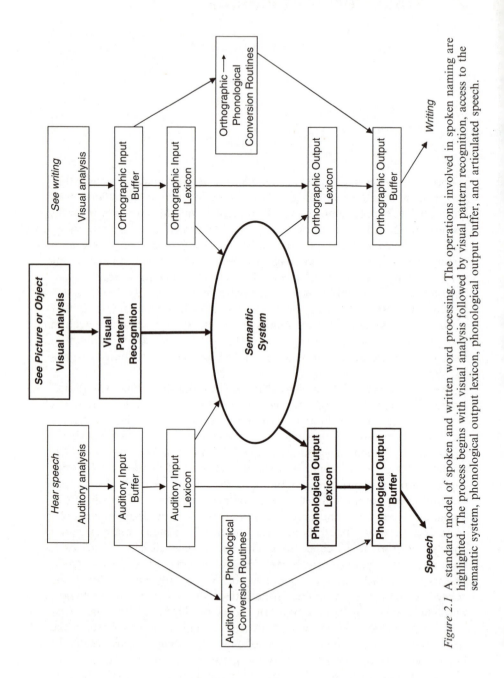

*Figure 2.1* A standard model of spoken and written word processing. The operations involved in spoken naming are highlighted. The process begins with visual analysis followed by visual pattern recognition, access to the semantic system, phonological output lexicon, phonological output buffer, and articulated speech.

neuropsychological approach that provided the theory and methods needed to detail the various forms. However, even the "pure" cases with well-circumscribed deficits described below are not totally intact in other respects, and the exact performance patterns vary from patient to patient even though they would all be under the same general heading of, say, semantic anomia. If one assumes that stages of word production interact with each other (see the interactive activation model presented in Chapter 1), it is of course questionable whether pure, isolated deficits where all symptoms relate only to a single lexical processing stage could even be theoretically possible. Here one should also take into account the nature of semantically driven word production: a functional damage to an early processing stage will have its reverberations throughout the production chain. As aphasic patients commonly have multiple deficits that simultaneously affect several subprocesses of naming and also other aspects of language, "pure" cases of specific anomia type remain relatively rare. These cases are nevertheless very valuable in revealing the functional components of naming, and they can also provide navigation points for hypothesis testing in clinical diagnostic work.

Naming can also be hampered by deficits that precede or follow the main stages of word production, as well as impairments of more general functions like maintenance of attention that underlie any conscious cognitive act. Confrontation naming can become impaired due to primary sensory or higher-level agnostic deficits in a single input modality (e.g., "optic aphasia", "tactile aphasia"), which lead to difficulties in meaning retrieval. On the other hand, peripheral problems (e.g., dysarthria, paralysis) can hamper word production in an output modality. However, here we focus on impairments in the central stages of word production. For a detailed recent review on visual object recognition and visual agnosia, the reader is referred to Farah (2004).

Detailed case studies of anomic patients have shown that the deficits may be limited to more or less specific semantic-syntactic categories. These categories include living vs. non-living things, different parts of speech, and different morphological operations (inflection, derivation, compounding). As the possible explanations for category-specific disorders encompass both semantic and post-semantic deficits, we will discuss these disorders in a separate section at the end of this chapter.

## SEMANTIC ANOMIA

Given that the overall functional architecture of naming entails major, functionally separable stages (meaning retrieval, word form retrieval, and phoneme assembly), it should be possible to identify patients whose word-finding deficits are based on an impairment of the semantic system. Assuming that the semantic representations used in word production are the same ones that are activated while identifying objects, a central semantically based naming impairment should be accompanied by comprehension difficulties with the same items that the patient finds hard to name. Moreover, these comprehension and production difficulties should be multimodal, i.e., affecting visual, auditory, and tactile object recognition, as well as production of both oral and written word responses and relevant gestures.

These predictions apply only to tasks that require access to semantics in order to retrieve a word. Some tasks such as repetition and oral reading can be achieved without accessing semantics. For example, preservation of sublexical grapheme-to-phoneme conversion (indicated by the patient's ability to read aloud pseudowords) would help the semantically impaired patient to avoid producing semantic errors in oral reading. On the other hand, in naming of familiar pictures there is no convincing evidence for the existence of a processing route that would bypass semantics. Thus, depending on the functionality of the sublexical processing mechanisms such as grapheme-to-phoneme conversion, a semantically impaired patient would show different rates of semantic errors across tasks and modalities (see Alario, Schiller, Domoto-Reilly, & Caramazza, 2003, for a recent analysis).

The term "semantic system" is used here rather loosely, as the nature of meaning representation is a matter of dispute. Some researchers have postulated separate conceptual and lexical-semantic levels in word production (e.g., Levelt, 1989; Butterworth, 1992) while others have put forth a single amodal central system (e.g., Caramazza, Hillis, Rapp, & Romani, 1990). Still others have argued for a multicomponent semantic system that separates visual and verbal semantics (Paivio, 1991) or is organised along the different sensory-functional domains (Warrington & Shallice, 1984). The controversy between domain-specific theories and those postulating a separate amodal semantic system reflects an age-old dispute in neuropsychology as to whether or not mental representations subserving recognition are separate from those subserving meaning. According to domain-specific theories, meaning emerges from learned multimodal (both perceptual and verbal) associations related to an object. The representations underlying this associative network are the same that subserve object recognition. In contrast, proponents of an amodal semantic system would argue that, for example, in visual object naming, access to meaning is preceded by object recognition that is based on separate structural representations of the object.

As regards aphasia, it is intriguing that there are patients whose verbal comprehension is impaired even though they can demonstrate understanding of concepts nonverbally. This performance dissociation could be taken as evidence for a distinction between conceptual and word-specific semantic representations. For example, Nickels and Howard (1994) studied categorisation performance with the verbal (word) and nonverbal (picture) versions of the Pyramids and Palm Trees task in a group of eight people with aphasia. They all produced semantic naming errors and evidenced word comprehension impairment on the verbal version of the Pyramids and Palm Trees test, but five of the eight patients also performed poorly on the nonverbal version. However, this difference could also reflect severity of the deficit in a single semantic system. The pictorial version may be easier as it provides rich information on the perceptual attributes of the object and thus a privileged access to semantics (Caramazza et al., 1990). A mild semantic deficit would thus be reflected as impaired performance on the verbal task, while impairment on both test versions would indicate a more severe semantic deficit. It has also been proposed recently that performance on semantic judgement tasks like the Pyramid and Palm Trees test is affected by limitations of short-term memory load of some aphasic individuals performing the test (Martin, 2005). This hypothesis claims that the difficulty lies in maintaining activation of words, images, and their corresponding semantic concepts in short-term memory long enough to compare concepts and make judgements of similarity. Milder impairments would affect short-term maintenance of words and their links to concepts, but not pictures and their links to concepts. More severe impairments would affect maintenance of both words and pictures and their links to conceptual representations.

The issue of test difficulty should be kept in mind while interpreting other test performances, too. For example, picture naming requires the retrieval of the specific meaning and form of a lexical item, but (depending on the exact task) picture categorisation could be accomplished with access to less precise semantic information such as superordinate category knowledge that may still be available to the patient.

Another issue that needs to be considered in understanding semantic anomia is whether such deficits reflect permanent erasure of conceptual-semantic representations from long-term memory or impaired access to still existing conceptual-semantic representations. The consensus is that either type of impairment can occur. Progressive neurological diseases can lead to what appears to be loss of actual representations (as in semantic dementia) or progressively impaired access to semantic or phonological representations of words (progressive fluent aphasia or progressive nonfluent aphasia). Aphasias associated with stroke or other nonprogressive neural impairment are more often thought to result in impaired access to intact representations but this issue remains open to investigation.

Warrington and Shallice (1979) proposed several diagnostic criteria for behavioural characteristics differentiating between impaired access and impaired semantic representations. Among others, a storage deficit would be reflected in consistency of item-specific performance, sensitivity to item frequency but not to presentation rate or priming, and hierarchical breakdown where superordinate knowledge is better preserved. Thus a damaged semantic storage is suspected if the patient demonstrates a consistent lack of knowledge of a specific concept across tasks, experimental setups, and modalities. This is difficult to show, of course, as the case rests on negative evidence, and performance variability is a common feature in brain-damaged patients. Rapp and Caramazza (1993) questioned the usefulness of this distinction because the definitions of access and storage deficits are not clear and some patients seem to exhibit features of both. Nonetheless, research on this issue continues, with a current interest in the so-called "refractory deficit" as an indicator of a semantic access problem. In the "refractory deficit", patients' performance on a semantic test such as word–picture matching is strongly influenced by temporal-contextual factors: stimulus presentation rate, repetition, or semantic relatedness (Warrington & Cipolotti, 1996). In contrast, patients with a storage deficit should not exhibit such performance features.

As may be apparent from our discussion thus far, semantic anomia may be broken down into several types, depending on whether access to and from semantic concepts is disrupted or the representations themselves are impaired. To exemplify the characteristics of semantic anomia and the means used to identify such patients, we will briefly summarise three cases presented in the literature. The first one, by Howard and Orchard-Lisle (1984), is an often-cited "classical" case. The second one, by Hillis, Rapp, Romani, and Caramazza (1990), presents a meticulous analysis of a semantically impaired aphasic patient, employing the same sets of stimuli with a number of input/output tasks. While the first two cases are patients suffering from aphasia as a result of a cerebrovascular accident (CVA), our third example is a carefully studied semantic dementia case with follow-up (Murre, Graham, & Hodges, 2001).

Howard and Orchard-Lisle (1984) reported a case study of JCU, a very severely aphasic patient with an extensive fronto-temporo-parietal haemor-rhagic lesion in the left hemisphere and a small one in the right. Spontaneous speech was limited to "yes" and "no" responses as well as to a small repertoire of recurrent utterances such as "I understand". The patient produced spontaneously only 5/30 correct responses on the Western Aphasia Battery (WAB) naming part. It appears that she mainly remained silent for the rest of the items. Given her severe language deficit, JCU was unusually sensitive to phonological cueing: she obtained 18 more correct responses on the WAB naming part when given a phonological cue. A separate test indicated that effectiveness of a phonological cue was positively correlated with target word frequency. When explored in more detail, it became evident that her sensitivity to phonological cueing extended even to false cues, particularly if they were semantically related to the target (e.g., /t/ for a picture of a lion). Besides semantic errors, cueing also elicited some unrelated word errors and neologisms. While JCU rejected most of the unrelated word errors, she accepted most of her semantic errors and also neologisms. With regard to comprehension, she had particular difficulty in rejecting category member names on an auditory word–picture matching task. No item-specific correspondences between this comprehension task and cued naming were observed. Nonverbal odd-one-out picture tasks provided counterintuitive results, as JCU performed within normal limits on the more difficult task calling for associative knowledge (e.g., *eskimo – igloo, house*) while being impaired on the easier task tapping superordinate category knowledge (e.g., *elephant – giraffe, dog*). Output phonology as measured by single word repetition was more or less preserved. All in all, semantic errors in comprehension (word–picture matching) and cued naming, as well as difficulties in recognising these as erroneous responses, suggested that JCU suffered from a semantic deficit. Howard and Orchard-Lisle (1984) hypothesised that JCU was using incomplete semantic representations in naming and word comprehension tasks. However, the lack of item specificity in JCU's semantic errors would indicate an access rather than storage deficit. Finally, the underlying mechanisms of her occasional neologistic responses in cued naming remained open.

Patient KE, reported by Hillis et al. (1990), was an aphasic man who had suffered an extensive fronto-parietal brain infarction 6 months before the initiation of the study. His spontaneous speech output was very nonfluent, consisting mainly of isolated nouns, and including semantic errors and overlearned phrases. Repetition of single words and nonwords was quite well preserved, with few phonological paraphasias that were often self-corrected. In speech therapy sessions, it was observed that KE made similar semantic errors in different tasks, and this prompted Hillis et al. (1990) to have a close look at his lexical processing. As the patient's sublexical reading and spelling mechanisms were severely impaired, it was assumed that his lexical performance patterns reflected the function of input and output lexicons and the semantic system. To ensure comparability across tasks, Hillis et al. were especially careful to employ the same items on all tasks used to examine KE's lexical performance. Naming performance and occurrence of semantic errors were evaluated in a number of presentation formats (word, picture, palpable object), input modalities (visual, tactile, auditory), and response types (naming, reading aloud, writing, matching words and pictures, gesturing, drawing). Similar rates of semantic errors were observed in all these tasks, accounting for as much as 21–45% of the total number of responses in each task. KE's semantic errors were mostly substitutions of one category exemplar for another (e.g., jacket → pants). Concreteness but not frequency was related to the probability that KE would make a semantic error. Furthermore, the item-specific probability for a semantic error was similar across the tasks, and performance accuracy did not differ on within-task (test-retest) vs. between-task comparisons.

These findings led Hillis et al. (1990) to conclude that KE suffered from damage to a single modality-independent semantic system that represents the perceptual, functional, and relational attributes of concepts. They hypothesised that KE had only partial semantic information available to him, either because of impoverishment of the semantic representations or because of impaired access to intact concepts. Hillis et al. (1990) do not discuss the access vs. storage deficit issue in any detail, but the item-specific consistency of KE's semantic errors within and across tasks could point to the latter alternative. KE's somewhat better performance with pictorial than word input was explained by the privileged access hypothesis discussed above, i.e., the perceptual features inherent in pictorial input provide direct access to semantics.

Semantic dementia, a term that was first coined by Snowden, Goulding, and Neary (1989), is one of the symptomatologies that can occur in frontotemporal dementia, a lobar neurodegenerative disease (see Chapter 4). Progressive aphasia of the fluent type with semantic emptiness of spontaneous speech, impaired naming ability, and verbal as well as nonverbal comprehension difficulties characterise this progressive condition (Hodges, Patterson, Oxbury, & Funnell, 1992; Neary, 1999). At the same time, syntactic and phonological aspects of speech output, repetition, reading and writing of orthographically regular words, nonverbal cognitive functions, and problem-solving skills can be initially remarkably spared. Also episodic memory is clearly better than in the most common form of dementia, i.e., Alzheimer's dementia.

A representative case of semantic dementia with a follow-up is described in Murre et al. (2001). Patient AM, a 64-year-old well-educated man with a work history as a works manager in an international company, was referred to clinical examination due to progressive word-finding and comprehension difficulties. Structural MRI revealed temporal atrophy particularly in the left hemisphere. Upon examination, his speech was fluent with preserved phonology and syntax but semantically empty. What follows is a part of the conversational speech sample provided by Murre et al. (2001, p. 651) that illustrates the severe word-finding deficit in his verbal output:

> *Examiner*: "Can you remember April last year?"
> *AM*: "April last year, that was the first time, and eh, on the Monday, for example, they were checking all my whatsit, and that was the first time, when my brain was, eh, shown, you know, you know that bar of the brain (*indicates left*), not the, the other one was okay, but that was lousy, so they did that and then doing everything like that, like this and probably a bit better than I am just now (*indicates scanning by moving his hands over his head*)".

The picture-naming ability of AM was severely compromised: he scored only 3/48 on a set of high-frequency familiar items (Knott, Patterson, & Hodges, 1997). Omission was the most typical response category, but occasionally he produced short circumlocutory responses. Most of the circumlocutions were very vague. Semantic naming errors were rare. No phonological paraphasias were observed in naming. AM's performance on a word–picture matching task employing the same items was impaired relative to normals' performance. The same was true for other word–

picture matching tests, where he also showed a frequency effect with better comprehension of high-frequency items. AM's errors on these tasks were overwhelmingly semantic, i.e., he selected semantic rather than phonological or visual distractors. He was also impaired on a semantic feature questionnaire based on simple yes/no questions (e.g., "Does an ostrich have a long neck?"). The nonverbal version of the Pyramids and Palm Trees test that taps conceptual knowledge was also difficult for him. Repetition of single words and nonwords was within normal limits for items up to three syllables in length, but there was some tendency for phonological errors in longer low-frequency words and in nonwords. Over the approximately 2-year follow-up, his performance on these two comprehension tasks dropped dramatically and reached chance levels. As a further evidence on the pro-grediating conceptual-level impairment, AM showed difficulties in selecting and using everyday items in an adequate fashion (e.g., placing a closed umbrella horizontally over the head in a rain storm; putting orange juice into his lasagne).

These three cases exemplify patterns of deficit that can all be labelled as semantic anomia. The performance features these patients shared were anomia coupled with comprehension difficulties and relatively preserved phonological abilities at a single word level. At the same time, all of them evidenced a "non-semantic" performance feature: JCU's naming as well as KE's and AM's word repetition showed occasional phonological paraphasias. On the assumption that their deficit was limited to the semantic level, this would support the idea of an interactive word production system where the integrity of semantics is of significance for the maintenance of corresponding word strings for production (see e.g., Martin & Saffran, 1997; Knott et al., 1997). Several differences in the patients' performance were evident as well. Two of them produced high rates of semantic errors in spontaneous (KE) or cued (JCU) naming, while the third one (AM) gave mostly "don't know" responses in spontaneous naming. However, we do not know if AM would have been sensitive to phonemic cues, as was JCE. Other differences are evident as well: KE showed a remarkable item-specific consistency in his semantic errors, while JCU reportedly lacked such a feature. KE's naming performance was sensitive to concreteness while word frequency affected JCU's cued naming and AM's word comprehension. Moreover, AM was the only one whose semantic deficits gradually extended to everyday object use as well.

These three cases are not directly comparable due to differences in task designs and items, but their diverging performance profiles nevertheless indicate considerable variability in the symptomatology of semantic anomia. We are not yet in a position to give a full theoretical account of this variability. For example, in the absence of other word substitution errors, the high rates of semantic errors in JCU and KE cannot be simulated by the interactive activation model of word production (Dell et al., 1997) described in Chapter 1. This is because in the IA model, semantic errors stem from dysfunctional mappings between semantic features and lexical nodes, leading simultaneously to formal paraphasias and unrelated word errors. In the anomia simulations with the IA model, the semantic representations themselves are assumed to be intact—an assumption that apparently does not hold for JCU and KE. It is evident that further empirical and theoretical work is needed to better understand the inner structure and dynamics of the semantic system and its disorders. For the time being, case descriptions such as those described above give guidelines in exploring the functionality of the semantic system in an anomic patient.

## PHONOLOGICAL ANOMIAS

### Impairment in access to output lexicons from the lexical-semantic system

In the general outline of the naming process that we follow in the present chapter, the first possible post-semantic locus of dysfunction leading to anomia would be the connections between semantics and output lexicons. Here one would expect anomia coupled with intact comprehension as well as normal performance on word production tasks that can be performed without semantic support, such as repetition and oral reading.

Perhaps the most clear-cut cases of such a deficit are provided by Lambon Ralph, Sage, and Roberts (2000). They reported two anomic traumatic head-injury patients, GM and JS. The anomic difficulties of GM were milder than those of JS: their scores on the Boston Naming Test were 31/60 and 16/60, respectively (there is no report on written naming for either patient). GM produced mainly circumlocutions that were quite accurate at least for more familiar items: PYRAMID → "the burial chamber for Egyptian kings . . . it's got three 'beats'". In addition, he produced occasional semantic errors that he always spontaneously rejected. As in the example above, GM also evidenced "tip-of-the-tongue" behaviour in that he was quite accurate in giving the syllable length of the target and identifying it as a compound word or not. For JS, omissions were the most common naming error type, and circumlocutions appeared only on request. He did also produce and spontaneously reject occasional semantic naming errors. Neither patient produced any phonological paraphasias in speech output tasks. Both GM and JS evidenced intact object recognition, and performed within normal range on an extensive battery of word comprehension and semantic-associative tasks (with the single exception of the PALPA Word Semantic Association task where GM had problems with the abstract items). Word and nonword repetitition and reading performances were also within normal limits, indicating intact phonological performance that was included in our criteria for a functional dissociation between meaning and form.

With regard to cueing, word-initial phonemic cues helped to bring GM's naming to normal levels. For JS, the beneficial effects of phonemic cueing were more modest. Phonemic miscueing by providing the first phoneme of a close semantic distractor (e.g., giving /v/ as a cue for the picture of a guitar) impaired JS's picture-naming performance and led to an increase of semantic errors that he immediately rejected. Besides phonemic miscueing, Lambon Ralph et al. (2000) also explored other ways to temporarily increase the patients' error rates. Presenting a semantically related word prior to the target picture, as well as blocking pictures category-wise, impaired GM's naming but did not have a statistically reliable effect on the naming performance of JS.

These data paint a picture of patients who have access to the meaning of the to-be-named object and, for GM, even partial phonological (and syllable) information about the corresponding word form. At the same time, they appear to be plagued by a selection problem where semantically close alternatives are competing for output. As discussed by Lambon Ralph et al. (2000), this pattern is best compatible with cascading or interactive activation models of lexical retrieval with temporally overlapping semantic and phonological processes (see Chapter 1 for a detailed discussion of the interactive activation models). In other words, in normal naming, semantic and phonological levels are involved in interplay that at a very fast pass narrows down retrieval to a single lexical candidate. If this interplay is disturbed by partial disconnection between semantics and output phonology, it becomes difficult to resolve the lexical-semantic competition for output that always takes place even in the naming of single isolated items.

One should note that other cases with similar patterns of naming deficit have been reported, but either their comprehension skills have not been extensively explored or, like the often-cited case EST published by Kay and Ellis (1987), the patients do not have intact phonological skills as measured by repetition or oral reading. Note also that in contrast to the previously described two patients, EST's naming errors were predominantly phonological paraphasias that were close to the target word he tried to produce. Phonological paraphasias were by far the most common error type in the semantically intact anomic patient reported by Bachoud-Lévi and Dupoux (2003). Similarly to EST, their patient also suffered from oral repetition impairment.

Lambon Ralph et al. (2000) do not report on their patients' written naming skills but Caramazza and Hillis (1990) analysed two anomic patients who evidenced a deficit in spoken naming only. Their lexical comprehension was reportedly preserved, and both produced mainly semantic errors as did GM and JS. A similar theoretical account as above could be applied to the Caramazza and Hillis (1990) patients, with the addition that such a deficit can be limited to spoken output only. This in turn means that the traditionally held idea of phonological mediation in writing, i.e., that orthographic output forms of words must be accessed via the phonological output system, would have to be abandoned. In support of this idea of autonomous orthographic and phonological output systems, Hillis, Rapp and Caramazza (1999) reported a case that had specific word production impairment affecting only written naming. Again, the predominant error type was a semantic substitution, like EAGLE → owl (so-called "deep dysgraphia"). The patient's oral picture naming of the same set of items was intact, and word–picture matching tasks with both written and spoken words were performed without errors. The impairment in this direction alone could be interpreted as a reflection of task difficulty. Writing has to have something extra when compared with speaking, be it sound–letter conversion or the longer time it takes to write, meaning that one has to hold onto output representations longer. Together with the dissociations of GM and JS, however, these data suggest autonomy of spoken and written output.

### Disordered phoneme assembly

A complex, hierarchically organised set of processes underlies speech motor output. The hypothesised processes are presented in detail in the lexical access theory by Levelt et al. (1999). In brief, their model assumes that the (morpheme-based) phonological code of the target word is "spelled out" as an ordered set of phonological segments that are incrementally strung together to form syllables. It should be noted that syllabification is created on-line as it is affected by the word's context. Syllables are then input to phonetic encoding where overlearned syllabic gestures are selected from a "mental syllabary" for motor execution. A smooth concatenation of the retrieved syllabic gestures is also needed. The final output of the word production system is the "articulatory score" for the phonological form of the target word that is then executed by the speech motor system.

Even a very brief description such as the one above indicates that our title, disordered phoneme assembly, does not do justice to the multifaceted nature of this cognitive-motor act, but rather serves as shorthand for describing various disturbances that fall under this domain. These processes could also be termed "post-lexical", with the reservation that interactions between lexical and segmental-phonological processes would in fact make these systems work as a well-orchestrated functional whole (e.g., Blanken, 1998). Although we are still short of fully understanding the mechanisms of phoneme assembly deficits, a commonly employed dichotomy is to categorise post-lexical word production deficits into phonemic and phonetic disorders. The former category is more or less synonymous to our title, disordered phoneme assembly, where substitutions, additions, exchanges, and omissions of phonemes or phoneme combinations appear in output. The latter refers to lower-level deficits in the articulatory planning of speech sound sequences that can also lead to distorted phonemes. This is nevertheless different from dysarthrias where the motor implementation of speech is disordered, leading to specific and quite consistent articulation problems irrespective of psycholinguistic factors such as word frequency and length, or the type of spoken word production task used. In this section, we will mainly discuss phonemic and not phonetic deficits, but will shortly comment on apraxia of speech that falls under the category of phonetic impairments.

Conduction aphasia is the clinical aphasic syndrome that has been related specifically to phoneme assembly deficits. It is a form of fluent aphasia where language comprehension is quite well preserved but the otherwise well-articulated speech output is characterised by numerous phonological paraphasias. These errors can be quite close to the target, and the patient may sometimes produce a sequence of errors when struggling to find the correct phonological form. Such instances suggest that the patient was able to retrieve the correct lexical-phonological representation but failed with prearticulatory planning (Kohn, 1984). Even though the term "conduction" refers to these patients' disproportionate difficulties in repetition when compared to fluency of output and comprehension skills, phonological errors appear in all speech output tasks. Conduction aphasics are typically very sensitive to word length, with longer words causing more production problems. A typical patient is reported in the case series of Laine, Kujala, Niemi, and Uusipaikka (1992), who explored the nature of oral naming deficits in 10 people with aphasia that represented the classical aphasia syndromes. C2, a 64-year-old CVA patient with the classical features of conduction aphasia, suffered from mild anomia, with 44/60 correct on the Boston Naming test and below normal performance on a 106-picture naming task and on a synonym production task. Over half of his naming errors were phonological errors. Only a single semantic naming error was noted, and even that particular error was coupled with correct super-ordinate category and semantic feature choice that was probed in con-junction with each error on the 106-picture naming task. His performance was flawless on a semantically based picture classification task, a word–picture matching task, and a purely visual odd-one-out semantic-associative task. Estimated familiarity of target pictures did not affect his naming success. Repeating the names of the items on the 106-picture naming task elicited a very similar error pattern as in naming, with over half of the errors being phonological. Laine et al. (1992) concluded that the patient's performance pattern was compatible with a phoneme assembly deficit that affects all phonological output tasks (here spontaneous speech, oral naming, and word repetition).

A recent case report by Larner et al. (2004) provides a more detailed view on a patient with a selective phoneme assembly deficit. This 55-year-old patient was referred for detailed neurological examination due to gradually progressive difficulties with speech output that the patient herself described as "sounding odd, as though I'm drunk", without suffering from slurred speech or word-finding deficits. She noted a loss of automaticity in speech output and felt that she had to concentrate on each word to avoid errors. Neurological examination revealed slowed spontaneous speech output with phoneme-level errors, and no signs of aphasia, dysarthria, or orofacial dyspraxia. Based on repeated structural brain imaging and biopsy, the patient was diagnosed as having a calcified haematoma affecting mainly the left precentral gyrus region.

Larner et al. (2004) report data from a 4-year follow-up during which the patient's verbal and nonverbal performance pattern was constant. For the whole follow-up period, the patient's overall neuropsychological status was more or less intact, with normal performance, for example in verbal and nonverbal memory and executive tasks. With regard to language functions, speech perception as measured by phoneme discrimination of words and nonwords was within normal limits. Spontaneous speech was slow, often syllable paced, with a tendency to make multiple attempts until coming up with the correct form of a word. Repetition of single phonemes was only mildly impaired while oral reading of letters posed more difficulties. In word repetition, multiple attempts were common. Accordingly, scoring by first attempt led to a 40% error rate in word repetition. Errors were either phonological paraphasias, abnormally slow syllable-by-syllable productions with stress on each syllable, or false starts. Her phonological paraphasias were mainly phoneme substitutions (e.g., democracy → temokracy, skimp → stimp, stream → strean) and additions; exchanges or omissions were more rare. Phoneme omissions occupied only middle and final positions in words. Repetition performance showed no word frequency effect but a strong sensitivity to word length, with more errors on multisyllabic words. Phoneme substitutions and additions were common in picture naming, but when one applied more lenient criteria for scoring (accepting responses with a single phoneme error), the patient's oral picture naming was in fact normal. Oral reading of words posed problems to the patient, too. In reading several attempts at the target (e.g., heroic → heroit, heroit, heroit, heroic) were noted, but the most prominent abnormality was particularly slow syllable-by-syllable reading of multisyllabic words. Spelling skills were intact. An overall analysis indicated that the proportion of phonological errors was similar in repetition, oral picture naming, and oral reading. With regard to phoneme omissions, both repetition and oral reading data indicated that they involved non-initial word positions.

The case reported by Larner et al. (2004) provides further support to the claim that brain damage can selectively impair a processing stage where the phoneme sequence of the to-be-produced word is being programmed. Lack of anomia, close target–error correspondence, and repeated attempts to correct her own phonological errors suggest that the patient had accessed the correct word form but failed with the assembly of its phonemes. If we hypothesise the action of this system as a memory buffer that keeps a phoneme string active while it is being transformed into articulatory gestures, sensitivity to word length could be interpreted as an overload in a damaged short-term memory store. The uneven clustering of phoneme omissions within words suggests that word-initial position has a special role in the phonemic output buffer. Phonological output buffer deficits have also been ascribed to other patients with solely phonological errors in speech production tasks (e.g., patient MM in Romani, Olson, Semenza, & Granà, 2002). In earlier theoretically driven analyses, Buckingham (1986) and Pate et al. (1987) examined the sources of phonological errors in conduction aphasia in the context of Garrett's model of normal language production (see Chapter 1). Within this model, they considered the positional level and later stages as the source of the patient's phonological output deficit.

Phonetic disintegration and motor speech disorders fall outside the scope of our review, and we note only briefly on the concept of apraxia of speech that has created considerable controversy in aphasia literature (for reviews see Ballard, Granier, & Robin, 2000; Buckingham, 1998; McNeil, Robin, & Schmidt, 1997). It involves a variety of speech abnormalities, including inconsistency in articulatory movements, slowed rate of speaking with accompanying lengthening in segments and segmental transitions, deviant stress patterns, voicing errors, and reduced coarticulation. One interpretation of these deficits, inspired by work on syllabic frequency effects on normals' naming performance (Levelt & Wheeldon, 1994), is that they represent impaired access to verbal-motor gestural automatisms that are normally employed in speech output (Whiteside & Varley, 1998). This would leave the patient with heavy on-line computation demands (in normal speech, the output is 10-15 syllables per second), and lead to the use of various compensatory strategies like slowing down of speech. Another interpretation, based on research on nonspeech actions in apraxia of speech, argues that it is a motor control disorder that is not specific to speech (Ballard et al., 2000).

## CATEGORY-SPECIFIC SEMANTIC-SYNTACTIC IMPAIRMENTS

Since the publication of seminal papers on category-specific naming impairments mainly by Elizabeth Warrington and her colleagues in the 1970s and early 1980s (Baxter & Warrington, 1985; McCarthy & Warrington, 1985, 1988; McKenna & Warrington, 1978; Warrington, 1975, 1981; Warrington & Shallice, 1984), these phenomena have stirred intense interest in neuropsychology and cognitive neuroscience. Warrington and colleagues reported patients with dissociations in naming and comprehension of abstract vs. concrete entities, proper vs. common names, animate vs. inanimate objects, and nouns vs. verbs, including modality-specific category-specific impairment. Since category-specific naming impairments were first identified, over

100 such cases of neurological patients with semantically relevant dissociations have been reported.

Before outlining the most prominent performance patterns that have emerged from this body of data and discussing their theoretical import, a few words on methodological issues are in order. As with most clinical case studies with performance dissociations, the category-related differences are relative rather than absolute. Moreover, it is not easy to draw definite general conclusions on the basis of existing data because studies vary with respect to tasks employed, control over test materials, use of normative data, and detail in reporting. For example, early reports of category-specific dissociations between living and non-living entities had not controlled for potentially important factors like familiarity and visual complexity of the pictorial stimuli used. However, later and better-controlled studies have been able to confirm that these dissociations are indeed real.

To give a concrete example of a category-specific semantic deficit, we will summarise a recent case report of patient KH by Lambon Ralph, Patterson, Garrard, and Hodges (2003). The case is somewhat unusual in the sense that the patient suffers from semantic dementia where well-established category-specific dissociations are rare. As we will see, KH's case illustrates quite well several challenges that the present theoretical models of category-specific deficits are facing. KH was a 59-year-old patient whose clinical symptoms were said to correspond well to the criteria of semantic dementia described in the previous section. His performances on tasks involving nonverbal problem solving (Raven's matrices), verbal working memory (WAIS-R Digit Span), visuoconstructive processing (copy of the Rey Complex Figure), and object recognition (four subtests of the Visual Object and Space Perception Battery including object decision) indicated that these abilities were well preserved. On the nonverbal Pyramids and Palm Trees test that taps conceptual knowledge, his performance was impaired when compared to normative data. Together with a "control group" of five other semantic dementia patients, KH was subjected to naming and comprehension tasks. On a naming task that included pictures of living things and artefacts, KH named 26/32 artefacts but only 16/32 living things correctly. With regard to word–picture matching, KH got 31/32 correct on the artefacts and 20/32 on the living things, again a significant difference. As the items were not controlled for familiarity, which tends to be lower amongst living things than man-made artefacts, another set of pictures matched for familiarity, imageability, word frequency, and length was administered to the patients for naming. KH was the only one of the six patients who showed a consistent effect of semantic category, naming this time 24/30 artefacts vs. 17/30 living things correctly. To explore the patients' naming and word–picture matching further, Lambon Ralph et al. (2003) administered the Snodgrass and Vanderwart (1980) set of 260 pictures to the patients both in a naming and in an auditory word–picture matching format. They then explored the determinants of success in test performance in each individual through logistic regression analyses where eight psycholinguistic factors served as independent variables: semantic category (artefact vs. living), visual complexity, imageability, frequency, familiarity, age of acquisition, name agreement, and length in phonemes. For KH, semantic category was the only factor that contributed significantly to success both in naming and in word–picture matching with the Snodgrass–Vanderwart picture set.

All in all, KH shows a systematically worse naming and comprehension performance with living entities than with artefacts, which is by far the most commonly observed pattern of category-specific impairment. How would the present models on category-specific deficits account for this? In their highly influential paper reporting a similar dissociation, Warrington and Shallice (1984) suggested that damage differentially affecting sensory vs. functional-associative semantic features that underlie concepts could give rise to such dissociation. The Sensory-Functional theory assumes that distinctions between living things are based heavily on sensory features (consider, for example, features that distinguish a tiger from a lion), but for man-made objects, functional features are relatively more important. This is consistent with the performance of one of Warrington and Shallice's (1984) patients who was also impaired on certain non-living categories like musical instruments, precious stones, and types of cloth, for which perceptual features appear to be particularly important. According to the Sensory-Functional theory, KH's deficit would thus be due to damage that particularly affects the sensory semantic features stored in the brain. To test this possibility, Lambon Ralph et al. (2003) explored their patients' naming and picture choices in response to spoken definitions that emphasised either sensory or functional-associative features of the target. KH was significantly worse in finding a name to sensory than functional definitions, but so were three other patients who did not exhibit living–nonliving dissociation. When asked to give descriptions to stimulus words, KH as well as the other patients produced fewer features overall when compared to a normal control group, with the lowest relative rate being for sensory features (see also Lambon Ralph, Graham, Patterson, & Hodges, 1999). Again, this is a problematic finding for the Sensory-Functional theory which predicts that especially KH should have been poor in producing sensory features in his responses. According to a recent critical review of 79 cases reporting dissociations within or between the biological and man-made (artefact) categories (Capitani, Laiacona, Mahon, & Caramazza, 2003), category-specific dissociations do not show any systematic relationship to difficulties with sensory vs. functional-associative features.

An alternative theoretical account suggests that category-specific effects reflect differences in intercorrelations of semantic features. With regard to the living–nonliving distinction, two opposing computational accounts have been presented. According to Gonnerman, Andersen, Devlin, Kempler, and Seidenberg (1997), living things have more intercorrelated features than artefacts, resulting in better initial resistance to brain damage. However, when a critical level of damage severity is reached, this same property produces the opposite dissociation as semantic knowledge for living things collapses. Semantic knowledge is still partly available for the artefacts that show a linear trend of impairment throughout the severity continuum. More recently, Tyler, Moss, Durrant-Peatfield, and Levy (2000) put forth a different computational account, according to which the intercorrelated features of living things are shared features (e.g., has eyes, sees) that do not specify a single category member. In contrast, artefacts would have highly intercorrelated function–form feature clusters (e.g., saw, blade, cutting) that define a concept. In effect, the predicted dissociations along the severity continuum would be opposite to those of Gonnerman et al. (1997), with artefacts showing initial resistance to damage as compared to living things but then collapsing in the face of a more severe dysfunction. Returning to KH's case, these accounts are not supported as, in terms of overall severity of semantic deficit, he fell at the middle of the sample, and neither the milder nor the more severe cases showed reliable living–nonliving dissociations in any direction. Also, a large-scale study of dementia patients (Garrard, Patterson, Watson, & Hodges, 1998) failed to verify a link between severity and direction of living–nonliving dissociation.

As a third account, Caramazza and Shelton (1998) argued that certain semantic categories have genetic underpinnings and cannot be reduced to differences in feature constellations, as suggested by the models that we have just reviewed. According to their domain-specific knowledge model, evolutionary pressures for survival have led to encoding of certain basic categories in the human brain. These categories are animals and plant life, and by contrast, artefacts. In support of their model, Caramazza and Shelton cite studies indicating dissociations within the category of living things: animals can be impaired or spared independently of fruits, vegetables, and plants. The category of fruits and vegetables can also be selectively damaged. Additionally, as discussed above, the evidence for the role of sensory and functional-associative features in category-specific deficits is inconsistent. Their model fits to KH's performance pattern, but it comes close to re-labelling his deficit, as there is nothing in terms of his structural brain damage or other test performances that would explain why he is the only one of the six patients who shows a consistent category-specific deficit. Caramazza and Shelton (1998) link their genetically rooted semantic categories to the functions of the limbic system, but KH's pattern of temporal lobe atrophy was not unique in the patient group.

Finally, Lambon Ralph et al. (2003) discuss the possibility that KH's category-specific impairment is somehow related to premorbid individual differences. Gender-related semantic category differences have been reported in normals, with females being better at naming living things while males are better on nonliving things (e.g., McKenna & Parry, 1994). Also, it has been noted that to date all reported patients having greater difficulty with plant life (fruits and vegetables) than animal categories have been males (Capitani et al., 2003). However, a possible gender effect in KH's case remains speculative, as there is no anamnestic information that would indicate that his premorbid knowledge of living things would have been unusually weak.

Through the case report by Lambon Ralph et al. (2003) we have reviewed major current theoretical models on category-specific deficits. This review indicates that none of these models is problem free. Nevertheless, the overall pattern of empirical findings that is emerging is as follows: the categories of animals, plant life, and artefacts can dissociate from each other. Within the category of artefacts, reliable fractionations do not exist (Capitani et al., 2003). This, together with lack of conclusive evidence for associations of specific types of semantic knowledge with category-specific impairments, is the empirical data set that a theory of semantic memory should be able to handle.

Before moving to word-class-specific impairments, we will dwell briefly on a semantic factor that is not categorical, but rather a continuum that is relevant for aphasic performance in lexical tasks. This dimension is concreteness/abstractness and it can affect lexical processing. It is closely related to the variable imageability that we will discuss in the next section in the context of noun–verb dissociations. A concreteness effect, with concrete words being significantly easier to read than abstract ones, is a well-documented feature of single word reading in deep dyslexia and is thought to reflect the semantic deficit these patients have (Coltheart, Patterson, & Marshall, 1980). However, it may also be that concrete words would show more "concept independence" and subsequently have fewer lexical competitors for output than abstract words (see Funnell, 2002). The use of picture naming to examine concreteness effects severely limits the variation one can have on this variable, but Nickels and Howard (1995) were nevertheless able to obtain significant (and partly independent) contributions of concreteness/imageability effects in some of their aphasic patients when they named pictures. However, a counterintuitive finding was published by Warrington (1975) who reported a patient showing a reversed concreteness effect, providing better definitions to abstract than to concrete words. Since that study, several patients with a reversed concreteness effect have been reported. One interpretation offered for this pattern is closely related to the Sensory-Functional theory: the reversed concreteness effect may be related to a more severe loss of sensory features that are more important for concrete than abstract concepts (Breedin, Saffran, & Coslett, 1994). However, the problem remains as to how to account for cases with presumably impaired sensory features that do not show the reversed concreteness effect.

## Word-class-specific impairments

Word class represents a basic grammatical property in language, but at the same time it has interesting parallels to semantics: for example, nouns and verbs play different roles in a sentence but their semantics are also different, with nouns referring to objects and verbs to actions. As we will see, this issue has been central to recent discussion of word-class-specific impairments.

First clinical observations on *noun–verb dissociations* date back to the middle of the 18th century (Denes & Dalla Barba, 1998; Östberg, 2003). Detailed case reports of such dissociations were not to appear until over 200 years later. While verbs could be considered as inherently more complex than nouns and thus more vulnerable to the effects of brain damage (e.g., Williams & Canter, 1987), performance dissociations in both directions have been described (for reviews, see Bird, Howard, & Franklin, 2003; Druks, 2002). Noun and verb production deficits can also appear together with a comprehension deficit affecting the same word class (for verbs: Daniele, Giustolisi, Silveri, Colosimo, & Gainotti, 1994; McCarthy & Warrington, 1985; for nouns: Daniele et al., 1994; Silveri & Di Betta, 1997) or without an apparent comprehension deficit (for verbs: Caramazza & Hillis, 1991; Silveri & Di Betta, 1997; for nouns: Miozzo, Soardi, & Cappa, 1994; Silveri & Di Betta, 1997). A word-class-specific impairment coupled with a corresponding comprehension deficit would suggest a central, semantic-syntactic deficit resembling the category-specific semantic deficits we have just reviewed, whereas a mere production deficit would indicate that the output lexicons or the incoming pathways would also represent the distinction between these two major content word categories. Further evidence for output-related word-class effects is provided by cases showing noun–verb dissociation in oral production or writing only (e.g., Caramazza & Hillis, 1991).

Nouns and verbs differ from each other syntactically, semantically, and even phonologically (Black & Chiat, 2003), and thus the underlying mechanisms of noun–verb dissociations can be quite complex and vary between patients. With regard to syntax, the commonly observed association between agrammatism and verb production impairment (e.g., Miceli, Silveri, Villa, & Caramazza, 1984) could suggest a syntactic impairment as a common denominator, but verb impairments have also been reported in aphasic patients who do not suffer from agrammatism (e.g., Daniele et al., 1994). Concerning semantics, it is worth pointing out that noun–verb production deficits have typically been studied with nouns corresponding to concrete objects and verbs corresponding to actions, enabling experimenters to employ picture-naming and picture–word matching tasks. The semantics of such selected sets of nouns and verbs would necessarily be different. Following the Sensory-Functional theory, one could thus argue that noun vs. verb impairments in single word processing tasks are related to underlying deficits in sensory vs. functional-associative features, respectively (Bird, Howard & Franklin, 2000). According to this view, noun–verb dissociations and living–nonliving dissociations (as well as abstract–concrete word dissociations) would be associated. A further point emphasised by Bird et al. (2000) is that hardly any of the previous studies on noun–verb dissociations have controlled for imageability, a dimension that reflects the overall richness of sensory features of a concept. It is unavoidable that picturable nouns and verbs that are typically used in these studies differ in their imageability, which is lower for verbs. To provide empirical support to their theorising, Bird et al. (2000) reported data from six patients with word production impairment: three were classified as "verb impaired" and the other three as "verb spared" patients (both groups had a similar degree of difficulty in naming nouns, i.e., objects). The "verb spared" patients showed more difficulty in naming living than nonliving things. Furthermore, when asked to produce definitions to living and nonliving things, a relative lack of sensory features was observed. As regards the "verb deficit" patients, controlling for imageability abolished their word-class effect, and no other relevant semantic effects were observed in this group.

Bird et al. (2000) were challenged for their semantic-conceptual account on verb vs. noun production deficits (Shapiro & Caramazza, 2001a, 2001b). Moreover, in response to the arguments on the role of imageability in noun–verb dissociations, Berndt, Haendiges, Burton, and Mitchum (2002) reported on five aphasic patients with significantly worse verb than noun production in picture naming. While imageability of the pictured action/object targets was not matched, Berndt et al. (2002) designed a spoken sentence completion task where the noun and verb targets were matched for imageability, frequency, and length. The sentence comprehension abilities of all the patients were sufficient to complete the task. In all five patients, the verb production deficit persisted even in this task. At the same time, imageability effects observed for two of the patients appeared to be unrelated to the word-class-specific effect. This study indicates that one cannot merely reduce noun–verb dissociations to an imageability effect. At the same time, there is a need for further studies on noun–verb dissociations that take into account all psycholinguistic factors currently deemed as relevant.

*Proper names* form an interesting subcategory of nouns, as they refer to unique entities. It is an everyday observation that the name is exactly the attribute of a person that is hardest to remember, and that proper name retrieval is particularly sensitive to the effects of ageing. Since the first detailed study on proper name anomia by Semenza and Zettin (1988), several case studies have reported a disproportionate impairment in the retrieval of proper names. This problem manifests itself as a severe difficulty in naming famous people and family members, while naming of various objects is significantly better. The more severe the difficulty in naming faces of familiar persons, the more probable it is that the patient has trouble with other proper name types such as the names of countries or cities as well (Hanley & Kay, 1998). Proper name anomia has been observed together with a difficulty in comprehending the same targets that the patient fails to name, a result that could suggest damage to a specialised domain in the semantic system (e.g., Miceli, Capasso, Daniele, Esposito,

Magarelli, & Tomaiuolo, 2000). However, it can also appear as a more or less output-related disorder (Harris & Kay, 1995). Proper name anomia as a phenomenon might be related to the fact that proper names are harder to recall even for normals, but there is recent evidence for a double dissociation that refutes a straightforward interpretation based on overall difficulty. Lyons, Hanley, and Kay (2002) reported a stroke patient with impairment in naming and comprehending common objects in the face of normal performance in naming familiar persons. They interpret the patient's performance pattern along the lines of the domain-specific knowledge model by Caramazza and Shelton (1998), joining with several authors who have suggested that knowledge of people should be added to the list of genetically determined semantic systems (animals and plant life vs. artefacts as a contrast) that would be subserved by dedicated neural circuits in the brain (Gentileschi, Sperber, & Spinnler, 2001; Kay & Hanley, 1999; Miceli et al., 2000; Valentine, Brennen, & Brédart, 1996).

Still another word-class-specific effect that has received attention in aphasia research is the *function word – content word* dissociation. In some anomic patients, function words are much better preserved than content words, and a simple explanation for this would be their high frequency (e.g., Ellis & Young, 1988). The opposite dissociation, specific difficulty with function words, has been observed in the context of agrammatic aphasia and deep dyslexia (e.g., Coltheart et al., 1980). Several reasons may underlie such a deficit. It may be related to syntactic problems (e.g., Druks & Froud, 2002) or to lexical-semantic deficits that impair function word processing, as these words are low on semantic content, imageability, and concreteness. Function word–content word deficits may also show complementary dissociations between oral and written output (Rapp & Caramazza, 1997), indicating a deficit downstream from central syntactic-semantic processing.

## Morphological impairments in word production

Words often consist of more than one meaning-carrying unit (morpheme). Main types of morphologically complex words include compounds (e.g., post+man), derivations (e.g., work+er), and inflections (e.g., work+s). Morphologically complex words, particularly inflections, are at the crossroads of lexicon and syntax: they signal information about the roles and relationships of lexical elements in an utterance. At issue here is the way in which multimorphemic word forms are produced. There are basically two alternatives (plus hybrid models that combine these): multimorphemic words are either assembled on-line from constituent morphemes (morphological composition), or they are stored and retrieved as full entities just like monomorphemic words (full-form retrieval). Prime candidates for morphological composition would be word forms that are most productive and semantically transparent, i.e., inflectional forms. On-line composition of such forms would save storage space, a significant issue in morphologically rich languages where multitudes of productive word forms are encountered and produced. Concerning full-form retrieval, semantically opaque (consider, e.g., the compound red+neck, the meaning of which is not the simple union of its constituents) and unproductive forms would appear to be the prime candidates. Besides opacity of meaning, phonological opacity in irregular forms like come → came instead of come+d could also prompt full-form storage at the phonological output level, rather than on-line phonological transformation.

In psycholinguistics, the role of morphology in speech production has been addressed mainly via analyses of speech errors in the selection and ordering of morphemes (see Chapter 1). Also in aphasia research, evidence for the mental organisation of morphological output has initially been derived from analyses of spontaneous speech. In neologistic jargonaphasia it is common to see nonword stems appearing with appropriate inflectional endings (Caplan, Kellar, & Locke, 1972). As regards agrammatism, Miceli, Mazzucchi, Menn, and Goodglass (1983) described two agrammatic Italian patients whose morphosyntactic problems were related to output only. One of the cases was described as more morphologically impaired, as he produced normal sentence structures but with omission of finite verb inflections and function words. At the same time, derivational forms appeared normally in speech output, suggesting dissociation between the processing of inflection and derivation that has also been reported in subsequent, more detailed case reports (e.g., Laine, Niemi, Koivuselkä-Sallinen, & Hyönä, 1995; Miceli & Caramazza, 1988). These case studies have documented substitutions of inflectional suffixes in various oral production tasks, together with more or less preserved derivational morphology. This would suggest that the linguistic distinction between derivation and inflection is psychologically real.

Aphasiological evidence for a distinction between inflection and derivation is not as clear-cut after all as it seems from a first look. Output errors dealing with derivational morphology have been reported in people with aphasia as well. Semenza, Butterworth, Panzeri, and Ferreri (1990) reported on three Italian neologistic jargonaphasic patients who came up with nonexisting forms employing both inflectional and derivational morphology (e.g., *fratellismo* "brotherness" instead of *fratellanza* "brotherhood"). Surprisingly, the majority of these errors employed derivations that were judged to be unproductive. One concern about these data is that for any single error it is difficult to rule out the possibility of a phonological error resulting in an affix-like string. Assuming that they were real affixes, why would they be the nonproductive ones? For normals, it is easier to come up with new productive than nonproductive derivational forms (Baayen, 1994). However, neologistic derivations have also been observed in such aphasic patients where the possible confound of phonological distortions can be ruled out. Laine et al. (1995) observed that their deep dyslexic and agrammatic Finnish speaker who had severe trouble in comprehending and producing inflected forms, occasionally produced non-existing stem + derivational suffix combinations as well. This patient almost never produced phonological paraphasias. Most of the derivational errors dealt with very productive derivational paradigms. This suggests that morphological composition may be employed for at least most productive derivational forms, but it remains open whether the composition process is a back-up procedure or routinely employed on-line. Laine et al. (1995) also noted that their patient's dramatic impairment with inflected words (as compared to monomorphemic and derived words) disappeared when one moved to a very high-frequency range. This suggests that very common inflected forms may enjoy full-form retrieval, pointing to the fuzziness of the boundary between inflection and derivation (see Luzzatti, Mondini, & Semenza, 2001, for similar evidence in Italian).

Within the domain of inflectional morphology, the distinction between regular and irregular English past tense forms (e.g., look – looked vs. run – ran) has received particular interest. Are irregularly inflected forms retrieved as full entities, while regularly inflected forms—possibly with the exception of high-frequent forms—would be compiled on-line (Pinker, 1998)? Ullman and his colleagues employed a simple sentence completion task to test this hypothesis with neurological patients (Ullman et al., 1997). Their results suggested a neuroanatomical differentiation in the processing of regulars vs. irregulars. Patients with predominantly anterior brain damage had more errors in producing regular than irregular verb forms. The opposite pattern (including over-regularisation errors like dig – digged) was observed for patients with predominantly posterior damage. However, the dual mechanism account has been challenged with connectionist models that are able to simulate regular–irregular dissociations within a single phonological-semantic network (Joanisse & Seidenberg, 1999). Specifically, irregulars were most sensitive to damage to semantic units (semantic-phonological links are needed to encode irregularity in the first place), whereas damage to phonological units was relatively more detrimental to regular forms, especially novel ones. Recent evidence from semantic dementia patients indicates a link between irregular past tense verb morphology deficit and semantic impairment (Patterson, Lambon Ralph, Hodges, & McClelland, 2001), but this is not a universal phenomenon (Miozzo, 2003).

Production of compound words is another source of information about morphological processes in lexical retrieval. It is not uncommon to observe aphasic naming errors on compound words that nevertheless retain the multimorphemic structure of the target word (e.g., Hittmair-Delazer, Andree, Semenza, De Bleser, & Benke, 1994). Here are some English examples of such errors: snowman → snow wheel, stopwatch → time clock, seahorse → horse something, trash can → can trash (Badecker, 2001). Such errors would suggest successful retrieval of the structural description of the compound with subsequent failure on phonological encoding. In order to study the effects of constituent frequency and semantic opacity of the compound on compound naming in aphasia, Blanken (2000) recently administered nominal compound naming tasks to altogether 40 German-speaking people with aphasia with at most mild phonological problems. Constituent frequency effects on naming success were found, especially for the first constituent. Such frequency effects suggest morpheme-based retrieval of the targets. With regard to semantic opacity, more opaque stimuli received less constituent substitutions and simplifications, suggesting an increasing use of whole-word retrieval with more opaque compounds.

## Category-specific semantic deficits limited to word production

The literature on category-specific semantic deficits also includes patients for whom the deficit is limited to word production, and a corresponding problem in comprehension is absent. Such cases include, for example, disproportionate naming difficulty for plant life (fruits and vegetables) (Hart, Berndt, & Caramazza, 1985) or for artefacts (Silveri, Gainotti, Perani, Cappelletti, Carbone, & Fazie, 1997). We have noted earlier that inherently different degrees of difficulty make comparisons between tasks like word–picture matching and naming tricky, but if these output-related category-specific effects are real, they have potentially important implications for the functional organisation of word production mechanisms beyond the central, semantic level. In theory, output lexicons could mirror the categorical organisation of the conceptual-semantic system, but one could also assume that semantic category effects are mediated by the mappings between meanings and forms. For example, in a discussion of category-specific output deficits within the context of a distributed computational model of lexical processing, Miikkulainen (1997) noted that the many-to-many mappings from semantic to phonological feature maps in such a model could be best conceived as consisting of interneurons that exhibit map-like organisation. In the proximity of the semantic map, this organisation is semantic, while at the other end it is phonological or orthographic.

## CHAPTER SUMMARY

Through a review of detailed case reports, this chapter exemplified aphasic performance patterns that can be ascribed to general and category-specific semantic deficits, difficulties in accessing output word forms, and problems in assembling the phonological string needed for articulation. With regard to general semantic deficits leading to anomia, we concluded that the performance features shared by these patients include lexical comprehension difficulties and relatively preserved phonological abilities at a single word level. A number of category-specific semantic-syntactic deficits were also described. With respect to the much-studied dissociations with the living and non-living categories, it appears that animals, plant life, and artefacts can dissociate from each other, while artefacts have not shown reliable within-category fractionations. For syntactic categories, dissociations between nouns vs. verbs, proper nouns vs. other words, and function words vs. content words have been reported, but as for the semantic dissociations, their underlying mechanisms are still unclear.

The tip-of-the-tongue phenomenon attests that the interface between semantics and phonology is a particularly vulnerable part of word production. We described representative aphasia cases whose functional impairment was located at this interface, as their lexical-semantic abilities and phonological skills were preserved but naming was impaired. These cases also exemplify the fact that one should not use a single symptom for making interpretations of the underlying deficits: it became evident that a patient may make semantic errors in naming even though there are no indications of a semantically based anomia. Rather, in patients with a semantics/phonology interface deficit, semantic naming errors appear to tell about interplay between semantics and phonology that is needed for normal lexical selection. Other cases with deficits below the semantic level have shown that the naming deficit can be limited to either spoken or written naming.

The last category of word production deficits we discussed, namely phoneme assembly disorders, covers several processing stages. In spoken word production, which we focused on, this entails syllabification, metrical encoding, and phonetic encoding. The patient suffering from a deficit at these levels may in fact not have anomia in the common sense of that term, but rather struggles with phonologically distorted outputs (more so with longer words) that can be quite close to the intended target. We can thus assume that the patient is targeting the correct word form but has problems in on-line assembly of the phonological output, a process that could also be described as a short-term buffer function. Finally, there are a variety of more peripheral speech abnormalities that we noted in passing, covered under the term apraxia of speech.

# 3    Neural basis of naming

What brain structures are critical for word production? The classical Wernicke–Lichtheim model (see Figure 1.1) gives a rather straightforward account. In any word production task, the auditory image of a word is retrieved at Wernicke's area in the left superior-posterior temporal lobe and fed to Broca's area (the posterior part of the third frontal gyrus) via a cortico-cortical pathway called the arcuate fasciculus. At Broca's area, the motor image for that word is evoked and used for guiding articulatory movements. If the word production task employed requires intentional/ conceptually driven communication (e.g., carrying a conversation or listing names of various animals on request of an examiner) rather than more automatic activity like repeating a heard word, a "concept centre" suggested by Lichtheim would take part in the process. This "center" was not localised in any specific area but was thought to be subserved by the regions outside the classical language zone. However, some early authors actually attempted to localise the "naming centre" in the posterior inferior regions of the (left) temporal lobe, following the assumption that it would serve as a convergence point for all incoming sensory information (Mills & McConnell, 1895).

In a revision of the classical Wernicke–Lichtheim model, Geschwind (1965) further assumed that the (left) angylar gyrus is a phylogenetically recent region which enables us to link word forms to concepts by serving as a polysensory convergence area. Note also that this region and surrounding temporal lobe tissue is typically, but by no means exclusively, cited as the locus of damage in the clinical syndrome of anomic aphasia (e.g., Goodglass & Kaplan, 1983). As we shall see, recent studies of lexical retrieval have challenged the classical model. The present evidence suggests a system that is distributed both functionally and anatomically, engaging areas within and outside the classical language regions. This accumulating evidence is heavily based on major developments during the last three decades in structural brain imaging (computerised tomography, CT; magnetic resonance imaging, MRI) that has enabled exact lesion localisation in brain-damaged patients, and in functional brain imaging (positron emission tomography, PET; functional magnetic resonance imaging, fMRI; magnetoencephalography,

MEG) that has given the opportunity to measure task-related local brain activity in the living brain.

## LESION STUDIES ON WORD PRODUCTION

Lesion studies are the traditional approach to the question of brain localisation of cognitive functions. Showing that lesions in area A impair lexical retrieval while lesions in area B do not, suggests (a) that the brain has developed some functional specialisation for this cognitive process, and (b) that area A is needed for lexical retrieval. This does not necessarily mean that lexical retrieval functions would "reside" in that area. It had already been emphasised by Hughlings Jackson in late 1860s that "while we may localise the damage which makes a man speechless, we do not localise language. It will reside in the whole brain (or whole body)" (Hughlings Jackson, 1867, cited in Harrington, 1987). Thus the deficient language performance of a brain-damaged patient tells primarily about the functionality of the remaining brain tissue. Nevertheless, the above-mentioned results suggest that at least one or more functional links or subprocesses necessary for intact word production are subserved by area A. In attempting to identify the subprocess(es) in question, one needs to proceed with more refined analyses of both the patients' naming performance and their lesion localisation.

It is important always to remember that human cerebral lesions are "experiments of nature" that follow physiological rather than functional divisions of the brain. Thus it may be that circumscribed lesions in, say, sub-areas A1, A2, or A3 are encountered very seldom at the clinic. Moreover, in patients with multiple brain infarcts, head trauma, cerebral tumour, or dementing illness, the localisation becomes less certain as the neural damage is more diffuse. These are some of the practical limitations of the lesion study approach. Moreover, a structural lesion seen on a CT or MRI scan does not inform us about the extent of preserved but hypometabolic and possibly malfunctioning neural tissue that typically surrounds a destroyed area.

On the behavioural side, a limitation is the "fuzziness" of patients' cognitive symptoms. In addition to naming-related subprocess(es), area A might also subserve other functions, the impairment of which could have secondary effects on naming. Moreover, the integrity of the entire cerebrum appears to be important for certain functions such as memory, attention, abstraction, and psychomotor speed. In other words, any brain lesion could induce these diffuse symptoms and, depending on the nature of the word production task employed, those effects could be reflected in lexical retrieval as well. Finally, patients with chronic aphasia may have developed compensatory strategies to overcome their word production difficulties, which could further complicate the interpretation of behavioural data. With

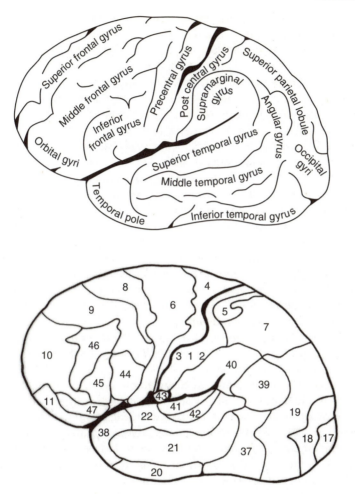

*Figure 3.1* The lateral side of the left hemisphere: main gyri (upper figure) and Brodmann's cytoarchitectonic areas (lower figure).

these cautionary notes, we will proceed to review lesion studies on naming disorders. For the convenience of the reader, we provide Figure 3.1, which depicts the lateral side of the left hemisphere with the major gyri and the Brodmann cytoarchitectonic areas (BAs).

## Lesion correlates of anomia

The assumption concerning a link between naming and temporal lobe function is an old one (for an early reference, see Mills & McConnell, 1895). Through an analysis of naming performance in World War II veterans with missile injuries to the brain, Newcombe, Oldfield, Ratcliff, and Wingfield (1971) found support for these claims. In their sample, impaired visual confrontation naming was related to left hemisphere and bilateral injury, and in the left hemisphere damaged group, all anomic patients (9 out of 57) had lesions in the left temporo-parietal region (lesion localisation without the current structural brain-imaging methods was of course crude). Further support was provided by similar lesion localisation studies (Coughlan & Warrington, 1978; McKenna & Warrington, 1980).

In the first systematic CT scan study on lesion localisation in anomia, Knopman, Selbes, Niccum, and Rubens (1984) examined and followed up 54 right-handed aphasia patients with single left hemispheric ischaemic infarcts. Large (> 60cm$^3$) infarcts always led to some impairment in visual confrontation naming. In more limited (< 60 cm$^3$) lesions with persistent anomia, two clusters of lesion sites were observed. The most severe impairments, with semantic naming errors as the most common error type, were associated with posterior superior temporal lesions, including most of the inferior parietal lobe and part of the middle temporal gyrus. The second cluster of lesions, with phonological naming errors as the main error type, included the insula and putamen, extending deep to the supramarginal gyrus. Individual variability was considerable, as neither type of lesion invariably resulted in poor naming.

Twenty years later, Damasio, Tranel, Grabowski, Adolphs, and Damasio (2004) published an extensive, mostly MRI-based lesion study on object recognition and naming deficits. Their final sample included 139 carefully screened neurological patients with unilateral brain damage mostly due to CVA. Naming and comprehension of pictures was probed by asking the patients to name objects from five different categories: famous faces, animals, tools & utensils, fruits & vegetables, and musical instruments. When failing to name the picture, the patient was prompted to provide a description of the object that was then scored for object recognition. In this way, Damasio et al. (2004) studied lesion correlates of both word retrieval (correct recognition but failed naming) and object recognition (failed recognition and naming). Naming error types were not analysed. Overall, more than half of the patients exhibited below-normal naming in at least one of the object categories. As one would expect, these were mostly left hemisphere damaged patients but about one third suffered from right hemisphere damage. Figure 3.2 shows a voxel-based rendering of lesion overlap in patients with a naming deficit. It indicates maximal lesion overlap in the classical language areas, inferior parietal and parieto-occipital regions, and in the whole anterior portion of the left temporal lobe in patients suffering from a naming deficit. In the brain-damaged patients with preserved naming ability (not shown in the figure), on the other hand, maximal lesion overlap was observed in right hemisphere regions. In contrast to the preponderance of left hemisphere lesions in naming deficits, picture recognition difficulties were associated with lesions that were more evenly distributed across the two hemispheres. We will return to the main

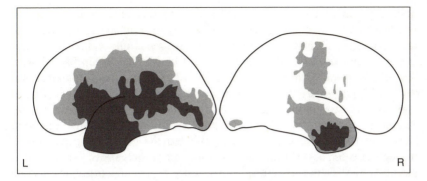

*Figure 3.2* Lesion overlap in unilaterally brain-damaged patients with a naming
deficit (*n* = 76) in at least one of five semantic categories tested. Voxel-
by-voxel analysis transformed to a normal brain template. Darker
areas show more lesion overlap in patients. Schematic drawing based
on Damasio et al. (2004).

issue of the Damasio et al. (2004) study, namely the lesion correlates of
recognition and naming of specific semantic categories, in a later section.

A comparison of the two structural brain-imaging studies of anomia that
we have just reviewed (Knopman et al., 1984, and Damasio et al., 2004)
indicates agreement that the left posterior lesion sites encompass
Wernicke's area and the adjacent inferior parietal regions. The differences
such as the role of the left anterior temporal regions in anomia most
probably relate to differences in the kinds of patients and lesion distributions included in each study, as well as to the types of semantic categories
included in the test materials.

Another approach to the study of the neural correlates of impaired
naming has been the use of direct cortical stimulation intraoperatively in
patients undergoing neurosurgery. While the awake patient is performing
a simple naming task, very weak and brief electric current is applied to
various patches in the exposed cortical tissue during the operation (often
temporal lobe regions, as temporal epilepsy patients form a significant
number of the patients undergoing such an operation). An interruption in
naming performance while stimulating a specific point indicates that the
stimulated site is related to naming function. In an overview of his extensive
work on language mapping by the cortical stimulation technique, Ojemann
(1991) notes that naming-related cortical regions these studies have identified are rather small (1–2 cm$^2$) spatially separated cortical patches. Interindividual variability is high, and naming disturbances have been observed
in stimulation sites ranging from middle temporal to superior temporal
areas, as well as from inferior to superior frontal regions in the motor,
premotor, and dorsolateral prefrontal parts of the frontal cortex. Amongst
these areas, stimulations of the middle and posterior parts of the left
temporal lobe have most consistently led to interruption in visual object

naming. Some studies using cortical stimulation have reported temporary disorders in both receptive and expressive language functions including also naming in the left inferior temporal region, sometimes called the "basal temporal language area" (Burnstine et al., 1990; Lüders et al., 1991; Lüders et al., 1986). It includes the inferior temporal gyrus, the fusiform gyrus, and the parahippocampal gyrus. When considering the interesting evidence from cortical stimulation studies, one should nevertheless keep in mind that the subjects are neurological patients with structural and functional changes in their brain that can have affected the cortical organisation of naming. Also the cortical area exposed for operation varies from patient to patient, and the clinical setting allows only for brief clinical testing like simple naming of pictures, without any further probing of the nature of the naming disturbance (semantic? phonological?) induced by stimulation of a specific site in a patient. In other words, neither these studies nor the early lesion localisation studies reviewed above can inform us about the brain–behaviour correlates of different types of anomia.

Recently a new method called transcranial magnetic stimulation (TMS) has enabled researchers to induce a local temporary disruption in cortical function in normals. The TMS apparatus delivers strong, localised magnetic pulses that can depolarise the membranes of cortical neurons underlying the coil. In other words, TMS can activate excitable cortical tissue and thus temporarily affect information processing in the brain. It has been shown that application of TMS over the left frontal areas can produce speech arrest (Pascual-Leone, Gates, & Dhuna, 1991), but there are still few systematic studies on naming with TMS. Stewart, Meyer, Frith, and Rothwell (2001) observed a temporary slowing in object naming but not in colour naming or word/nonword reading during stimulation over the posterior part of the left BA 37. This effect was interpreted as an indication of posterior BA 37 role in object recognition rather than in semantics or phonology.

To sum up, left temporal/temporo-parietal damage is most consistently associated with anomia. In addition, word-finding deficits have also been observed in many other lesion loci, including left frontal/frontobasal (Jacobs, Shuren, Bowers, & Heilman, 1995; Newcombe et al., 1971; Ojemann, 1991), left thalamic (Raymer et al., 1997a), left insular-putaminal (Knopman et al., 1984), left parietal (Newcombe et al., 1971) lesions or stimulations, and rarely even after right temporal or parietal lesions (crossed anomic aphasia; Ferro, Cantinho, Guilhermina, & Elia, 1991; Hadar, Ticehurst, & Wade, 1991; Larrabee, Holliman, Doreen, & Zachariah, 1991). The neuroanatomically widespread but mainly left-sided lesion loci related to naming difficulty were established in the recent extensive study by Damasio et al. (2004) as well. Also in the clinical syndrome of anomic aphasia, in which lexical retrieval difficulties are the most prominent feature, lesion loci vary from left angular gyrus damage to left posterior middle/inferior temporal gyrus lesions and occasionally to subcortical left frontal lesions (Goodglass, 1993). In fact, the overwhelming majority of aphasic patients, with lesions encompassing various parts of the left perisylvian region both cortically and subcortically, suffer from lexical retrieval difficulties (Goodglass, 1993).

In conclusion, these results suggest that *the functional integrity of extensive left hemisphere areas, forming a closely interconnected system, is important for successful naming.* At the same time, lesion studies indicate that some areas in this neuroanatomically distributed network (particularly the left posterior temporal and temporo-parietal regions) are more crucial than others. In addition, differences in aetiology and individual brain organisation lead to variability in brain–behaviour correlates of anomia. It is no wonder that although anomia has been considered a sensitive sign of left hemisphere damage, it is the least localising of such markers (Goodglass & Kaplan, 1983).

As we discussed in the previous chapter, in accordance with the major stages of naming, there are functionally dissociable types of anomia. Are semantic anomias, phonological anomias, and phoneme assembly disorders associated with different lesion loci? We will review next the available evidence, but need to point out that one cannot give any definite answers to these questions as the carefully examined "pure" cases representing specific anomia types are rare.

## Lesion correlates of semantically based anomias

In semantic dementia, across-the-board semantic-conceptual impairment leading to dense anomia takes place. Due to the progressive, diffuse neurodegenerative nature of the disease, structural neuroimaging data from these patients cannot provide very detailed information on lesion localisation. Nevertheless, there is a consistent pattern of temporal lobe atrophy that is often more dominant on the left side. This is exemplified in the structural MRI results in Figure 3.3, showing the regions of significantly reduced grey matter density (i.e., neuronal loss) in four patients with semantic dementia (Mummery, Patterson, Wise, Vandenbergh, Price & Hodges, 1999). Galton et al. (2001) recently performed a careful volumetric analysis of the subregions of the temporal lobe on structural MRI images of 18 semantic dementia patients. The subregions included the temporal pole (mainly BA 38), amygdala, hippocampus, parahippocampal gyrus, fusiform gyrus, inferior and middle temporal gyri (BA 20 and 21), and superior temporal gyrus (BA 22 with some of 41 and 42). Elderly controls and Alzheimer patients were also included in the study. In comparison to the controls, the semantic dementia patients showed highly significant atrophy on all these temporal lobe regions except the right hippocampus and the superior temporal gyri. Correlation analyses (semantic dementia and Alzheimer patients combined) indicated that the degree of atrophy in the left fusiform gyrus was significantly associated with patients' scores on tests

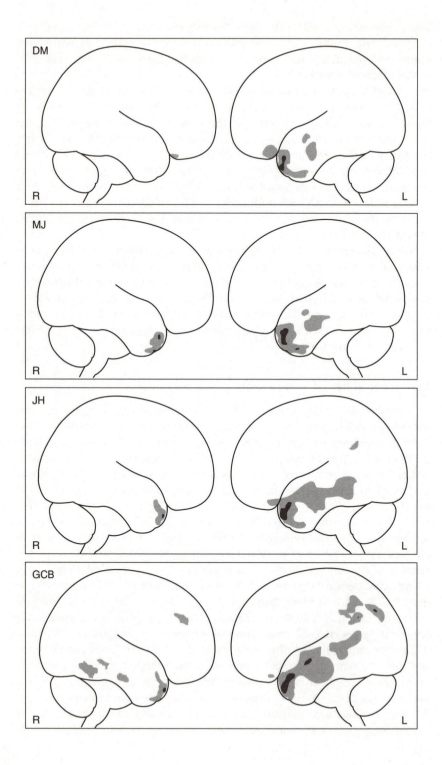

that tap semantic processing (the Pyramids and Palm Trees test, semantic category-based word generation, picture naming). Moreover, degree of atrophy in the left temporal pole as well as in the inferior and middle temporal gyri correlated with the scores on the two naming tests.

The few neuropsychologically well-studied CVA patients whose anomia is based on a general semantic impairment unfortunately do not enable one to draw any definite conclusions on brain–behaviour relationships. This is because their lesion loci are not described in detail and/or they had suffered from extensive damage affecting more than one lobe. Patient JCU reported by Howard and Orchard-Lisle (1984) had an extensive left hemisphere lesion involving the inferior-posterior frontal region, the superior temporal lobe, and the inferior parietal lobe. In addition, a small right parietal lesion was present. Patient KE by Hillis et al. (1990) is only said to suffer from a large left fronto-parietal infarct.

With regard to classical aphasia syndromes, the rather rare syndrome of transcortical sensory aphasia is of interest here as it could be viewed as a disturbance in the mapping between semantics and phonology (e.g., Hickok & Poeppel, 2004). These patients show a comprehension impairment and paraphasic speech output that may include semantic errors, unrelated word responses, and neologisms. Naming is severely impaired and may show grossly irrelevant responses (Goodglass & Kaplan, 1983). However, the ability to repeat words and sentences indicates that the phonological systems are largely preserved in these patients. Lesion sites vary, but posterior temporo-parietal regions are most commonly affected. In their lesion localisation study on transcortical sensory aphasia, Kertesz, Sheppard, and MacKenzie (1982) reported two loci with lesion overlap: medial inferior temporo-occipital region and the more lateral superior parieto-occipital "watershed" area.

## Lesion correlates of phonologically based anomias

In the more or less clear-cut cases of phonologically based anomias discussed in the previous chapter, accurate lesion localisation is not possible as the patients had either traumatic head injury (Lambon Ralph et al., 2000) or a massive brain tumour (Kay & Ellis, 1987). The case reported by Bachoud-Lévi and Dupoux (2003) had a large left temporal lobe infarct that encompassed the superior, medial, and inferior temporal gyri. Raymer

*Figure 3.3* Lateral brain templates showing regions with significantly decreased grey matter density in four patients diagnosed with semantic dementia. Darker areas show more significant atrophy. Semantic dementia is associated with conceptual-semantic disorders, including semantically based anomia. Note that these images depict structural, not functional changes. All four patients evidence predominantly left-sided anterolateral temporal lobe atrophy. Schematic drawing based on Mummery et al. (1999).

et al. (1997a) reported a case similar to those by Lambon Ralph et al. (2000), i.e., showing impaired naming with preserved comprehension and repetition, and interpreted as an impaired access from semantics to output phonology. The patient had suffered a brain infarct that had damaged the posterior part of the left inferior temporal lobe, corresponding to the superior-lateral portion of BA 37 (older, small lesions were noted, too). In line with Raymer et al. (1997a), Foundas, Daniels, and Vasterling (1998) reported a case with phonologically based anomia with a BA 37 lesion. Their other anomic patient with relatively preserved lexical-semantic abilities suffered from damage in the inferior-lateral part of the prefrontal cortex (BA 6).

The importance of BA 37 lesion in phonologically based anomias was examined further by Antonucci, Beeson, and Rapcsak (2004) who analysed naming performance and lexical-semantic abilities in eight CVA patients sustaining focal left inferior temporal lesions. Naming performance of the patients varied from normal to severely impaired. Their patients were reported to have no or at most mild lexical-semantic impairment, but as lexical comprehension was not examined in great detail, the possibility of subtle semantic deficits cannot be excluded. The patients showed the most lesion overlap in the ventromedial section of the left temporal lobe, including areas BA 20, BA 37, BA 36 and BA 28 (note that the latter two structures are not visible in Figure 3.1 as they lie medially in the temporal lobe). Interestingly, the youngest, 49-year-old subject with considerable damage in BA 37 and BA 20 was not anomic at all. Partial anterior involvement of the left temporal lobe did not change the quality of the naming deficit, but similarly to temporal lobe ablation effects in epileptic patients (Herrman et al., 1999), the anterior extent of the lesion correlated with the degree of anomia. Taken together, these results, albeit based on limited data, suggest that left mid-ventromedial temporal lobe lesions would be associated particularly with "pure" forms of phonological anomia.

### Lesion correlates of phoneme assembly disorders

As we noted in Chapter 2, conduction aphasia represents a clinical aphasia syndrome that has been related to phoneme assembly deficits. In this syndrome, phonological paraphasias are the predominant error type in different language production tasks. It has been argued that the critical lesion site in this syndrome is the left supramarginal gyrus (Palumbo, Alexander, & Naeser, 1992). Other lesion sites include the white matter tracts deep to sensory cortex or the subinsular extreme capsule, and also the posterior part of the superior temporal gyrus (Damasio & Damasio, 1980). With lesions extending partly to the superior temporal gyrus, an initial syndrome of Wernicke's aphasia may evolve into conduction aphasia with severely paraphasic output and dense anomia (Alexander, 2000). Large lesion extensions to the parietal lobe are also associated with more severe anomia. According to Alexander (2000), these data suggest the existence of a regional functional network that communicates via temporo-parietal short association pathways in order to support the phonological output structure in spontaneous speech, repetition, oral reading, and naming.

In addition to a posterior phoneme assembly network, an anterior motor-articulatory network has been postulated. The "phonemic output buffer" deficit case by Larner et al. (2004) that we described in some detail in Chapter 2 had a white matter lesion in the left precentral gyrus, extending partly to the posterior portion of the middle frontal gyrus but sparing Broca's area. This overlaps with the lesion sites related to phonetic disintegration: inferior precentral gyrus (face area), Broca's area, and adjacent white matter (Lecours & Lhermitte 1976; Schiff, Alexander, Naeser, & Galaburda, 1983). Larner et al. (2004) suggested that Broca's area may be important for encoding of both serial structure and articulation of speech output, which would then be transmitted to the inferior precentral gyrus for motor execution. Depending on the site and extent of lesion in these areas, either phonological, phonetic, or a combined disturbance would then appear. Lesions of the anterior insula have also been implicated as the key location in patients suffering from apraxia of speech (Dronkers, 1996), but the unique role of insula in articulatory planning was recently questioned by Hillis, Work, Barker, Jacobs, Breese, and Maurer (2004), who argued that this lesion overlap may simply represent a general vulnerability of the insular cortex in large middle cerebral artery infarcts.

With regard to the frontal cortical areas related to the anterior motor-articulatory network, their connections with the basal ganglia and the cerebellum have also been implicated in motor speech output. For example, patients with Parkinson's disease, a common neurodegenerative illness affecting the basal ganglia, can exhibit monotonous and somewhat hastened speech that is imprecise with respect to consonant production (e.g., Schirmer, 2004). On the other hand, cerebellar damage can lead to slowed speech tempo, tendency towards equalised syllable lengths, and increased variability in voice onset time when producing voiced vs. unvoiced stop consonant–vowel pairs such as /ba/ vs. /pa/ (e.g., Ackermann, Mathiak, & Ivry, 2004).

## Lesion correlates of category-specific semantic-syntactic impairments

Damasio, Grabowski, Tranel, Hichwa, and Damasio (1996) studied the neural correlates of category-specific naming by administering a visual confrontation naming task with pictures of familiar faces, animals, and tools to 127 patients with a focal brain lesion. The dependent variable was the number of naming errors in each noun category, and a score was considered abnormal if it fell more than two standard deviations below that of a matched control group. In an attempt to focus on deficits in word form retrieval, Damasio et al. (1996) scored only those errors where the response indicated that the stimulus had been recognised correctly (e.g., skunk → oh, that animal makes a terrible smell if you get too close to it, it is black and white, and gets squashed on the road by cars sometimes). This modified scoring procedure does not inform us about the status of lexical-semantic processing of the patients, as the number of discarded semantically vague error responses is not reported. Thus one should be cautious in interpreting the origin of any category-specific effects in this study. All patients with impaired naming (*n* = 30) had a left hemisphere lesion affecting the temporal lobe, with the exception of a single case suffering from right temporal damage. Of greater interest, it was found that (1) impaired naming of familiar faces was correlated with a lesion in the left temporal pole, (2) impaired animal naming was correlated with left inferior temporal damage, and (3) impaired naming of tools was correlated with a left posterolateral temporal lesion along with a posterior extension.

Damasio et al. (1996) suggested that these left temporal regions play an intermediary role in lexical retrieval. Functionally, they would thus be related to a lexical level between a concept and a phonological realisation of a word (see Chapter 1). According to the authors, the category-specific neural organisation of this level may be due to differences in sensorimotor features associated with the category members. However, as we noted above, the modified error-scoring procedure used by Damasio et al. (1996) does not enable one to rule out a semantically based disorder underlying these category-specific naming difficulties. To reach that conclusion, one should be able to show intact performances on tests measuring both general and item-specific semantic knowledge.

In a subsequent study, Damasio et al. (2004) returned to the issue of category-specific naming difficulties by analysing lesion loci in 139 focally brain-damaged patients, with a stimulus set that included pictures of animals, tools & utensils, fruits & vegetables, and musical instruments. As discussed in the previous section, in this study a separate score for comprehension (based on the patient's descriptions of the object that were prompted by the examiner if needed) and naming was calculated. With regard to *recognition deficits*, the following maximal lesion overlaps were observed. For familiar faces, recognition deficits were associated with right temporal pole and right angular gyrus damage. In recognition problems with tools and utensils, maximal lesion overlap was located in the left posterior-inferior temporal lobe. Impaired recognition of animals was related to bilateral, mostly mesial occipital lesion loci. Deficient recognition of fruits and vegetables correlated with bilateral, mostly lateral and ventral anterior-inferior temporal lobe damage as well as extensive right temporo-parietal damage. Lesion overlaps associated with impaired recognition of musical instruments also showed bilateral involvement, encompassing the right angular gyrus and patchier, widespread areas in the left hemisphere. Thus recognition deficits affecting three out of five picture categories indicated bilateral lesion correlates for recognition deficits, but *naming deficits* showed more localised left hemispheric lesion correlates (Figure 3.4). Disturbed naming of famous faces was associated with left temporal pole lesions. Impaired animal naming was linked to damage in the left anterior-inferior temporal areas, anterior insula, and dorsal temporo-occipital junction. Tool naming failures occurred with lesions of the temporo-parieto-occipital junction area, the inferior pre- and post-central gyri, as well as the insula. Problems in naming fruits and vegetables were related to lesions in the inferior pre- and post-central gyri and the anterior insula. Finally, deficits in naming musical instruments were associated with lesions in the temporal polar regions, the anterior-inferior temporal areas, the posterolateral temporal cortex, the insula, and the inferior pre- and post-central gyri.

We should note that there are two issues that complicate the interpretation of the results obtained by Damasio et al. (2004). First, the stimulus sets were not matched for factors such as visual complexity, word frequency, and imageability. In fact, the authors argue that control for these factors can lead to non-representative stimulus sets. While some (but not all) of these factors indeed correlate with semantic category type, it is a fact that they can affect recognition and naming. Controlling for these factors might even have wiped out the category-specific effects in some patients. It is thus not totally clear what the relative naming deficits and their lesion correlates reflect in this study. The second issue is the way in which the naming scores were obtained. The naming score included only those stimuli to which the subject had produced a correct recognition response, meaning that the items on which the naming score was based varied from patient to patient. While there had to be at least 50% correct recognitions to obtain a naming score, in this scoring system patients could obtain similar naming scores (e.g., 30% correct) even though their recognition performance varied. In other words, the naming deficits and their neural correlates described above are not pure indices of word retrieval difficulty. In fact, Damasio et al. (2004) addressed this issue in a separate analysis where they contrasted patients with naming-only deficits with those having both naming and recognition deficits. In this analysis, only the tools & utensils and the musical instruments categories showed significant differences between these two groups. For tools & utensils, maximal lesion overlap for naming-only defect was in the left frontal operculum and the inferior motor region, while for combined recognition and naming deficit it was in the left posterior-middle temporal lobe. For musical instruments, a naming-only deficit was correlated with damage to the posterior part of the superior temporal gyrus, while a combined recognition and naming deficit showed a lesion overlap in the inferior regions of the left temporal pole. For the rest of the categories, the lesion overlaps were in the same areas that were described above.

We have reviewed the lesion studies by Damasio et al. (1996, 2004) extensively, but there are also several other lesion analyses of patients

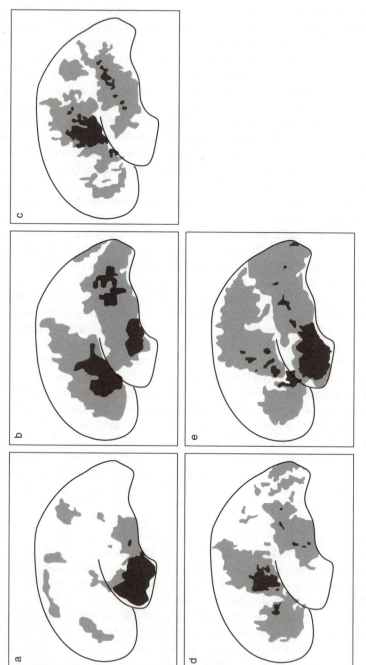

*Figure 3.4* Lesion-difference maps showing maximal lesion overlaps in patients showing deficits in naming (a) famous faces, (b) animals, (c) tools & utensils, (d) fruits & vegetables, and (e) musical instruments. Darker areas show more lesion overlap in patients. Schematic drawing based on Damasio et al. (2004).

suffering from category-specific semantic deficits. Gainotti (2000) presented a literature review of 47 patients with category-specific impairments for whom some information on lesion localisation was available. The most common type of category-specific semantic impairment, living things (animals and plant life) deficit, offered the opportunity to compare aetiology and lesion sites in output-related deficits vs. clearly semantically based deficits. Note however that it is difficult to rule out the possibility of a mild semantic problem in the case of output deficits (cf. Capitani et al., 2003). The eight subjects whose impaired naming of living things was classified as an output deficit were typically CVA patients with more restricted, left hemispheric lesions affecting inferior temporo-occipital structures. Those patients with clearly semantically based deficits with living things suffered from aetiologies that tend to cause bilateral damage and affect the anterior parts of the temporal lobes, i.e., herpes simplex encephalitis, head trauma, and semantic dementia.

An analysis of those cases where more detailed neuroanatomical information was available indicated that the living things deficit was associated with anterior-mesial and inferior temporal lobe damage that spared the lateral posterior temporal areas. The damage was bilateral but more prominent on the left side. Lesion correlates for a naming deficit limited to plant life were explored further as there were three such cases providing more detailed lesion localisation. All three CVA patients suffered from left inferior-mesial temporo-occipital lesions. Lesions associated with a semantic deficit with animals appeared to be more bilateral than those associated with plant life deficits. Detailed neuroanatomical information was available for only two patients with a semantically based deficit for animals, and both were herpes simplex encephalitis patients with massive bilateral temporal lobe damage that left only the posterolateral temporal cortex and the temporo-occipital regions intact. The six patients with a semantically based deficit specific to man-made objects had large middle cerebral artery infarcts encompassing fronto-temporo-parietal areas in the left hemisphere. Three cases with an output-related artefact naming deficit also had left hemisphere lesions, affecting anterior temporal areas in two patients, and the middle temporal gyrus, hippocampus, and the inferior parietal lobe in the third one.

The lesion studies reviewed above point to neural differentiation of semantic category knowledge and naming especially within the left temporal lobe. When comparing the two large-scale lesion studies by Damasio et al. (1996, 2004), the most consistent finding appears to be the clustering of lesions in the left temporal pole in a naming deficit with famous faces. Their 2004 study of an animal-naming deficit indicates three sites of damage instead of a single left inferior temporal lesion cluster, one site being in the left inferior frontal operculum. The same left inferior frontal lesion overlap site was now present for a tool-naming deficit as well. Also the two semantic categories not employed in the 1996 study, fruits &

vegetables and musical instruments, were associated with a combination of left temporal and frontal lesion clusters. The data base in the review by Gainotti (2000) is not directly comparable to that of Damasio et al. (2004), but both studies indicate that semantically based deficits for living things are related to a bilateral injury, while man-made artefact/tool deficits are associated with unilateral left hemisphere lesions. A recent cortical stimulation study provided some additional support to this finding, as left-sided frontotemporal stimulation sites elicited more pronounced anomia for tools than for animals (Ilmberger, Rau, Noachtar, Arnold & Winkler, 2002). With regard to possibly output-related category-specific naming deficits limited to plant life, the results by Gainotti (2000), although based on three patient reports only, suggest a more posterior, temporo-occipital lesion site than the maximal temporal lesion overlap in Damasio et al. (2004). Given these discrepancies and the variability in the materials, methods, and criteria used to establish category-specific knowledge and naming deficits, one should be careful in drawing far-reaching conclusions on the basis of the lesion data. We will return to the theoretical implications of these findings after discussing the results of functional imaging studies of category-specific processing in normals.

## Word-class-specific impairments

Analyses of lesion localisation in word-class-specific retrieval difficulties were prompted by earlier studies showing selective impairments in the production/comprehension of nouns in anomic aphasia (typically suffering from left posterior damage) and of verbs in agrammatic aphasia (typically suffering from left anterior damage) (Goodglass, Klein, Carey, & Jones, 1966; McCarthy & Warrington, 1985; Miceli et al., 1984; Zingeser & Berndt, 1990). Damasio and Tranel (1993) reported a study of three patients with focal left hemisphere damage, in which they examined their ability to name actions, objects, and familiar faces. Their lesions were outside the classical language area and none was clinically aphasic. One patient had extensive bilateral damage and evidenced a conceptual deficit, while the other two patients exhibited deficits limited to lexical retrieval. The two patients with left anterior/middle temporal damage were impaired in naming proper nouns and objects but action naming was intact. The third patient with a left frontal lesion showed exactly the opposite performance pattern. This pattern was reported to be stable and similar in both oral and written naming. Daniele et al. (1994) reported a similar double dissociation in noun/verb processing in three patients with progressive language deterioration and left hemisphere focal atrophy. The two patients with left frontal lobe atrophy were impaired in naming and comprehension of verbs, while the third one with left temporal lobe atrophy was disproportionately impaired in naming and comprehension of nouns.

While noun-specific retrieval difficulties appear to be strongly (but not solely) associated with left middle/inferior temporal lesions, there are also patients with verb retrieval difficulties who evidence lesions outside the left frontal lobe. Both Baxter and Warrington (1985) and Miceli, Silveri, Nocentini, and Caramazza (1988) reported a case having left temporo-parietal damage and a specific difficulty in verb retrieval. Variability in left hemisphere lesion loci in verb deficits could perhaps be accounted for by assuming several underlying mechanisms. Verb production impairments in anterior lesions might be related to syntactic deficits, while verb impairments in posterior lesions may be associated with phonological-morphological deficits (Silveri, Perri, & Cappa, 2003).

We noted above that there is considerable evidence that impairments in naming famous faces cluster to left temporal pole lesions (Damasio et al., 1996, 2004). However, one should add that focal brain lesions associated with *proper name* retrieval deficits have not been limited solely to damage to the left temporal pole. There are case reports of CVA patients with proper name (person name) retrieval deficits with left-sided lesions in other parts of the temporal lobe (posterior middle temporal in McKenna & Warrington, 1980; mesial temporal in Verstichtel, Cohen, & Crochet 1996), parieto-occipital regions (Semenza & Zettin, 1988), occipital lobe (Miozzo & Cappa cited in Semenza, Mondini, & Zettin, 1995), and thalamus (Cohen, Bolgert, Timsit & Cherman, 1994; Lucchelli & De Renzi, 1992).

## The right hemisphere and lexical retrieval

As far as language is concerned, the right hemisphere has traditionally been considered to be nondominant. However, split brain studies and subsequent experiments with both normals and right hemisphere damaged patients have revealed important information on the language capabilities in the right hemisphere. They indicate that the right hemisphere shows semantic abilities and a vocabulary limited to concrete and common words but is unable to effect oral output without left hemisphere mediation (for reviews, see Baynes, 1990; Chiarello, 1991; Zaidel, 1998). There are cases of right-handed right hemisphere damaged patients with aphasia, including more or less pure anomia (Ferro et al., 1991; Hadar et al., 1991; Larrabee et al., 1991) but those can be argued to reflect "anomalous" language dominance (for a recent review of crossed aphasia, see Coppens, Hungerford, Yama-guchi, & Yamadori, 2002). A tachistoscopic visual confrontation naming study by Bergego, Deloche, Pradat-Diehl, Robineau, and Lauriot-Prevost (1993) indicated that most of right hemisphere damaged patients' errors were predominantly visual (visual-semantic or purely visual) and semantic errors were lacking. Such a pattern indicates a perceptually based deficit rather than an involvement of language-related mechanisms. The lesion studies reviewed above indicate that category-specific difficulties with living things are associated with bilateral temporal lobe lesions, indicating a right hemisphere contribution to the recognition of animals and plants.

Case studies by Rapcsak and his colleagues (Rapcsak, Comer, & Rubens, 1993; Rapcsak, Kaszniak, & Rubens, 1989) suggested that the right hemisphere may make a unique contribution to the naming of facial expression. They reported two cases with right temporal damage who showed a selective visual-verbal disconnection between facial expressions and their names in spite of intact language functions, visuospatial functions, and recognition of familiar faces. Their findings are in line with studies reporting specific difficulties in the processing of emotional content of facial expressions after right-sided perisylvian damage (Adolphs, Damasio, Tranel, Cooper, & Damasio, 2000).

## Subcortical involvement in naming deficits

The contribution of subcortical nuclei to language is a controversial issue. Various left-sided subcortical lesions including the basal ganglia (striato-capsular damage) have been associated with aphasic symptoms. However, large variability in symptomatology, associated white matter lesions that can lead to disconnections, and possible direct or indirect effects on cortical function complicate the interpretation of these results. After considering the available evidence, Nadeau and Crosson (1997, p. 387) concluded that "the basal ganglia have very little to do with language function" and that the very variable aphasic symptoms reported in these patients reflect concomitant left cortical hypoperfusion (see e.g., Hillis et al., 2002b), structural damage not detected in the scans, and/or thalamic disconnection.

With regard to aphasia following left thalamic damage, Nadeau and Crosson (1997) argue that it reflects a true subcortical involvement in language mechanisms through disruptions of a cortico-thalamo-cortical network that is important for modulating cortical function. They suggest that the pulvinar and the lateral posterior nucleus of the thalamus are particularly important here, as their major projections are to the temporal and parietal cortices. The symptomatology following left thalamic damage appears to be more consistent than in basal ganglia lesions, namely fluent speech output with semantic paraphasias, naming difficulties, and sometimes comprehension deficits. Raymer, Moberg, Crosson, Nadeau, and Gonzalez-Rothi (1997b) studied two patients who had sustained thalamic infarct and evidenced the clinical pattern of anomic aphasia. The patients' anomia appeared to be of the output type as lexical comprehension tasks were performed well. Both oral and written naming were affected, with semantic-visual and semantic naming errors being the most common error categories. The patients showed a strong frequency effect in naming, performing much better with higher-frequency items. Why would left-sided thalamic lesions lead to this kind of anomia? One possibility that Raymer et al. (1997b) entertain is that disrupted thalamocortical connections lead to a degradation of the lexical-semantic representations supported by cortical networks. These representations would still be sharp enough to manage comprehension tasks like word–picture matching, but would lead to increased errors in naming where the single target item has to be chosen for production amongst competing, closely related alternatives. Specific nuclei in the left thalamus would thus be important in selectively engaging cortical networks that subserve semantic and lexical knowledge.

Assuming that naming is based on a well-concerted activity of anatomically distant regions, the integrity of long axonal connections between these areas must also be important to successful naming. In animals, cortico-cortical connectivity can be identified with autoradiographic techniques, but until the recent development of MRI-based diffusion tensor imaging technique (a technique that utilises the restricted motion of water molecules in white matter axonal bundles and thus enables visualisation of white matter tracts), the data from humans have been derived from postmortem examination or, more commonly, ordinary CT/MRI imaging of white matter lesions. The earlier structural imaging studies have suggested that the location and extent of white matter lesions are important for the symptomatology and recovery of aphasic patients (Naeser, Palumbo, Helm-Estabrooks, Stiassny-Eder, & Albert, 1989) but have not allowed direct identification of the fibre bundles.

Duffau et al. (2002) performed intraoperative stimulation of brain tumour patients' left hemispheric subcortical language pathways, and could show that stimulation of a white matter tract called *subcallosal fasciculus* induced anomia and reduced spontaneous speech. The medial part of this fibre bundle connects the supplementary motor area and the cingulate gyrus, related to initiation of speech, to the caudate nucleus. This tract is part of a larger fronto-striato-thalamic-frontal feedback circuit that is important for higher cognitive functions. Stimulation of another subcortical area, *periventricular white matter* below the lower sensorimotor mouth area, induced dysarthria or even loss of speech, apparently by disrupting efferent (corticospinal) and possibly also afferent connections of the face motor area that is crucial for articulatory movements. The third stimulated fibre bundle, *the arcuate fasciculus*, has traditionally been implicated particularly in conduction aphasia. It connects various parts of the temporal (the inferior-lateral, medial, and posterior-superior regions) and the parietal lobe to the frontal cortex via extreme capsule around the insula. It is the major pathway linking the classical posterior and anterior language areas. Stimulation of the arcuate fasciculus at various points induced transient inhibition of language output. Due to the nature of the study by Duffau et al. (2002), the effects listed here may have partly reflected the disruption of other pathways as well. These include insular pathways that have extensive connections to cortical and limbic regions and have been related to speech output planning (Dronkers, 1996), and the uncinate fasciculus that connects the orbitofrontal cortex with the anterior temporal lobe. It has recently been suggested that the uncinate fasciculus would be part of the neural circuitry for propositional speech (Blank, Scott, Murphy, Warburton, & Wise, 2002).

## Summary of the lesion studies

The lesion studies cited above indicate that word production engages a widespread network in the left hemisphere, extending outside the classical perisylvian language zone and encompassing also cortico-thalamo-cortical connections. Within this network, the most sensitive region to anomia is the left temporal lobe. It must thus play a central role in the word production network, but its contribution may of course be augmented by the fact that anomia is mostly assessed with visual confrontation naming tasks that employ concrete objects. The ventral processing stream that is crucial for object recognition runs from the visual areas to the inferior temporal regions. Different regions of the temporal lobes have been associated with all the major processing stages in naming—semantic processing, word form retrieval, and phoneme assembly. Depending on object category, there may be more (cf. living things) or less (cf. tools) need for bilateral temporal lobe contribution in object recognition. The anterior regions of the left temporal lobe have been implicated on the one hand in general semantic processing (semantic dementia), and on the other hand in retrieval of proper names. Middle inferior left temporal regions have been linked with access from meaning to word form, and the left superior-posterior regions (Wernicke's area) to phoneme assembly. Other major regions involved in anomia include the left inferior parietal lobe, which has also been implicated in phoneme assembly as well as in verb retrieval, together with left premotor and prefrontal regions. Finally, an anterior motor-articulatory cortical network has been hypothesised, encompassing Broca's area, lower part of the premotor cortex, and possibly the insula. Besides these cortical regions, the integrity of several white matter tracts is important to the act of naming: fibre bundles connecting the frontal and temporo-parietal cortical areas, forming the cognitive-motor fronto-striato-thalamic loop, and mediating articulatory commands via efferent connections to brainstem nuclei that are connected to the vocal tract.

This rough summary is based on the most common symptom–lesion correspondences. From this review, it should be clear that there are no one-to-one correspondences with specific naming-related deficits and restricted anatomical regions in the left hemisphere across patients. Rather, these lesion–deficit associations represent statistical probabilities or clusters. This is hardly surprising, as we deal here with extremely complex biological systems that have been damaged. Individual variability in naming-related functional brain organisation may be considerable, as has been suggested by cortical stimulation studies.

# FUNCTIONAL BRAIN IMAGING OF WORD PRODUCTION IN NORMALS

Functional imaging methods have recently opened up new possibilities for studying brain–behaviour relationships. Importantly, these methods allow us to study the functioning of the intact brain. With these measures, one can track physiological changes in the brain while the subject is engaged in a cognitive task. The physiological changes that have been measured in conjunction with naming include indices of cerebral blood flow and metabolism and electromagnetic brain responses. Even though the colourful "images of the mind" produced by these techniques are quite striking, it should be remembered that the data obtained are of correlative nature. Moreover, as with any experimental approach, there are technical and experimental limitations that affect the interpretation of any set of functional neuroimaging results obtained during cognitive processing (for a detailed introduction, see Frackowiak et al., 2003).

In spite of this note of caution, fMRI, PET, and MEG have the power to provide us with information on the brain regions involved in word production, and MEG can even provide the evolvement of the activation patterns during the fleeting moment it takes for a normal adult to produce a word. This is a crucial addition to the traditional lesion study approach, which has its own limitations. Lesions are experiments of nature that follow physiological rather than functional neuroanatomical boundaries, and their behavioural effects are modulated by whatever compensatory mechanisms the patient is using. What we want to find are the points of convergence in lesion and functional neuroimaging data that could enable us to identify the neural substrates of the main components of word production. Among other things, this knowledge can help to constrain cognitive models of naming/anomia.

Brain activity measurements by the two most commonly used techniques, PET and fMRI, are based on the fact that the normal brain autoregulates its blood flow according to metabolic demand. This demand depends on neuronal activity in the regions that are engaged in a task, e.g., in picture naming. In PET, these measures require an injected radioactive tracer to identify task-related local blood flow/metabolic changes in the brain. In fMRI, the signal is based on oxygenation of brain tissue, reflecting blood flow to the local vasculature and thus indirectly local neural activity. Note that in both methods "local" activity refers to a population of many tens of millions of synapses. MEG, on the other hand, measures the extremely weak magnetic fields created by synchronised neuronal activity in the brain. The primary currents causing the signals are the same in MEG and EEG but, in contrast to EEG, MEG provides not only excellent temporal (at the millisecond level) resolution but also good spatial resolution for localisation of the magnetic sources.

Indefrey and Levelt (2004) recently reported a meta-analysis of altogether 82 word production studies including picture naming, word generation, word reading, and pseudoword reading experiments. The overwhelming majority were PET, fMRI, or MEG studies, but some cortical stimulation studies and a single lesion study (Damasio et al., 1996, see above) was included as well. Indefrey and Levelt employed the spoken word production model of Levelt et al. (1999; see Chapter 1) and made predictions regarding which stages of word production should or should not be shared between the tasks used in the various production studies. They then attempted to identify reliable neural correlates for conceptual preparation and lexical selection, word form retrieval, syllabification, phonetic encoding, and articulation, as well as self-monitoring.

*Conceptually driven lexical selection* was assumed to be shared by picture naming and word generation but not by word reading, which is perceptually driven (even though semantics are certainly involved in normal reading). Following this logic, the meta-analysis indicated only a single consistent locus of activation that was shared by the two conceptually driven tasks. It was found in the mid-section of the left middle temporal gyrus. Indefrey and Levelt (2004) interpret this as the neural substrate for lemma selection rather than conceptual preparation, as conceptual processing may take place in widespread areas that could vary between semantic categories.

*Word form retrieval* should be shared by picture naming, word generation, and word reading, but not by pseudoword reading. Common, reliable areas of shared activation for only the first three tasks included the left posterior superior and middle temporal gyri (Wernicke's area), the right supplementary motor area, and the left anterior insula. With regard to the right supplementary motor area and the left anterior insula activation, Indefrey and Levelt (2004) speculated that they may be related to articulatory planning rather than word form retrieval.

*Syllabification* (included in phoneme assembly in the terminology we have employed earlier) is shared by all spoken language production tasks. Indefrey and Levelt (2004) hypothesised that as this processing stage operates on an abstract segmental representation, its neural substrates should be insensitive to overt vs. covert word production. The only area that was both common to the four word production tasks and insensitive to the covert/overt distinction was the left posterior inferior frontal gyrus, corresponding to Broca's area. Their earlier meta-analysis had also linked the left mid-superior temporal gyrus for this processing stage (Indefrey & Levelt, 2000), but they now considered this as less probable due to its sensitivity to the overt/covert production distinction. However, one can question whether the syllabification stage should be totally unresponsive to the phonetic encoding and articulation demands. Other consistent loci across all the tasks that appeared at least twice as often in overt than in covert production were the left ventral precentral gyrus, the left posterior fusiform gyrus, the left thalamus, and the right medial cerebellum.

For several reasons, *phonetic encoding and articulation* was considered to be the most difficult stage to identify in the functional neuroimaging results:

it can also take place in covert production, and overt responses can be used for self-monitoring. Moreover, overt vs. covert production was not evenly distributed by task type in the data base. Nevertheless, Indefrey and Levelt (2004) searched for areas activated at least twice as often in overt than in covert production across all the tasks, and not being reliably activated in the word perception studies (possibly reflecting self-monitoring) that they also analysed. These criteria revealed altogether 17 loci throughout the brain. Most of these areas are known to be related to motor functions: bilateral ventral sensorimotor regions, right dorsal motor region, right supplementary motor area, left and right cerebellar regions, bilateral thalami, right midbrain.

With regard to *self-monitoring*, Indefrey and Levelt (2004) noted that the data base they analysed allowed only the localisation of the external loop (acoustical input from own voice) of self-monitoring, not the internal loop that takes the end result of syllabification as input. However, they assume that the neural substrates of these two loops may overlap to a considerable degree. To identify the external loop, Indefrey and Levelt (2004) searched for brain areas that showed consistent activations in word listening and were also more strongly activated during overt than covert production tasks. This analysis revealed the bilateral superior temporal gyri with the exception of the right anterior part.

Besides searching for neuroanatomical loci for the major stages of word production, Indefrey and Levelt (2004) considered time frames for each of these stages based on reaction time and evoked potential studies. The only functional brain-imaging method that can simultaneously provide excellent temporal and good spatial resolution over the cortical mantle in cognitive activation studies is the magnetoencephalography (MEG). However, there are only a handful of published MEG studies on naming of familiar pictures (Levelt, Praamstra, Meyer, Helenius, & Salmelin, 1998; Maess, Friederici, Damian, Meyer, & Levelt, 2002; Salmelin, Hari, Lounasmaa, & Sams, 1994; Sörös, Cornelissen, Laine, & Salmelin, 2003). We will shortly review three of these studies that came from the same laboratory and used similar methodology to identify cortical activation patterns during naming of single pictures (Salmelin et al., 1994; Levelt et al., 1998; Sörös et al., 2003). It will be of interest to attempt to relate the results to the scheme provided by Indefrey and Levelt (2004). The first two of these MEG studies are actually included in the data base of Indefrey and Levelt (2004).

Overall, all three MEG studies on picture naming indicate a mainly (but not solely) feedforward wave of activation that starts early on from the occipital lobes and spreads to temporal and parietal regions and to motor areas. During the first *150-200 milliseconds* after picture onset, all the three studies found bilateral occipital activations. These fit to early visual processing and pattern recognition.

In the *200-400 millisecond time window*, activation patterns diverge within and between studies. In the Salmelin et al. (1994) study, half of the six subjects exhibited bilateral cortical activation around the temporo-parieto-occipital junction, whereas the other half at the same time showed bilateral temporal lobe activation close to the auditory cortices. Sörös et al. (2002) also found a bilateral spread of activation mainly around the posterior part of the Sylvian fissure. Levelt et al. (1998), on the other hand, observed shorter overall oral naming latencies in their subjects and divided this time period into 150–275 and 275–400 millisecond time windows. In the first time window they observed a strong activation cluster in seven out of eight subjects in the right parietal cortex along the posterior end of the superior temporal sulcus. In the latter time window, they reported a clear activation cluster (six of eight subjects) close to the posterior third of the left superior temporal gyrus and the temporo-parietal junction, corresponding to the Wernicke's area. The MEG study by Maess et al. (2002), which used a different analysis method and focused on a semantic interference effect in object naming, reported the neurophysiological indices of this interference in the time window of 150–225 milliseconds post-stimulus, the location being in the left temporal lobe. Of these data, the results by Maess et al. (2002) fit best to the lemma selection stage in the scheme by Indefrey and Levelt (2004), as it is assumed to take place by 250 milliseconds after picture onset and to be subserved by the mid-section of the left middle temporal gyrus. The other MEG studies did not show any strong cluster of activations in the left middle temporal lobe. Consistent with the hypothesis that word form retrieval is linked to Wernicke's area activity and should take place around 300–350 milliseconds post-stimulus, Levelt et al. (1998) observed a clear-cut source cluster that corresponded to this location and time frame. Half of the subjects in the Salmelin et al. (1994) study also evidenced spatiotemporally similar sources, while in the study by Sörös et al. (2003), only 2 out of 10 subjects showed a left posterior superior temporal source in this time window.

In the Salmelin et al. (1994) study, the final *400–600 ms time window* revealed more anterior, bilateral activation around the motor cortex, Broca's area, and its homologue in the right hemisphere. Results of the final time window in the Levelt et al. (1998) study showed scattered activations, including the sensory-motor cortex as well as parietal and temporal regions. Sörös et al. (2003) also observed a large scatter of source clusters in the fronto-temporo-parietal cortices bilaterally, as well as a cluster in the left occipital lobe. In the Indefrey and Levelt (2004) scheme, this time window would be linked to syllabification as well as phonetic encoding and articulation, the former one being associated with Broca's area and the latter with motor areas. All three MEG studies showed at least some sources in the left inferior frontal regions and in the sensorimotor areas that would fit these processing stages, but the scatter in source locations was large. In the Sörös et al. (2003) study, there was also evidence for an occipital reactivation after word form retrieval.

All in all, we can conclude that the available spatiotemporal data from MEG measurements on picture naming provide partial support for the scheme put forth by Indefrey and Levelt (2004). Variability within and between studies is considerable, and it may be related to differences in the experimental designs, stimulus materials, small samples, as well as to individual differences that are also evident in the intraoperative cortical stimulation studies on naming that we discussed above.

As the Indefrey and Levelt (2004) review focused on word production from lexical-semantic retrieval onwards, we should briefly comment on functional neuroimaging results with picture naming that also entails earlier processing stages. Based on a comparison of nine PET activation studies of picture naming and object identification, Murtha, Chertkow, Beauregard, and Evans (1999) concluded that the most consistently activated structures during these task performances were in fact the bilateral superior/middle occipital gyrus and the left fusiform/inferior temporo-occipital gyrus. This corresponds well with the functional neuroanatomy of the ventral processing stream dedicated to object recognition (e.g., Ungerleider & Haxby, 1994). Some researchers have associated the left fusiform activation with semantic processing (e.g., Simons, Koutstaal, Prince, Wagner, & Schacter, 2003), while others consider it to be related to higher-level visuoperceptual processing that may only show task-dependent secondary "top-down" semantic effects (Whatmough, Chertkow, Murtha, & Hanratty, 2002). The difficulty in identifying the functional roles of these areas in terms of presemantic vs. semantic processing is also due to lack of specificity in visual object recognition theories (Murtha et al., 1999).

## Category-specific semantic effects in normals' brain activations

Inspired by the category-specific deficits identified in neurological patients, there have been an increasing number of published functional neuro-imaging studies with normal subjects in the last decade that have addressed category-specific processing with various production (e.g., picture naming, word generation) and comprehension tasks. In conjunction with their lesion localisation study, Damasio et al. (2004) presented summative data on their PET activation results on normals' naming performance for the categories of famous faces (person names), animals, and tools. Their earlier PET naming data (Damasio et al., 1996), with the search volume in the temporal lobe, indicated overlapping but separable activation foci for these categories. The category-specific separable activation maxima included the left ventrolateral temporal pole for famous faces, and the left posterior infero-temporal region for tools and animals, with a more posterior and lateral maximum for tools than for animals. These sites corresponded reasonably well with their 1996 lesion results. Besides these temporal lobe activations, the summative whole brain level analysis by Damasio et al. (2004) indicated several category-specific activation loci outside the temporal lobe, including bilateral frontal activation maxima for naming famous faces, bilateral occipital activation foci for animals, and right-sided supramarginal gyrus activation for tools.

Other category-specific semantic processing studies with PET or fMRI have provided variable results. Possible reasons for the variability include differences in baseline measures (for example, Damasio et al., 2004, employed an unusual baseline task with unfamiliar faces either in correct orientation or upside down), experimental tasks, control of stimuli (e.g., visual complexity, familiarity, imageability of items), subject groups, and analysis methods (more liberal statistical criteria used in part of the relevant studies are more prone to false positive errors in activations). Based on the variable and partly negative results, some researchers have concluded that there is no evidence for regional category-specific organisation. Instead, conceptual-semantic tasks as a whole activate a large primarily left hemisphere network involving the temporal pole as well as the middle and inferior temporal gyri, suggesting a distributed organisation of conceptual knowledge (Tyler & Moss, 2001). Other reviews, while also assuming that object categories are represented in a distributed semantic feature space, argue that there are nonetheless consistent category-specific activation patterns in the brain. According to Martin and Chao (2001), for example, in various semantic tasks such as picture naming and picture–word matching, living things (animals, faces) and artefacts activate partly different areas in the ventral temporo-occipital cortex. Specifically, living things activate more lateral aspects of the fusiform gyrus, while artefacts activate more medial aspects of the fusiform gyrus. Martin and Chao (2001) relate these activations to processing of object form. They also entertain the hypothesis that in processing terms, the posterior-to-anterior temporal axis represents increasing specification and thus has higher demands in object processing, with faces as unique entities being subserved by the most anterior part of the temporal lobe (Damasio et al., 1996). Other types of features such as object-related motion and use-associated motor patterns with tools may be linked to lateral posterior temporal (just anterior to motion perception area MT/V5 that is located at the boundary of BA 19 and BA 37) and left ventral premotor (BA 6) activations, respectively (Johnson-Frey, 2004; Martin & Chao, 2001).

In summary, category-specific brain activations in normals have been hard to replicate across studies. Moreover, as most of these studies have employed verbal tasks, it is not clear to what extent the effects have been semantic as opposed to lexical (Thompson-Schill, 2003).

## Word-class-specific effects in normals' brain activations

As with category-specificity, the neuroimaging studies on noun vs. verb processing in normals have yielded conflicting results. Some studies have indicated regionally specific activation patterns for verbs. For example, Perani et al. (1999) employed a lexical decision task with Italian verbs and nouns, and reported increased left inferior frontal activation for verbs. Other studies, however, have failed to find activation differences between nouns and verbs. These studies have employed diverse methods, including verb vs. noun generation (Warburton et al., 1996), lexical decision and semantic categorisation (Tyler, Russell, Fadili, & Moss, 2001), and visual confrontation naming of actions vs. objects (Sörös et al., 2003). Tyler, Bright, Fletcher, and Stamatakis (2004) recently drew attention to the possibility that verb vs. noun effects in brain activation may be related to inflectional morphology. In their fMRI study, subjects made semantic decisions on regularly inflected verb and noun triads. Both word types elicited left frontotemporal activation increases, but the verb task was associated with significantly stronger activation in the left inferior frontal cortex (BA 44, 45, and 47). Tyler et al. (2004) attribute this effect to morphosyntactic aspects of inflected verbs rather than differences in lexical-semantic representation between verbs and nouns. Note that the Perani et al. (1999) study reporting verb–noun differences was performed in Italian where free-standing word forms are always inflected.

As regards processing of proper names, lesion data indicate an association between left temporal pole damage and proper name deficit, albeit we have noted that several other lesion loci have also been reported. Functional neuroimaging results in normals have also indicated some variability, with semantically loaded familiar face processing tasks activating, e.g., ventromedial temporal regions and the temporal poles bilaterally (Sergent, Ohta, & MacDonald, 1992), the left hippocampus and the inferior parietal regions bilaterally (Kapur, Friston, Young, Frith, & Frackowiak, 1995), or the temporal poles bilaterally (Damasio et al., 1996). In a recent review, Haxby, Hoffman, and Gobbini (2000) put forth an anatomically and functionally distributed model of human face perception where the anterior temporal regions are assumed to subserve personal identity, name, and biographical information. Further fMRI evidence has also associated retrieval of people's names with activity in the left temporal pole (Tsukiura et al., 2002). Finally, Gorno-Tempini and Price (2001) recently reported equal activation in the anterior part of the left middle temporal gyrus during identification of both famous faces and famous buildings. This suggests that the left anterior temporal regions respond to semantically unique items rather than to the single category of familiar faces.

## Functional brain imaging in anomic patients

A highly interesting application of functional neuroimaging is the scanning of anomic patients while they are performing word production tasks. This is still a little-studied area, as the structural and functional brain changes in the patients make the analysis and interpretation of their functional neuroimaging results difficult. While lesion information helps to delineate brain regions that are necessary for successful lexical retrieval, functional neuroimaging can reveal ways in which damaged brains try to accomplish the task that has become a very difficult one. In principle, the possible neural substrates of residual naming in an anomic patient include immediate perilesional regions that may partly share the capacities of the damaged area, intact right hemisphere homologues (less likely due to the left-sided lateralisation of language production mechanisms), and subcortical systems connected to the lesioned area.

Using fMRI in a cross-sectional design, Cao, Vikingstad, George, Johnson, and Welch (1999) examined the neural correlates of covert object naming and verb generation in seven left hemisphere damaged recovered aphasic patients 5 months post-onset. In comparison to controls, the patients showed the same total activated volumes during the two lexical tasks. Yet there was a difference in the lateralisation of the activated volumes, as the patients exhibited decreased left-sided and increased right-sided brain activation. This was interpreted as hemispheric interaction during recovery from aphasia. Within the left hemisphere, anterior and posterior activation shifts away from the locus of lesion were observed. Moreover, the patients failed to activate left inferior parietal regions that were usually activated in the control subjects, even though these regions were spared. This was related to possible functional disconnection caused by the lesions. A regression analysis indicated that the more even the distribution of the activated volumes over the two hemispheres, the better was the naming score at the time of the study. Thus a bilateral activation pattern, assumedly based on partial restitution of the damaged left hemisphere and compensatory activation in the right hemisphere, implicated better recovery.

Gorno-Tempini, Wenman, Price, Rudge, and Cipolotti (2001) measured brain activation by PET in a densely anomic brain tumour patient and six controls. Structural MRI of the patient's brain revealed left frontal and left posterior temporo-parietal cystic lesions. In the PET measurement, a same-different matching task was employed, and the stimuli were pairs of pictures depicting famous and non-famous faces and buildings. A naming test following the PET session verified that the patient was very impaired in naming the famous items, but could nevertheless provide uniquely defining biographical information for most of them (e.g., picture of Princess Margaret → she is the sister of the Queen). Given that the patient's anomia was assumedly post-semantic, it was of interest to examine whether he would activate the left anterior temporal cortex in the same fashion as normals when matching famous stimuli. Normal-like activation of the left anterior temporal cortex would suggest that this region is related to semantic processing of famous entities rather than to retrieval of their names. Indeed, both the patient and the normals activated the anterior temporal cortex when matching famous items.

Two further brain activation studies have examined single patients with word-category-specific naming disorders. Sörös et al. (2003) studied the dynamics of action vs. object naming in JP, a chronic aphasic patient suffering from anomia that was significantly more severe with objects than with actions. The patient had sustained left posterior temporoparietal damage due to CVA, and exhibited moderate anomia that had both a semantic and a phonological component (Cornelissen, Laine, Tarkiainen, Järvensivu, Martin, & Salmelin, 2003). Ten normal controls tested for the study showed a similar chain of MEG activations in both action and object naming, advancing from occipital cortices to temporo-parietal areas and further to the left frontal regions without consistent involvement of the classical Wernicke's and Broca's areas. JP's activation chain for the better-preserved category, verbs, was similar to those of the normals, with the exception of a relatively stronger verb- than noun-related activation in the left perilesional angular gyrus area and lack of sensorimotor area activations. Activation in the angular gyrus area was followed by activation in Broca's area. In contrast, in object naming the left angular gyrus activation was accompanied with strong simultaneous activation of Broca's area and the left superior parietal lobe, followed by a late left middle temporal gyrus activation that was lacking in the action-naming condition. These findings indicate that the dynamics of naming-related cortical activation in JP changed significantly for items that had become difficult to name following his left posterior brain damage. The interpretation of the early activation in Broca's area and the late left middle temporal lobe activation remains open, but in the light of the Indefrey and Levelt (2004) neurocognitive model of word production, they could reflect deranged/compensatory processes of phoneme assembly and lexical-semantic retrieval.

Grabowski et al. (2003) studied face-naming-related brain activation by fMRI in eight epilepsy patients who had undergone left temporal pole and partial hippocampal removal. The patients were not aphasic but experienced proper name retrieval problems with intact recognition of familiar faces. Compared to normals, the patients showed decreased rather than increased naming-related brain activations in bilateral temporal, left frontal, and left cingulate areas. Grabowski et al. (2003) suggest that these decreases indicate a functional disruption of a large-scale neural network engaged in proper name retrieval. The only relative activation increase in the patients was observed in a mesial occipital region, interpreted as compensatory intensified visual processing.

## CHAPTER SUMMARY

We began this chapter by referring to classical neurological views of naming. According to a view presented by Lichtheim, conceptual input in word production is provided by widespread cortical areas outside the classical language regions. Some earlier authors have also argued for special multimodal convergence zones that serve as gateways from concepts to words—according to Mills & McConnell (1895), the left inferior temporal region; according to Geschwind (1965), the left inferior parietal lobe. Word production would then proceed by retrieval of corresponding auditory (Wernicke's area) and motor word images (Broca's area) to motor implementation by the lower part of the motor strip.

It is interesting to note that many of these elements appear even in current models of naming. With regard to the semantic system, both lesion studies and functional neuroimaging experiments implicate a bilateral network outside the classical language areas, mainly located in posterior brain regions and encompassing anterior, middle, and inferior temporal regions, as well as temporo-parietal cortices. While both patient data and functional neuroimaging in normals suggest fractionation of semantic and grammatical knowledge, one-to-one correspondences between categories and specific anatomical areas remain elusive. This could be due to any or all of the following reasons: (a) differences in methods and subjects being employed, (b) uncontrolled psycholinguistic factors that can affect many studies (e.g., imageability and morphosyntactic effects in verb retrieval), (c) considerable interindividual variability in the cerebral organisation of higher cognitive functions, or (d) some as yet poorly understood aspects of the dynamic, distributed nature of information storage and retrieval in the brain. Nevertheless, converging evidence is accumulating for certain categories. For example, both lesion studies and functional neuroimaging experiments indicate that the left anterior temporal cortex is a "hotspot" for processing of unique semantic entities such as famous faces.

With regard to the gateways from semantics to the lexicon, recent evidence has implicated the left middle temporal cortex, but the left inferior temporal and parietal areas suggested earlier have also figured prominently in both lesion and functional imaging studies. According to some lesion studies, the left mid-ventromedial temporal area would be important in linking lexical semantic information to the corresponding word form. Wernicke's area and adjacent inferior parietal regions have been associated with a posterior phonological assembly network, and preparation for word output is assumed to continue in an anterior motor-articulatory network, encompassing Broca's area, lower part of the premotor cortex, and possibly the insula.

# 4 Clinical assessment of anomia

In this chapter, we take a clinically oriented approach to anomia. At any medical facility working with gerontological and/or neurological patients, word-finding deficits are commonly encountered. Given anomia's significance in differential diagnosis, its localising value as a nonspecific but sensitive indicator of left hemisphere dysfunction, and its importance for everyday living and communication, diagnosis of naming disorders is an integral part of neurobehavioural assessment. Here we will list some important subject characteristics that should be taken into account when evaluating naming abilities of an individual, summarise the manifestations of anomia in some common neurological conditions, and outline diagnostic procedures for the clinical assessment of anomia.

## SUBJECT CHARACTERISTICS AFFECTING NAMING

### Age

It is a common experience that word-finding problems increase as we age. In conversation, they show up as an increase in pauses, greater use of circumlocutions and empty phrases, indefinite terms, and pronouns without antecedents. Because many common neurological conditions may also be present in the elderly, it is important to be able to differentiate normal age-related changes in naming ability from pathological conditions. Although many basic language functions are less sensitive to age-related changes than, for example, performance in speeded nonverbal and psychomotor tasks, there is evidence suggesting a decline in picture-naming performance in the normal elderly, but it is not consistent. In a review of 25 studies addressing age-related naming performance, Goulet, Ska, and Kahn (1994) noted that only 15/25 studies reported statistically significant differences between younger and older subjects. Moreover, in 2 of these 15 studies older subjects performed better than younger ones. As all but one of the 25 studies was cross-sectional, the results indicating decline in naming by increasing age could be counfounded by cohort effects such as differences in education and socioeconomical level. However, the few existing longitudinal studies that circumvent cohort effects indicate age-related decline in picture naming (e.g., Au, Joung, Nicholas, Kass, Obler, & Albert, 1995; Connor, Spiro, Obler, & Albert, 2004). Moreover, a recent cross-sectional study that included a subsequent 2-year follow-up of elderly subjects indicated that the association between age and picture-naming performance cannot be explained by increased prevalence of incipient dementia in older individuals (MacKay, Connor, & Storandt, 2005). The onset of naming impairment is controversial: some authors claim that there is a sharp decline after age 70 (Nicholas, Barth, Obler, Au, & Albert, 1997) while others have emphasised individual variability in the onset of age-related naming problems (Goulet et al., 1994).

In sum, the majority of studies suggest that on average, picture-naming performance is worse in older than in younger subjects. This finding is enough to warrant the use of age-appropriate norms in differential diagnosis when such norms are available. In conjunction with an overall decline, individual variability in naming performance (as well as in other cognitive functions) increases with advancing age. There are most probably multiple reasons underlying age-related decline in naming. Physiological changes take place in sensory-motor systems as well as brain structure and function. At the cognitive level, executive functions can become more compromised, and spontaneous retrieval from long-term memory may be less effective. An elderly person may also show less active use of vocabulary, and become increasingly cautious when faced with cognitive tasks.

## Education

In several studies, more extensive schooling has been shown to associate with better naming performance (e.g., Ardila & Rosselli, 1989; Henderson, Frank, Pigatt, Abramson, & Houston, 1998; LeDorze & Durocher, 1992; Nicholas, Brookshire, MacLennan, Schumacher, & Porrazzo, 1989; Welch, Doineau, Johnson, & King, 1996; Worrall, Yiu, Hickson, & Barnett, 1995) but reports with no significant effect of education exist as well (Béland & Lecours, 1990; Farmer, 1990; LaBarge, Edwards, & Knesevich, 1986). Age and education are easily confounded in cross-sectional studies. Schooling is typically defined as years of education, but the functional significance of equally long education in, say, the 1940s or 1980s may be different. Nevertheless, the positive correlation between naming success and educational level leads to the plausible conclusion that individuals with more extensive education possess larger vocabularies and that education-adjusted norms should be used if available.

## Overall health status

Even when neurological illnesses are excluded, it is important to pay attention to the general health of an elderly person. Various health problems accumulate in older age, and they can be linked to impaired cognitive performance of an individual, although results from group studies have been controversial (e.g., Ylikoski et al., 2000). Concomitant use of medication in elderly individuals with failing health may further exacerbate their impairments, as some drugs have adverse effects on cognitive performance. The presence of major depression may also affect cognitive performance, including picture naming (Georgieff, Dominey, Michel, Marie-Cardine, & Dalery, 1998). In addition, the incidence of dementing illnesses of various origins (discussed later in this chapter) increases sharply in old age.

## Premorbid performance level

Anamnestic information is crucial when the premorbid cognitive level of an individual is estimated. Among other things, in the interview it is important to pay attention to early development and school performance. Specific learning difficulties, such as problems in learning to read, write, or acquire mathematics, may have a far-reaching impact on language-related performance well into the adult years. In dyslexic children, naming difficulties, e.g., in so-called rapid automatised naming tasks, are a rather common symptom even though their receptive vocabulary skills can be intact. Subtle naming impairments are reported in adult dyslexic readers as well (e.g., Felton, Naylor, & Wood, 1990). Evidence from naming to definition experiments involving long low-frequency words suggests that the reason for the naming difficulty in dyslexic readers may lie in poorly specified phonological representations (Snowling, 2000).

## Language and cultural background

In an increasingly multicultural and multilingual world, clinicians are more and more often encountering individuals having different language and cultural backgrounds. Evaluation of such individuals can be problematic, because most picture-naming tasks or other language measures have not been validated with culturally diverse populations. This can lead to false positive diagnoses of impaired cognitive performance (e.g., Fillenbaum, Huber, & Taussig, 1997; Roberts & Hamsher, 1984). Besides basic language proficiency, multilingual subjects' performance on language tasks can also reflect quality of education, literacy level, and overall acculturation. Even for multilinguals' dominant language, norms based on monolingual native speakers' performance are not necessarily adequate (Kohnert, Hernandez, & Bates, 1998; Touradj, Manly, Jacobs, & Stern, 2001). When evaluating multilinguals with language tasks, one should include language history questionnaires and self-assessment forms of everyday language skills in the test battery. Information from these measures should be considered in conjunction with performance on quantitative measures when making a final diagnosis. The situation is further complicated when the clients are multilingual aphasic patients who can show a variety of language recovery patterns (Paradis, 2001).

In summary, a number of subject-specific background factors need to be considered when diagnosing lexical retrieval difficulties. Age and education exert effects on naming performance, and for certain test instruments these factors are taken into account in the available norms. A clinician should also be aware of the possible effects of general health status and medication on a patient's linguistic performance, even though in practice the role of these effects may be difficult to pinpoint. Careful analysis of patient history helps to avoid the possible misdiagnosis of behaviours related to a developmental language disorder as symptoms of more recent cerebral dysfunction. Finally, considerations of culture- and language-related effects in language tasks like picture naming provide additional challenges to the clinician.

## ANOMIA IN COMMON NEUROLOGICAL DISEASES

Although there is a wide variety of neurological conditions that can lead to the occurrence of anomia together with other neuropsychological impairments, we will focus on those that are clinically most common. These conditions include cerebrovascular disorders, primary dementias, and head trauma. Even though the nature and severity of anomia varies considerably within these aetiologies, it is clinically useful to characterise the features of anomia in each of these conditions.

### Cerebrovascular disorders

Cerebrovascular disorders figure prominently in cognitive neuropsychological research, as most of the evidence for highly specific neuropsychological disorders (including pure forms of anomia and other language deficits) comes from focal cerebrovascular accidents, i.e., acute strokes and intracerebral haemorrhages. In those cases, specific symptomatology typically emerges after the generalised cerebral dysfunction at the acute stage has dissolved. However, highly specific neuropsychological syndromes are rather rare, and the majority of hospitalised patients suffering from aphasia have either very severe (global aphasia) or very mild disorders (residual aphasia). In mild cases, the diagnostic value of anomia is particularly important, as it is one of the hallmarks of left hemisphere dysfunction. The common occurrence of naming problems in stroke (together with other cognitive deficits) is exemplified by a recent clinical study on 209 consecutive acute stroke cases where 45% of the patients scored below cut-off point on a short naming screening test (Riepe, Riss, Bittner, & Huber, 2004). Although aphasic symptoms may dissolve over time (in stroke patients, most marked spontaneous recovery typically takes place within the first months post-onset), there are possible chronic after-effects, typically including occasional word-finding deficits coupled with reading and writing problems.

The majority of CVAs leading to language problems affect the distribution of the left middle cerebral artery. This artery supplies the perisylvian language region located in the frontal, temporal, and parietal cortices. Some clinical types of aphasia (Broca, Wernicke, conduction, anomic) tend to follow the occlusion of one of the several main pial branches of the middle cerebral artery. This artery also supplies certain subcortical structures (left striatum and white matter pathways) which when damaged sometimes result in aphasia. Infarction of the anterior cerebral artery, feeding inferior and medial frontal regions, may cause language production problems characteristic of transcortical motor aphasia (verbal adynamia). In this syndrome, naming is typically quite well preserved, but when difficulty in naming does occur, phonemic cueing is very effective in eliciting the elusive word. The territory of the posterior cerebral artery includes inferior temporal regions. Left-sided infarction in these zones can affect the so-called basal language area (see Chapter 3), which may lead to disturbances in naming and other language-related functions. Small penetrating branches of the posterior cerebral artery also supply the thalamus, and infarction or haemorrhage in the left thalamus may cause aphasic symptoms.

In Chapter 3 we reviewed studies on the neural basis of naming. As most of this evidence comes from CVA patients, that chapter informs the reader about the correlations between specific anomia subtypes and the location of damage in CVA. As will be emphasised later in this chapter, diagnosis of anomia subtypes requires additional testing. Anomia as such is the least localising sign among the symptoms of aphasia, and its presence merely suggests probable left hemisphere dysfunction, which can, of course, be a clinically very valuable observation.

## Alzheimer's disease

Primary dementias are associated with more global cognitive impairments where language disturbances are only rarely the single dominant feature. The most common form of primary dementia, Alzheimer's disease (AD), accounts for approximately half of the cases. Besides increasing age, risk factors for AD include family history of dementia, head injury, Down's syndrome, and the presence of ApoE-4 allele on chromosome 19 (possibly facilitating the aggregation of amyloid in the brain) (Cummings, 1995). Early AD is characterised by slowly progressive cognitive impairment, affecting several functions such as memory and learning, attention, visuoconstructive abilities, and language. Disorders of language appear in the form of fluent aphasias. Anomic aphasia is commonly present, and naming difficulties may be, in fact, the earliest sign of language impairment (Bowles, Obler, & Albert, 1987). Occasionally, a specific cognitive deficit such as a language disorder or a visuoconstructive deficit can appear as an early dominant symptom. As the disease progresses, language and other communicative functions become increasingly compromised, finally leading to total breakdown of communication.

Initially, AD-related pathology typically affects medial temporal structures, which explains the predominance of episodic memory impairment in the symptomatology. As the pathology gradually spreads into posterior cortical areas, language functions including word retrieval become impaired. The nature of lexical retrieval deficit in AD has been explored in a number of studies. Most researchers have emphasised the role of a semantic impairment in AD. Mild-to-moderate AD patients produce mainly semantically related errors in picture naming, and evidence difficulty in other semantic tasks such as semantically based word generation (e.g., producing as many animal names in a minute as possible), semantically based word and picture classification, word–picture matching, object attribute ranking, description of the function of objects, and generation of verbal definitions (Butters, Granholm, Salmon, Grant, & Wolfe, 1987; Chertkow, Bub, & Caplan, 1992; Flicker, Ferris, Crook, & Bartus, 1987; Grober, Buschke, Kawas, & Fuld, 1985; Hodges, Salmon, & Butters, 1992b; Martin & Fedio 1983; Ober, Dronkers, Koss, Delis, & Friedland, 1986; Schwartz, Marin, & Saffran, 1979). Additionally, item-specific comprehension and naming impairments have been documented in AD (Chertkow et al., 1992; Chertkow, Bub, & Seidenberg, 1989), as well as altered semantic priming (Chertkow, Bub, Bergman, Bruemmer, Merling, & Rothfleisch, 1994; Salmon, Shimamura, Butters, & Smith, 1988). Category-specific impairments have been described as well (e.g., Garrard et al., 1998).

In addition to semantic impairment, word form anomia may also play a role in AD: impaired naming in AD is not always associated with impaired identification of corresponding semantic features (Sommers & Pierce, 1990), and there are priming data indicating that mild AD patients have impaired inhibitory control over phonological competitors in picture naming (Faust, Balota, & Multhaup, 2004). Finally, as some dementia patients produce numerous visually based naming errors (e.g., can → "drum"; Rochford, 1971) and perceptual quality of stimuli affects naming in AD (Goldstein, Green, Presley, & Green, 1992; Kirshner, Webb, & Kelly, 1984), visuoperceptual impairment cannot be ruled out as a factor in their naming difficulty. Nevertheless, most researchers would agree that semantic impairment plays a predominant role in anomia associated with AD. At the same time, phonological processing of words is typically preserved, as attested by intact repetition skills.

### Vascular dementia

Vascular dementia (VaD), the second most common form of dementing illnesses, has received less attention in neuropsychological studies. As this syndrome encompasses a variety of ischaemic, hypoxic, or haemorrhagic brain lesions, both cortical and subcortical, it is understandable that specific symptomatologies of individual patients vary considerably. As a group, however, VaD patients suffer from widespread cognitive impairment that is not markedly different from that observed in AD (Almkvist, Bäckman, Basun, & Wahlund, 1993). White matter damage may be more common in VaD than in AD, and in some studies it has been related to more marked psychomotor slowing and motor speech output problems in VaD (Almkvist et al., 1993; Powell, Cummings, Hill, & Benson, 1988). A direct comparison of performances on picture naming and other related tasks in mild-to-moderately demented matched AD and VaD patients indicated that semantic impairment underlies anomia in both conditions (with a tendency for more severe semantic deficit in AD) even though individual variability was considerable (Laine, Vuorinen, & Rinne, 1997).

## Fronto-temporal lobar degeneration

Fronto-temporal lobar degeneration (FTD) is a previously underdiagnosed condition: as the name implies, FTD affects frontal and temporal lobes, and atrophic changes are bilateral and more or less symmetrical (The Lund and Manchester Groups, 1994). Cases with asymmetric pathology affecting predominantly the left frontal and/or temporal regions evidence the syndrome of primary progressive aphasia (PPA). Such patients lack the widespread intellectual deterioration of dementia. Both fluent and nonfluent forms of PPA have been reported, and word retrieval difficulties are part and parcel of the symptomatology. Frontal involvement in PPA leads to characteristic behavioural changes as well as verbal adynamia, perseveration, echolalia, and even mutism. On the other hand, purely anomic forms of PPA with predominantly left temporal lobe damage are hard to differentiate clinically from early AD (Kertesz, Hudson, Mackenzie, & Munoz, 1994; see Graham, Patterson, & Hodges, 1995, for a case analysis and follow-up of progressive pure anomia). FTD confined to the left inferolateral temporal cortex can also lead to a syndrome coined as semantic dementia that was discussed in Chapter 2. This syndrome is characterised by an isolated breakdown of semantic memory coupled with marked anomia and surface dyslexia (e.g., Hodges et al., 1999).

## Traumatic brain injury

Traumatic brain injury (TBI) can lead to a complex pattern of behavioural and cognitive impairment, including problems with attention, memory, psychomotor speed, and higher-level language. TBI also differs from cerebrovascular illnesses and dementia by the fact that it affects a wide age-range with a peak of occurrence in adolescence. TBI varies depending on the nature and severity of the damage-inducing factor, but it commonly includes diffuse axonal damage which may be coupled with focal lesions. Language disorders do not dominate the symptomatology of TBI, except in cases with concomitant focal lesions in the left perisylvian regions. While frank aphasias are uncommon, impairments of conversational fluency and naming are often observed in TBI patients (Dalby & Obrzut, 1991; Hartley & Jensen, 1991).

Reports of naming error patterns in TBI have indicated a predominance of semantically related and circumlocutory errors (Levin, Grossman, Sarwar, & Meyers, 1981). According to a naming study with TBI patients and matched controls (Kerr, 1995), overall error patterns were quite similar in these two groups, although quantitatively the TBI group performed more poorly. In both normals and TBI patients, the majority of picture-naming errors were semantically related to the target. Also in a study comparing naming error patterns in mild-to-moderately anomic stroke patients, AD patients, and TBI patients, semantically related errors (associates, subordinates, or superordinates of the target) represented the most common error category (Boles, 1997). The only significant difference between the TBI group and either of the other two groups was in the occurrence of visual misperceptions: such errors were produced by the TBI group (and the AD group) but their rate was close to zero in the stroke group.

## COGNITIVE MODELS IN THE CLINICAL ASSESSMENT OF ANOMIA

In principle, cognitive models should provide a blueprint for clinicians to identify the source of a patient's language impairment. They have successfully been applied to accounts of both normal and abnormal word production, as detailed in Chapters 1 and 2. It should follow that these models could serve as a framework within which to diagnose acquired impairments of language.

What does a cognitive model offer to clinicians trying to diagnose a language disorder? Berndt (1987) notes that a cognitive model allows us to reach beneath surface symptoms and consider underlying processing problems. Basso (1993; Basso & Marangolo, 2000) views a cognitive model as a series of hypotheses about the structure and functioning of mental processes such as those mediating word retrieval. Basso adds two reservations to keep in mind when using a model to help diagnose a word-processing deficit. First, identification of a functional lesion in such a model can only be as specific as the detail of the model allows. A disorder cannot be defined in terms that are not represented in the model. The more detailed the model, the more detailed the diagnosis. If a model indicates merely that word production is a two-stage process of retrieving semantic and phonological representations of words, then the anomic impairment can be identified as a disturbance of one or both of those stages. If a model adds further details about, for example, semantic organisation or phonological encoding, the diagnosis can be more explicit. Greater detail in a model allows for finer, more accurate descriptions of a disorder. Cognitive models have become increasingly detailed in their description of the psycholinguistic structures and operations that underlie word production, a progression that reflects our increased understanding of these operations. As was discussed in Chapter 2, we know from several case studies of anomia, for example, that although aphasia can affect semantic processing of words selectively, semantic errors in aphasic speech do not necessarily correspond directly to damaged semantic processes (e.g., Caramazza & Hillis, 1990).

Basso's (1993) second reservation in using a model to diagnose language disorders concerns the functional overlap among some components of a cognitive model. Some components will have functions that are utilised in more than one task. If behaviour is the primary clinical means of identifying a functional lesion in a cognitive model, care must be taken to evaluate any language process in all of the tasks that engage that process. This concern can be clarified with the following example. Lexical retrieval involves at least two access stages, each followed by retrieval of a representation: access to the lexical-semantic representation of a word and access to the corresponding phonological representations of that word. The second stage of lexical retrieval is common to at least two tasks: naming and repetition (also oral reading). The first stage of lexical retrieval is mandatory in naming and optional in repetition and reading. If the naming disorder involves the first stage of lexical retrieval, we would expect to observe errors in naming but not in repeating or reading aloud those same words (barring any additional deficits). If the naming disorder is due to problems in retrieving the phonological form, errors should be observed in naming, repetition, and possibly reading. It is this sort of reasoning (based on a structural model of word retrieval such as the one in Figure 2.1) that helps in choosing the proper tasks to diagnose naming disorders in psycholinguistic terms.

As an example of the application of cognitive models to the diagnosis of naming disorders, consider the following two anomic patients, GL and VP (reported in Martin & Saffran, 1997, 2002). Each achieved similar scores on the Philadelphia Naming Test (Roach, Schwartz, Martin, Grewal, & Brecher, 1996). However, this does not necessarily mean that their individual naming impairments arise from the same underlying word-processing difficulty. Table 4.1 lists the kinds of naming errors that they made and also their performances on measures of semantic and phonological aspects of word-processing ability. These measures provide clues to the functional locus of the word-processing deficit.

The first two measures, types of naming errors and the score on repetition of single words, provide some insight into the condition of the output processes. Good repetition and the lack of phonological errors in VP's naming indicate that output phonological processes are relatively intact.

*Table 4.1* Patterns of word-processing deficits underlying word retrieval
failure in two anomic patients

| Language measure | Proportion correct GL | VP |
|---|---|---|
| Picture Naming (Philadelphia Naming Test, *n* = 175) | .29 | .28 |
| Naming error types | phonemic, semantic, formal | semantic, no response, whole-word perseveration |
| Repetition of single words | .56 | .93 |
| Phoneme discrimination | .86 | .95 |
| Rhyme recognition | .88 | .96 |
| Auditory lexical decision | .94 | .91 |
| Peabody Picture Vocabulary Test (standard score) | 96 | 78 |
| Word-to picture matching (in context of three semantic distractors) | 1.00 | .88 |
| Synonymy Judgements (word meanings) | .93 | .66 |

Semantic errors, coupled with the tendency to perseverate on a previously
uttered name, and a tendency to give no response at all ("I don't know the
name" or "I know it, but can't say it") indicate difficulty in activating the
word's lexical representation on the basis of conceptually driven semantic
processes.

The rest of the measures listed in Table 4.1 involve primarily input
processes, and their relationship to output processes involved in naming is a
controversial issue (e.g., Martin & Saffran, 1999). There are models which
postulate that lexical and semantic information accessed comes from the
same "store" of information whether the tasks is input or output (see
Monsell, 1987, for discussion). At the same time, many models assume
separate stores of phonological information for input and output processing (R. Martin, Lesch, & Bartha, 1999). That issue aside, we can at least
examine performance on input measures with respect to the similarity to the
output measures.

Phoneme discrimination and rhyme recognition both measure phonological processing ability. GL's performance on these tasks is relatively poor
compared to VP's. In contrast, GL's performance on lexical semantic tests
(word to picture matching including the Peabody Picture Vocabulary Test
and synonymy judgements) is quite good and much better than that of VP.
Both subjects do fairly well on the auditory lexical decision test, a measure
of word recognition ability. This indicates that despite GL's phonological
input processing deficits and VP's semantic deficits, they are each able to
recognise a word. In GL's case, she probably uses semantic information

accessed on the basis of "fuzzy" phonological input to help her discriminate words from nonwords. In VP's case, we can assume that input processing is sufficient to activate a word-level representation, but less sufficient in activating its meaning. The important aspect of these input measures is that they are consistent with the output measures. We can conclude on the basis of these measures that GL's naming impairment is related primarily to a breakdown of phonological encoding, and VP's naming impairment is primarily of semantic origin with problems in mapping between a semantic representation and the corresponding word form.

## CLINICAL ASSESSMENT METHODS FOR WORD-FINDING DEFICITS

The assessment of word-finding ability in a neurobehavioural examination is particularly important, as anomia is among the most sensitive indicators of left hemisphere damage. Several test instruments are available, and we will shortly review some of the most common ones. As with any diagnostic test measure, the user should have knowledge about the main psychometric features (validity and reliability) of the test and become acquainted with previous relevant research that can provide information about its sensitivity and specificity in neurological patients.

To an attentive examiner, anomic problems (e.g., circumlocutory, halting, informationally "empty" speech) and possible paraphasic responses may be apparent in an initial interview. However, mild word-finding deficits can be concealed by use of stereotypical phrases and multiple ways of expression which characterise everyday language. Thus, mild anomia may be revealed only on naming tests or in more demanding communication situations that require retrieval of specific words. The most common test instrument to assess word retrieval ability is the picture-naming task because it provides a fairly well-controlled situation in which a specific lexical item must be retrieved. This minimises the chances for concealing an existing deficit with circumlocutory responses. Alternative assessment methods include narrative speech tasks like description of the events in a cartoon or story retelling, and analysis of conversational speech samples (see, e.g., Mayer & Murray, 2003; McNeil, Doyle, Fossett, Park, & Goda, 2001; Pashek & Tompkins, 2002; Prins & Bastiaanse, 2004). This important research field is still in its early stages: for example, there is no consensus on the lexical retrieval measures used with these complex contextual tasks. Accordingly, we postpone discussion of these approaches until the final chapter.

One of the most widely used clinical picture-naming tasks today is the Boston Naming Test (BNT; Kaplan, Goodglass, & Weintraub, 1983). It consists of 60 line drawings of objects, presented in an order of increasing naming difficulty. If spontaneous naming fails, the subject is provided with semantic cues (e.g., "it tells time" for a clock) and/or phonemic cues (initial phoneme or phonemes of the to-be-named target word). In addition to an analysis of a patient's naming error pattern, cueing effects may provide valuable information about the underlying mechanisms of a naming deficit. An extensive body of research literature exists on the BNT, ranging from normative studies to results in various patient populations. Other relevant clinical picture-naming tests include the 30-item Graded Naming Test (McKenna & Warrington, 1983; Warrington, 2002) and the 175-item Philadelphia Naming Test (Roach et al., 1996) which is a non-published test available from the authors. With regard to category-specific naming disorders, the Object and Action Naming Battery (Druks & Masterson, 2000) and the Category-Specific Names Test (McKenna, 1998) are available. Besides specific picture-naming tasks, aphasia test batteries like the Boston Diagnostic Aphasia Examination (BDAE; Goodglass, Kaplan, & Barresi, 2001), the Western Aphasia Battery (WAB; Kertesz, 1982), the Psycholinguistic Assessments of Language Processing in Aphasia (PALPA; Kay et al., 1992), the Aachen Aphasia Test (for an English language version, see Miller, Willmes, & De Bleser, 2000) and the Comprehensive Aphasia Test (Swinburn, Porter, & Howard, 2004) include visual confrontation naming tasks as well as other tasks tapping lexical processing such as naming to definition, naming in response to questions, and word comprehension.

As noted earlier, in order to draw conclusions about the underlying mechanisms of patient's anomia, naming tests (preferably tested separately for oral and written naming as they can dissociate) should be complemented with word comprehension tasks, as well as tests that tap the integrity of phonological output with repetition and reading. For example, in order to establish the diagnosis of a semantically based anomia, objective evidence for impaired semantic comprehension and relatively well-preserved phonological abilities at the single word level is needed. Test batteries such as the PALPA provide suitable subtests for these purposes but other tests are also available. The PALPA also provides single word processing tasks that explore the effects of important psycholinguistic variables such as word length, frequency, and imageability on patient's performance. However, careful task analyses such as the one done by Cole-Virtue and Nickels (2004) on the PALPA spoken word-to-picture matching subtest suggest that clinicians should exercise caution when interpreting results on single tests in terms of underlying impairments.

With regard to more detailed tests of word comprehension, many researchers use their own experimental tasks, but there are also commercially available tests for probing word comprehension, including the Peabody Picture Vocabulary task (Dunn & Dunn, 1997) using spoken word-to-picture matching, and the Pyramids and Palm Trees test that taps access to semantics from both spoken (or written) words and pictures (Howard & Patterson, 1992). Additionally, there are tests designed to identify possible difficulties in visual object recognition, such as the Birmingham Object

Recognition Battery (Riddoch & Humphreys, 1993). Other sources of normative data on various sets of pictorial and word stimuli in different languages are available in the psychological research literature (see, e.g., the Psychonomic Society Archive of Norms, Stimuli, and Data currently at http://www.psychonomic.org/archive). These can be quite useful when designing word production tests for experimental purposes.

## CLASSIFICATION OF NAMING RESPONSE PATTERNS IN ANOMIA

In order to reach an adequate clinical diagnosis of anomia, both quantitative and qualitative data on naming need to be considered. Age-stratified normative data provided by, for example, the BNT helps the clinician to estimate whether a patient's naming success is quantitatively poorer than would be expected. As regards qualitative data, naming response patterns (for example, the types of errors that are made in naming) provide important information about what stages of the word retrieval process are disrupted. However, an analysis of naming errors is not sufficient information to draw conclusions about the mechanisms underlying anomia: the existence of both "central" semantic errors (coupled with a comprehension problem) and "output" semantic errors (coupled with intact comprehension) is a case in point. Semantic errors in naming predominate in both of these disorders and thus, the output pattern is not sufficient to discriminate between the two impairments. Tests of word comprehension and a closer look at the qualitative features of naming (e.g., are semantic naming errors spontaneously rejected by the patient?) are needed to narrow down the anomia diagnosis in such patients.

An important issue in naming research (and in the clinic) concerns how to score naming responses. For example, should one score the first word-level response? Or should one only take into account the final one? Or should one score the full naming attempt, sometimes including several response types? There is no single accepted schema for the scoring of naming errors. It varies depending on what kind of information one needs about the patient's performance. If we are interested in noting how stable word retrieval is, we might score only first attempts. But if we are measuring progress after therapy, we might take special note of naming accuracy even after multiple responses. It may be that at one point in time a patient has been unable to name a picture after multiple attempts, but after treatment can now name the picture after more than one attempt. Whatever the choice, in testing it is important to record the responses in full. The taxonomy in Table 4.2 presents one possible system for the classification of naming errors in a picture-naming task. This taxonomy is applicable to object naming, which is the most common way to probe word retrieval in clinical settings. For action naming, additional factors need to be considered, including the fact

*Table 4.2* An example of a scheme for classification of responses in
visual confrontation naming

---

## CORRECT RESPONSE

Besides the targeted names, correct responses include synonyms, dialectal and
colloquial names, and so-called augmented correct responses where the subject
provides additional information on the target item. In some languages, areas, and
subject groups, dialectal variation is so marked that if the examiner does not master
the dialects in question, consultation may be needed to avoid classifying a dialectal
variant as a paraphasic response.

Example: TAPE RECORDER → cassette recorder, magnetophone, portable
tape recorder, tape deck

## INCORRECT REAL WORD RESPONSE

### Semantically related to the target (semantic paraphasia)
This error class includes erroneous responses exhibiting different kinds of semantic
relationships (category-based, associative) between the target and the response. In
order to examine whether a semantic error is of a "central" type (coupled with
impaired comprehension of the target) or of an "output" type (the target is
identified correctly), one should probe the subject's semantic knowledge of the item
in conjunction with naming. Possible additional information provided by the subject
like immediate rejection of the own semantically incorrect response (e.g., "cucumber
no it's not, something else") is also useful here.

(1) *Semantic-visual*
This response is related to the target both in terms of meaning and visual features. It
is not uncommon in normal naming responses.

Example: VIOLIN → guitar, BEAVER → squirrel

(2) *Category member*
The response is derived from the same category members but does not carry an
apparent visual similarity with the target.

Example: APPLE → banana, HELICOPTER → rocket

(3) *Superordinate*
Instead of the target name, its superordinate category name is offered as a response.

Example: CORN → veggie, CAR → vehicle

(4) *Associative*
These errors represent various sorts of associative relationships that go across
category boundaries.

Example: MOUSE → cheese, ICE SKATES → hockey

(5) *Featural or functional description*
These are often circumlocutory responses where some conspicuous aspect of the
target is described.

Example: TRUMPET → you blow in it, PEACOCK → it has fantastic colours

### Phonologically related to the target (formal paraphasia)
The response shares phonological features with the target. The degree of
phonological similarity required for labelling an error as formal paraphasia varies

*(continues)*

*Table 4.2 (continued)*

between studies. With lax criteria, there is an increased risk of classifying random relationships as formal paraphasias if appropriate base level probabilities for this are not calculated and related to the patient's error rates.

Example: HORSE → house, BAT → mat

**Semantically and phonologically related to the target (mixed error)**
The response is related to the target both in meaning (associate, categorical) and in phonology. As discussed in Chapter 1, the occurrence of these errors in normals has been used as evidence for the interdependence of meaning and form retrieval in word production. With regard to the operational definition of phonological relatedness, same words of caution apply as for formal errors.

Example: CAT → rat, SACK → bag

**Unrelated word**
These are real word responses with no evident target–response relationship. Either they are random or represent some idiosyncratic relationship unknown to the examiner.

Example: HAMMER → sun, PYRAMID → wheel

**Morphological variant of the target**
Morphological variants of the target can represent three distinct morphological operations: inflection, derivation, or compounding. The latter two operations change the meaning of the word stem.

Example: CAR → cars, SURF → surfer, CHALKBOARD → chalk

**Other response**
There is always a heterogeneous group of responses that is not covered by a given error classification. Here such responses include for example different perseverative responses (immediate or so-called intrusions that appear after some intervening stimuli), egocentric comments ("we have that stuff at home"; "I used to have it"), and semantically irrelevant sentence-level utterances.

## NONWORD RESPONSE

**Over 50% phonological similarity with the target (phonological paraphasia)**
A commonly used criterion to classify a nonword error as target-related is that it has at least 50% phonological overlap with the target word. This criterion for overlap is arbitrary and can vary between studies. It is also possible to lump phonological and neologistic paraphasias together as phonologically distorted responses and treat the degree of target–error phonological similarity as a continuous variable that is calculated for each target–error pair. However, in clinical use, the differentiation between milder (phonological paraphasias) and more severe (neologisms) may serve as a characterisation of the degree of the patient's phonological output disturbance. Phonological paraphasias appear in different subtypes, and the affected units may vary from subsyllabic units (syllabic constituents, phonemes, sometimes perhaps even single phonemic features) to syllables.

Examples:
CAMEL → /cametel/ (addition)
BRAIN → /bain/ (deletion)
KITE → /kaim/, /mait/ (substitution)
GUITAR → /tiga:r/ (exchange)

*(continues overleaf)*

*Table 4.2   (continued)*

---

***Phonological similarity with the target 50% or less (neologistic paraphasia)***
These are the more far-fetched nonword responses, varying in their phonological structure, sometimes including perseverative phoneme strings as well. Neologisms may include real morphemes as well. The term "abstruse neologism" is used for nonword responses with no identifiable relation to the target (some of these may in fact be lexical-then-phonological errors, rendering the substituted and phonologically distorted word unrecognisable)

Example: TENT → /mek/

***Multiword response including neologisms (neologistic jargon)***
Sometimes neologisms appear as parts of longer uninterrupted utterances, making it difficult to determine which single product, if any, is meant to be patient's answer.

Example: ELEPHANT → this memory, getting on /ko/ /ne/ /flan/ but maybe, I don't see

***Illegal combination of existing morphemes (morphophonological paraphasia)***
As these kinds of errors are by definition non-existing combinations of bound and free-standing morphemes, they reveal the productive aspects of morphology and can involve inflection, derivation, or compounding. Inflection is a productive morphological operation but for derivations, productivity and semantic transparency varies, and it is of interest to relate these factors to the patient's morphophonological paraphasias.

Examples: TEACHER → she's teachering; TILE → brickment; MIRROR → loopmirror

### OMISSION

Omissions take various forms: either the patient remains silent (often showing by gestures that s/he does not have the answer) or indicates the inability to name by comments like "I don't know it", "pass", "I know what it is but cannot get it"). As omission can represent a processing failure at any stage of word production (and possibly a conscious choice to stay quiet), further probing may reveal whether semantic or phonological information of the unnamed target is nevertheless available.

---

that responses like "that's swimming" may represent gerunds, which belong to the grammatical category of nouns. For a classification of action-naming errors, see e.g. the schema employed by Kemmerer and Tranel (2000). For a detailed classification of nominal compound errors, the reader is referred to Blanken (2000).

### CHAPTER SUMMARY

In this chapter we have taken a clinical view on the diagnosis of anomia. We first noted several background factors that can affect the naming performance of a subject: age, educational level, overall health status and medication, premorbid cognitive level, as well as language and cultural background. These factors should be controlled for by a careful interview and by using adequate age- and education-adjusted test norms when available. Then we reviewed briefly the occurrence of anomia in most common neurological conditions including cerebrovascular disorders, primary dementias, and head trauma. With regard to testing, a comprehensive evaluation of naming, word comprehension, and lexical-phonological processing is called for if one wants to reach a diagnosis on the underlying mechanisms of a patient's anomia. Here we have provided a list of commercially available test instruments suitable for these purposes. Additionally, we recommended that evaluation includes a qualitative analysis of a patient's naming response pattern, and have provided an example of a naming error classification scheme. However, mere testing for the presence of anomia can also be clinically useful for screening purposes, as anomia is a non-localising but sensitive sign of left hemisphere dysfunction.

# 5 Therapeutic approaches to word-finding deficits

In Chapter 1 we reviewed the recent and rapid development of cognitive modelling of normal and impaired language processing. On the virtual heels of that movement, clinicians and scientists interested in rehabilitation began to apply these models to treatment of speech and language disorders (e.g., Howard, Patterson, Franklin, Orchard-Lisle, & Morton, 1985a, 1985b; Nettleton & Lesser, 1991; Nickels, 1992). Much of this chapter will focus on that enterprise because it shows promise of expanding our knowledge of aphasia treatment in significant ways. However, the use of cognitive models to guide treatment is a relatively recent development, and thus we will begin with a brief history of aphasia rehabilitation and factors leading to the current interest in model-based approaches to treatment. Following this, we will discuss applications of cognitive models to therapy, current limitations on this endeavour, and future directions.

## A BRIEF HISTORY OF APHASIA REHABILITATION

Aphasia rehabilitation is a relatively young discipline which first emerged after the catastrophes of the World Wars in the first half of the 20th century that created the need for rehabilitation of a large number of brain-injured war veterans. To take an early example, in 1916 Kurt Goldstein founded a military hospital for head-injured soldiers in Germany, with the intention of integrating medical, psychological, and occupational interventions for their impairments, including aphasia (Goldstein, 1919). In the United States, following World War II several army hospitals started programmes for treatment of post-trauma patients. Wepman (1953) is credited for extending the scope of rehabilitation programmes for returning veterans to the larger population of untreated civilians who could also benefit from therapy. The post-war developmental course of aphasia rehabilitation was similar in some other countries such as Great Britain (Butfield & Zangwill, 1946; Byng, 1993), while for others, e.g., Poland (Pachalska, 1993) and Japan (Sasanuma, 1993), the profession emerged a few decades later.

In its early years, research in rehabilitation of aphasia addressed questions about whether treatment of neurogenic language disorders could be effective. What kind of recovery was possible? Could impaired language abilities be repaired? Could other neural systems assume functions of the impaired language system? Several philosophies of speech therapy emerged in the 1940s and 50s that embody differing views about these questions. One approach to rehabilitation assumed that *restoration* of impaired language processes was possible and that therapy would aid in returning an impaired ability to its normal state. Hildred Schuell, one of the pioneers of aphasia rehabilitation in the United States, combined restorative and functional approaches in treatment. She advocated direct stimulation of auditory comprehension (which she considered central to language functioning), but also recommended that the content and extent of treatment be tailored to the patient's personal agenda (Schuell, 1974).

A second philosophical approach to aphasia treatment, *reconstitution*, is based on the view that recovery of behaviours results from functional reorganisation of neural circuitry. Luria (1969), an advocate of this approach, maintained that although impaired processes will remain so, function can be restored by means of integration and adaptation of other unimpaired neural processes. Luria defined a functional system as a group of interconnected acts carried out by a network of brain structures that cooperate to perform a given task. He proposed that the initial and final links of these functional systems are fixed, but that the intermediate steps involved in carrying out a particular task are modifiable within broad limits. If one component is lost or impaired, the functional system presumably undergoes reorganisation in order to perform the task, albeit somewhat differently.

Restorative and reconstitutive philosophies differ in their assumptions about the nature of the neurological changes that occur as a consequence of treatment and recovery (restoring neural circuits vs. reorganising them). However, they both aim to re-establish function, and it is this goal that brings them together as the foundation of current impairment-based therapies.

A third approach to aphasia treatment is best described as *compensation*. Advocates of this approach (Byng & Duchan, 2005; Holland, 1991; Holland & Hinckley, 2002; Worrall, 1995) acknowledge that some recovery of function is possible, but focus rehabilitation efforts on helping the patient to adapt to his or her disability and make use of whatever functions remain in order to communicate. The goal of therapy within this framework is to facilitate verbal and nonverbal communication within the environment of the individual. In the domain of naming therapy, goals and activities would focus less on directly restoring word retrieval abilities and more on helping the patient to find alternative means to communicate. For example, a person with anomia would be encouraged to develop circumlocutory skills, rather than struggle with retrieval of an elusive word.

There is no single right or wrong approach to therapy, but the choice should be based on the individual's personal circumstances, and most often both approaches are employed to some extent. That is, a person may work directly on improving their verbal output, but at the same time will be encouraged to find ways to communicate needs nonverbally in conjunction with verbal efforts.

## THE "SEEDS" OF COGNITIVE MODEL-BASED TREATMENTS OF ANOMIA

Both restorative and reconstitutive approaches to treatment attempt to directly manipulate the impaired language system via tasks designed to stimulate specific language operations. It is this aspect that links them quite naturally to cognitive models. Thus, as the use of models of word processing for diagnostic and research purposes increased, treatment researchers who advocated restorative and reconsitutive therapies were ready to explore the application of these models in the domain of treatment. Hildred Schuell's restorative approach to therapy was not based on a formal cognitive model of language, although her methods were described mostly in terms of functional components of a language processor (e.g., auditory comprehension). In this respect, her approach, along with Luria's ideas of functional plasticity, can be considered antecedents of current model-based treatment programmes. Each philosophy assumes that the language processor can be decomposed into functional components (e.g., auditory comprehension or word retrieval) although Schuell believed that in aphasia all modalities were affected by a unidimensional impairment. Luria viewed treatment as an aid to functional neural reorganisation (assuming that it stimulated development of cognitive strategies). Schuell advocated direct stimulation of auditory processes to help a patient regain access to language abilities that she believed were intact, but unstable. Auditory processes were considered by Schuell to be the ideal route for stimulation and she believed that other modalities should be stimulated in conjunction with the auditory stimulus. The influences of each of these approaches remain strong and widespread today. What these two approaches share is a fundamental belief in neural plasticity that is influenced by external stimulation.

Schuell's focus on stimulation of the auditory input channel to revive unstable language processes and representations is shared by others who advocate direct stimulation methods. Huber, Springer, and Willmes (1993) note that auditory comprehension often appears to be the least impaired modality in aphasia. This appearance, however, may be due in part to compensatory guessing strategies based on the use of contextual information. Weigl (1961) also advocated the use of direct and indirect stimulation, but did not limit that stimulation to the auditory modality. He used a method called "de-blocking" to stimulate word retrieval. This method incorporated the assumption that accessing a word in an unimpaired task (e.g., reading or repetition) would make that word temporarily more accessible for retrieval via an impaired modality (e.g., as in naming). Once produced in the impaired modality, the response would remain available for some period of time following the stimulation. Moreover, Weigl felt that effects of de-blocking access to one word could spread to a whole semantic field. Reading or repeating the word "dog", for example, could facilitate access to words semantically associated to dog (e.g., puppy, kennel, bone, and cat). This technique is more currently known as "priming" and is used in treatment, but also in research to determine whether different types of aphasic impairments are more or less sensitive to phonological and semantic input (e.g., Baum & Leonard, 1999; Milberg, Blumstein, & Dworetzky, 1988; Milberg, Blumstein, Katz, Gerschberg, & Brown, 1995). The work of Schuell, Luria, Weigl, and others during the 1950s, 60s, and 70s stimulated an appreciation of the value of using a model of language operations as a framework for conceptualising and treating language impairments. The adoption of the idea that mechanisms underlying language processing in the brain were not fixed, but could be manipulated to some extent by external stimuli and demands, led to a need for more precise definition of the functional organisation of language. This sentiment in the rehabilitation community contributed to the interest in cognitive models of language being developed by psycholinguists and cognitive psychologists, as reviewed in Chapter 1.

## USING A COGNITIVE MODEL TO GUIDE THERAPY

In earlier chapters, we reviewed how cognitive models of word processing are used in research and in clinical work to determine the nature and severity of language impairments. This approach was illustrated ideally in a case study published by Howard and Franklin (1988). They administered a comprehensive set of measures to assess numerous language skills (spoken and written language) of their subject, MK, who demonstrated numerous impairments of the word-processing system. Their case report provides an excellent example of how a cognitive model of word processing can be used to guide one's evaluation of language impairment. Howard and Franklin (1988) administered a carefully designed battery of tests to pinpoint within the word-processing model those functions that were still operational and those that were impaired. The information gained from these tests enabled them to identify which functions or pathways in the model were impaired or available to MK, enabling them to devise strategies that exploited intact processes to treat impaired processes.

Although the detailed assessment used by Howard and Franklin is well beyond the scope of what can be accomplished in a busy clinical setting, knowledge of cognitive models can guide a clinician's intuitions about what aspects of client's language impairment warrant more detailed diagnosis. The *Psycholinguistic Assessments of Language Processing in Aphasia* (*PALPA*, Kay et al., 1992) described earlier, is intended for a more in-depth analysis of impairments identified in screening tests of language function. For example, if reading is determined to be impaired in a screening test, the PALPA provides numerous subtests which will pinpoint the specific stages of reading that are affected (e.g., grapheme–phoneme conversion or sound blending).

In the next section, we discuss research on the use of cognitive models to guide treatment. This line of research is currently entering its second phase. The first phase, discussed below, explored how models could tell us what impairment to treat. This focus was due largely to the fact that functional models of language were limited to descriptions of the structure of the language system. The second and current phase of treatment research emphasises the "how" of treatment. This development has been made possible by advances in computer and neurological sciences. There are now computer models that can address questions of dynamics of the therapeutic processes and learning in normal and damaged brains. Additionally, recent research in neuroscience has yielded new and promising information about neuroplastic processes that underlie recovery of brain function.

## USING A COGNITIVE MODEL TO GUIDE TREATMENT, I: WHAT NEEDS TO BE TREATED?

As noted, cognitive models have been most useful as guides to diagnosis and they are still used often for this purpose. For example, the PALPA test is based on a functional cognitive model of word processing (Kay et al., 1992). Early efforts to base treatments on theoretical models did not go far beyond their use as diagnostic mechanisms. The models would indicate what needed to be treated and would characterise the deficit in psycholinguistic terms, but could not indicate how to treat the deficit.

Despite these limitations, the use of a model to identify what to treat represented a major advance in the field. In Chapter 1 we noted that word retrieval is a process of translating a nonverbal concept into a sequence of articulated sounds. Words have meanings, sounds, and syllabic and morphological structures that are computed over several stages. Brain damage does not typically affect all of these stages uniformly, but rather results in what appear to be selective functional lesions affecting one or more of the retrieval stages. A model provides a framework within which to characterise the deficit, which in turn should ultimately make therapy more effective (Ellis, Franklin, & Crerar, 1994). The profile of spared and impaired representations and processes that results from a model-based diagnosis of a word-processing disorder can be used to identify possible cognitive strategies which would provide an alternative means of performing a task that can no longer be performed (e.g., writing instead of naming, as suggested in the case study of MK by Howard & Franklin, 1988) or facilitate the impaired naming processes by means of self-cueing (e.g., Nickels, 1992).

Huber et al. (1993) also note that processing models support decisions about the kind of therapeutic intervention techniques to use by guiding a more precise definition of the problem. Perhaps the impairment involves primarily transmission of information by a certain modality, in which case treatment should involve development of strategies to improve that transmission. Impairments based on loss of linguistic knowledge would require a different, more linguistically oriented approach.

Models also provide theoretically motivated predictions of the outcome of a therapy approach (Byng, 1993) and thus a more precise basis on which to measure the effectiveness of therapy. This is an important asset to treatment research. With a clear definition of the means by which a therapy approach aims to address a specific impairment, it is easier to measure the effects of that particular treatment. In this way, model-based treatment protocols serve as a testing ground for theories of language organisation. Indeed, model-based treatments of naming have been referred to as hypothesis testing (Byng, 1993; Caplan, 1992). That is, based on a model of word-processing and diagnostic tasks that presumably tap word-processing functions from each part of the model, we should be able to identify the locus of impairment, and design our therapy tasks to treat the impaired processes accordingly. The effectiveness of our therapy would be used, in part, to verify our hypothesis about the site of functional lesion in our model and, in this sense, therapy would serve as an ongoing assessment tool (Howard & Hatfield, 1987).

If we use a cognitive model to develop hypotheses about a disorder and we test those hypotheses via therapy, what happens when the therapy does not work? We might conclude that our model is wrong, but this would be premature for several reasons. A number of factors contribute to the success or failure of treatment, including severity of impairment, choice of stimuli, or the training task. And although the failure may be due to some aspect of our hypothesis of what the impairment is, it is just as likely that our model is insufficiently detailed to identify the problem. For example, the box-and-arrow models that are most often used to diagnose language disorders do not readily address dynamic aspects of treatment techniques used in the clinic. If the therapy does not work, we would formulate another hypothesis about the underlying impairment, again using the model or a modified version of the model. Although therapy often takes on this trial-and-error approach whether a model is used or not, the framework of a model allows for more accurate diagnosis of the language deficits and therefore increases the probability that therapy will be directed towards the deficit.

## Treatment studies of anomia based on functional cognitive models of word retrieval

Numerous studies testing the efficacy of anomia treatments have been based on psycholinguistic functional models of naming. One of the issues that these treatment studies addressed in the 1980s was whether naming ability would benefit more from semantic therapy or from phonological therapy. Recall that word retrieval in naming involves at least two stages before a word is phonologically encoded and articulated: retrieval of a word's meaning (its semantic representation) and retrieval of its word form (the word's phonological form). We know from studies of speech errors and other disruptions to normal speech output (e.g., tip-of-the-tongue states) that the word retrieval process can break down because of dysfunction at one or both of these stages. Thus, apart from determining whether there were differences in effectiveness of semantic and phonological treatments, there is the related question of whether their effectiveness was related to the impairment underlying the naming disorder (Nettleton & Lesser, 1991). That is, would it be better to match a semantic impairment with a semantic treatment and a phonological impairment with a phonological treatment? On the surface, this question might seem rather straightforward to answer. Conventional wisdom might suggest that it would be most effective to target the locus of impairment directly with tasks and materials that stimulate the processes and representations that are impaired (Code & Müller, 1995). However, this inclination does not consider the dynamics of processes that mediate language and their role in the various tasks that are used in therapy.

There have been a fair number of treatment studies that address this question of whether it is necessary to match the treatment to the deficit. Nettleton and Lesser (1991) reported a study of six anomic patients whose naming impairments they attributed to three different sources: semantic impairment ($n = 2$), lexical-phonological impairment ($n = 2$), and impairment in phoneme assembly ($n = 2$). Four of the subjects, those with semantic impairment and with lexical-phonological impairment, were given treatment appropriate to the presumed source of their deficit. The two subjects with a deficit affecting phoneme assembly were also administered the semantic treatment, as a test of the hypothesis that semantically based treatment is beneficial to naming regardless of the source of the naming impairment. The results suggested that the four patients who received therapy suited to their particular deficit benefited more from treatment than the two patients whose treatment was not matched specifically to their deficit. However, as Nickels and Best (1996a) note, we cannot know for sure if the lack of improvement of these two phonological patients was because the treatment did not match their deficit or because they were too severely impaired.

## Treatments for semantic disorders

There have been several approaches to rehabilitation of anomia that is due to semantic processing impairment. Most models of language agree that there is a single semantic system serving both input and output processes.

How does a semantic impairment affect naming? In semantic dementia, the deficit appears to be one of gradual loss of conceptual semantic knowledge (as discussed in Chapter 2) leading to erosion of semantic support of the word production system. In the case of aphasia, the semantic deficit is typically characterised as a processing deficit and involves impaired access to semantic representations and/or impaired ability to access word representations from semantics. We will discuss treatment approaches to semantic processing impairment associated with aphasia, and then discuss some recent approaches to treatment of anomia when conceptual semantic knowledge is deteriorating (as in semantic dementia). In terms of current spreading activation models, in the former case activation of semantic representations is weak or decays too quickly, but the underlying conceptual knowledge that connects with these representations is presumed to be intact. This deficit may affect both input and output activation of semantic representations and consequently can affect both comprehension and production of words. Thus, many therapies for semantically based naming disorders include input and output tasks to stimulate semantics and strengthen the ability to access and maintain activation of these representations sufficiently to process language.

There have been a number of studies investigating the effects of semantic treatment for individuals with a semantic processing deficit (Byng, 1993; Davis & Pring, 1991; Marshall, Pound, White-Thomson, & Pring, 1990; Nickels & Best, 1996a). "Semantic" tasks employed in these studies include spoken and written word-to-picture matching, using semantically related distractors, responding to yes/no questions about pictures, and picture categorisation. These studies have shown that the comprehension training led to improved naming ability irrespective of whether the impairment was semantically or phonologically based. From these findings, however, we cannot conclude that semantic treatment leads to improvement for all types of naming impairments because these treatments were not purely semantic. That is, the tasks that were used to probe semantics or encourage semantic processing often also engaged phonological processes. Word-to-picture matching tasks, for example, require processing of the phonology of a word as well as its semantics.

Two studies carried out during this time frame examined effects of semantic training with and without accompanying phonological production of the words (Drew & Thompson, 1999; LeDorze, Boulay, Gaudreau, & Brassard, 1994). These studies used comprehension tasks with and without accompanying spoken words to treat the naming deficit. Thus, they were able to compare semantic treatment (comprehension task) with and without engaging phonological processes. The results of these studies indicated that maximal benefit was achieved when both semantic and phonological processes were engaged in treatment.

Two other approaches to treating semantically based naming impairments are worthy of mention here. The first one is an approach that uses training of semantic features (e.g., Boyle, 2004; Boyle & Coehlo 1995; Lowell, Beeson & Holland, 1995). A matrix of semantic features about a particular to-be-named object is used to cue the speaker's retrieval of the word. This technique is intended to improve naming of individual target words, but also to facilitate development by the speaker of a strategy to retrieve other words. In keeping with these goals, subjects have demonstrated improvement on trained words as well as some generalisation to untrained words.

Hillis (1991) used an approach to rehabilitating semantically based naming impairments that she called "semantic distinctions" training. It was thought that this approach should be effective when it appeared that semantic representations are underspecified. The use of the term "underspecified" implies that the representations themselves are somehow degraded. In terms of today's processing models, however, language patterns that reflect apparent underspecification of semantic representations could be due to weak activation or too rapid decay of representations that affects their ability to compete with other similar representations. Training involved contrasts of semantic features of one object with a closely related object, thus encouraging the speaker to make finer and finer distinctions among concepts. This approach proved successful with Hillis's (1991) patient who suffered from a semantic impairment and also with another patient whose naming impairment was attributed to impaired access to the output lexicon from semantics (Ochipa, Maher, & Raymer, 1998).

## Treatment for anomia in progressive neurological disease affecting conceptual semantic representations

One of the first symptoms to appear in semantic dementia and other progressive diseases affecting language is anomia. In cases of progressive semantic impairment, it is semantic knowledge (the content of semantic memory) that is affected. This is in contrast to semantic impairment in aphasia which presumably affects access to semantic knowledge (Jefferies & Lambon-Ralph, 2005; Martin, 2005). Therapy for anomia that is due to degraded knowledge representations will necessarily depend on utilising intact morphophonological representations of language and other forms of memory, such as episodic memory, to assist in comprehension and production of words. Although research in this area is scarce, there have been a few recent reports of "treatments" for anomia related to degenerative language disorders. These studies have aimed to enable the affected individual to maintain accessible vocabulary for longer than might normally be the case as the disease affects the language system. Some of the techniques for word retrieval training that have been used with some success in dementia (Grandmaison & Simard, 2003; Hopper, 2004), include spaced retrieval training and errorless learning. Reilly, Martin, and Grossman (2005) studied the effects of massive repetition priming on short-term learning and found that this approach to learning was not effective by itself. Other studies have demonstrated that individuals with semantic dementia can recognise recently viewed objects, pictures, faces, and words (Graham, Becker, & Hodges, 1997; Simons & Graham, 2000).

A study by Graham, Patterson, Pratt, and Hodges (2001) suggests that maintenance of vocabulary can be supported by a combination of intensive drill and use of episodic memory. They reported a longitudinal study of DM, a patient with semantic dementia and progressively worsening word-finding difficulties. DM attempted to maintain his vocabulary by studying the *Oxford English Picture Dictionary* (Parnwell, 1977) daily for as many as 6 hours per day (the intensive drill). Additionally, he kept a journal that included pictures of famous faces and their associated names (the input of episodic memory). Graham et al. observed that DM's performance on tests of category fluency (naming as many members of a category as possible in a specified period of time) improved following this extensive exposure and practice of vocabulary. Unfortunately, DM needed to maintain this practice in order to reap the benefit. His performance declined soon after he stopped his daily vocabulary training. This suggests, as Graham and colleagues (2001) conclude, that DM's word learning was short-lived and did not reflect full comprehension of the words. Nonetheless, the observation that vocabulary can be maintained with the use of techniques that draw on episodic memory and knowledge systems other than semantic knowledge is an important one that deserves further investigation.

Overall, what these and other studies suggest is that learning in dementia is based more on skill acquisition that does not rely on conceptual knowledge, and that this learning can be further facilitated by episodic memory (if it is intact) and perceptual salience.

## Treatment for impaired access to the output lexicon

Word retrieval deficits can result from a breakdown in the ability to access output word representations from semantics. One possible source of this problem is the strength of the signal coming from semantics. Because several models assume that connections between the lexicon and semantics are shared by input and output processes, the effects of weakening these connections on comprehension and production would vary based on severity of the deficit. Milder semantic processing impairments would affect production more than comprehension, at least on the tasks commonly used to clinically assess these two abilities. Whereas word comprehension tasks usually involve mapping a single spoken word onto one of four pictures, word production tasks involve mapping a single concept onto one of thousands of potential word forms. Thus, a weakness in a single semantic system that serves both input and output would have different consequences for input and output pathways, depending on the severity of the impairment and the nature of the task (Martin & Saffran, 2002). This kind of deficit should benefit from therapy techniques that strengthen the semantic signal (spread of activation) to the lexicon.

The second kind of breakdown in accessing representations in the output lexicon would be that the word representations themselves are not reaching threshold when activated or are not remaining active long enough to be phonologically encoded. This kind of deficit should be amenable to treatment that involves priming of these representations. Thus, when there is a breakdown in the transmission of semantic information to the lexicon, it is important to determine whether it is based on weakened spread of semantic activation or a difficulty within the lexicon itself (weak activation of word representations). A comprehensive diagnostic exam will help to a certain extent to pinpoint the breakdown, but responses to particular therapy approaches aimed at strengthening semantics or strengthening lexical representations will also confirm or disconfirm the hypothesised deficit.

In 1993, Raymer, Thompson, Jacobs, and Le Grand reported results of a therapy programme for four individuals whose anomia resulted from a difficulty in accessing the phonological output lexicon from semantics (impaired picture naming) and from graphemic input (impaired oral reading). More specifically, for three of them, naming difficulties were attributed to moderate semantic impairment, and in the case of the fourth participant, to impairment at the phonological output lexicon. The stimuli used in their phonologically based treatment programme consisted of two sets of 30 pictures. In each set, there were 10 pictures that would be trained directly, 10 pictures whose names rhymed with the words in the training set, and 10 pictures of objects that were semantically related to the picture names to be trained. The treatment method used a cueing hierarchy that began with an attempt to spontaneously name the target word. If that attempt was unsuccessful, there were three types of cues provided as needed: a rhyming word cue, an initial phoneme cue, and an auditory model of the word. Once the word was elicited (and with whatever level of cueing), the participant repeated the word five times. Each target word was treated in this way two or three times per session. Raymer et al. (1993) set the criterion for treatment success at 80% correct on two consecutive sentences. If criterion was not reached after 15 sessions, treatment was terminated.

The results of this treatment were mixed. Although all subjects demonstrated acquisition of the target names, no subject reached criterion within the 15 sessions. Generalisation to the semantically and phonologically related sets was observed in two patients, although Raymer et al. (1993) do not report specific rates for one or the other type of relationship. While the generalisation results are promising, the lack of an unrelated control set makes it difficult to evaluate the role of the specific relationship between trained and untrained picture names. Raymer et al. also evaluated generalisation to reading and writing of the same names, which they observed in two participants. Finally, although none of the participants reached criterion for correct naming, effectiveness of the treatment was evident in changes in the error patterns of all four subjects. After treatment, Subject 1 made fewer unintelligible responses, Subject 2 made fewer no-responses, Subject 3 made fewer semantic errors, and Subject 4 made fewer perseverative errors. This kind of in-depth evaluation of error patterns provides good evidence of change following treatment, even when that change is not necessarily evident in correct output.

## Treatments for phonological impairments

Some naming impairments are due primarily to impairment at the stage of phonological encoding. The semantic activation of lexical forms has been successful, but there is a breakdown in the selection and/or ordering of the phonemes of the word. Some treatments for these impairments have emphasised repeated practice of the words' pronunciations through reading, repetition, and picture-naming activities (Miceli, Amitrano, Capasso, & Caramazza, 1996). Other treatment approaches have emphasised the development of increased awareness of the phonological make-up of words, using tasks requiring judgements of initial phonemes of words and number of syllables (Robson, Marshall, Pring & Chiat, 1998). Both of these approaches have resulted in improvements and some generalisation to untrained items.

### Cueing hierarchies

Phonological cueing hierarchies have also been used to improve phonological retrieval (Greenwald, Raymer, Richardson, & Rothi, 1995; Hillis, 1993; Raymer et al., 1993). This procedure requires the participant to attempt to name a picture without any cue. If unsuccessful, a series of cues with increasing amounts of phonological information are provided. The phonological cueing approach has met with some success for patients with semantic or phonological impairment, but it has been argued that it is less effective than semantic treatment, at least in some patients (Hillis, 1998).

Another cueing approach that is more semantic in nature than phonological cueing is the personalised cueing technique. This approach has been developed by Marshall and colleagues (Freed, Celery, & Marshall, 2004; Marshall, Freed, & Carow, 2001). Its central aim is to enable individuals with anomia to facilitate retrieval of words with a cue word that they create. The therapist works with the client to identify words (and associated concepts) that will be linked by some personal association to a particular object (or action) name. The training then proceeds to help the person practise retrieving these names when given this personalised cue. This approach is appealing because it engages the client in a personal way that other cueing hierarchies do not. This aspect could serve to better motivate the client's participation in therapy.

The personalised cueing technique encourages a depth of processing that is likely to be longer lasting than phonological cueing. Although there is little research on this question, the evidence thus far suggests that this may be true. Marshall et al. (2001) compared this method with a phonological cueing technique in a study that examined the ability of 30 aphasic individuals to learn and recall unknown subordinate category names of dogs. Recall was tested 1 week, 1 month, and 6 months after training was completed. Results indicated that personalised cueing led to significantly greater levels of naming accuracy than phonological cueing treatment. In a related study, Freed et al. (2004) used this technique with picture materials more typically used in a clinical setting. That study compared the effects of personalised cueing and phonological cueing on three aphasic individuals' long-term naming accuracy, using stimuli that are typical of those used in clinical treatments. The study also included a control condition with no training. Here again, post-treatment assessment indicated significantly higher levels of naming accuracy in the personalised cue condition than in the phonological cue condition and the untrained control condition up to 3 months post-training.

## Computerised cueing programs

Among the many studies employing cueing hierarchies in anomia treatment, there have been a number in recent years that have administered the cueing systems on computer programs. Bruce and Howard (1987) used a computer-generated treatment approach that facilitated the use of self-generated cues by converting letters to sounds. This program was aimed at individuals who benefited from initial phoneme cues. Five patients were trained with this program and all of them improved on both treated and untreated items with the use of this aid. Additionally, one subject eventually was able to name the pictures without the cueing program. This program was later found to be successful in a case that had a more severe word retrieval deficit and limited letter knowledge (Best, Howard, Bruce, & Gatehouse, 1997). Despite this cognitive limitation, the treatment for this individual was very successful and led to improved naming for both treated and untreated items without dependence on the cueing aid.

Another programme that used computer-generated phonological cueing hierarchies to facilitate naming was reported by Fink, Brecher, Schwartz, and Robey (2002). They used the Moss Talk Words program (Fink, Brecher, Montgomery, & Schwartz, 2001) to examine the effects of a phonological cueing hierarchy under two training conditions: fully guided by a clinician and partially self-guided. The six subjects enrolled in the study had moderate to severe phonologically based naming deficits. Those subjects in the clinician-guided treatment participated in three weekly sessions with the clinician assisting in selecting cues and providing feedback. The three subjects in the partially self-guided group worked with a therapist once a week. In that session, the clinician guided use of the cueing hierarchy in the same manner as in the first condition. In the other two sessions, subjects in the partially self-guided group practised the treatment protocol independently, but with instructions to follow the cueing hierarchy as trained. Results of this training programme were mixed. Naming abilities of two subjects in each group improved for items trained and these gains were maintained after six weeks. Generalisation to untrained items was mixed across patients.

There are also computer-supported cueing programs that offer both semantic and phonological cues. Van Mourick and Van de Standt-Koenderman (1992) examined the efficacy of one such program, called Multicue, in a study of four aphasic subjects. Multicue provides a variety of semantic and phonological cues and the therapy participant is encouraged to identify which cues are most facilitating for them. Of the four people with aphasia receiving the treatment, three showed improvements in naming.

Doesborgh, Van de Standt-Koenderman, Dippel, van Harskamp, Koudstaal, and Visch-Brink (2004) tested the efficacy of this same cueing program in a study of 18 individuals with aphasia. Eight of the subjects received the treatment and ten did not. Performance on the Boston Naming Test before and after treatment was the critical measure. Following treatment, all eight individuals who received the treatment showed gains on the BNT and the group that received no treatment improved only slightly. Overall, the mean improvement for the treated group was not significantly different from that of the subject group that did not receive treatment.

## Directions of research in treatment approaches to word-finding disorders

From the research reviewed above, it can be seen that there is no strong evidence suggesting a clear relationship between impairment and type of treatment. Despite failures to answer this question absolutely, the issue warrants further investigation for several reasons. One factor that has impeded progress in this area is the fact that case reports have varied considerably with respect to the thoroughness of their evaluation of semantic and phonological abilities of the subjects in their studies (becoming more thorough in later studies). This inconsistency makes it difficult to compare case reports. Much of treatment research is carried out in the context of single or multiple case studies. On the one hand, the single case study approach encourages a thorough analysis of a participant's language abilities and yields a more precise definition of the impairment within a model of language processing. On the other hand, pooling data from many case studies requires synthesising varieties of diagnostic and treatment tasks. Extracting a unified interpretation of data from multiple studies using similar, but certainly somewhat varied, training tasks and diagnostic procedures is difficult at best. This problem is gradually resolving itself as researchers strive for more replications of studies and uniformity of diagnostic and therapeutic procedures across studies. Additionally, there is now a stronger emphasis in the clinical community on using evidence-based treatments. Treatment approaches are being held to higher standards in terms of the research that has been used to evaluate their efficacy. The single and multiple case study research carried out to date has served to generate hypotheses about patterns of response to treatments that can now be explored further in larger-scale clinical trial studies.

A related concern in clinical research is a need to include a critical analysis of treatment tasks and the likely effects of the training tasks on lexical access. How does a particular task stimulate semantic processes or access to the phonological lexicon? Question–answer tasks are very different from repetition priming tasks with respect to the levels of representation that are activated and the way in which information flow through the word retrieval network is stimulated. A critical task analysis of the methods used in therapy is essential for understanding their effects on a damaged system. This type of analysis—the "how" of therapy—is rarely incorporated into therapy studies (Horton & Byng, 2002).

Related to this, we need to know more about how stimulation of semantic or phonological processes affects access to semantic and phonological representations in intact systems as well as impaired systems. Cognitive models used to guide treatment studies have not been able to address the dynamics of treatment techniques and their interaction with the normal and damaged brain (Basso & Marangolo, 2000; Hillis & Heidler, 2005), issues about learning new information or relearning of lost information (Huber et al., 1993), or how other cognitive processes, such as attention and short-term memory, work with linguistic processes to enable word retrieval (Martin, Laine, & Harley, 2002). These elements of treatment dynamics, the task components, the content (semantic, phonological) of therapy, and the nature of the impairment, need to be investigated systematically. This need is currently being met in the aphasia research community. In the next section, we discuss current research that is beginning to address the "how to" aspects of therapy.

## USING A COGNITIVE MODEL TO GUIDE TREATMENT, II: HOW DO WE TREAT THE IMPAIRMENT?

Although much of the treatment research to date has failed to satisfactorily address questions about how to treat language impairments, we have every reason to be optimistic about the future of this line of research. We now have computational models of language (e.g., Dell & O'Seaghdha, 1992; Plaut, 1996) and other cognitive capacities such as short-term memory (e.g., Gupta & MacWhinney, 1997) that are being used to test hypotheses about learning dynamics which play a role in treatment. Additionally, empirical studies of naming deficits in aphasia are more focused on the dynamic processes that control retrieval. There has been much interest in recent years about the dynamics of learning and whether it is better to retrain via "errorless" learning or "errorful" learning. Errorless learning techniques, which minimise opportunities for error during the learning process, have proven somewhat successful in treating memory impairments (Wilson, Baddeley, Evans, & Shiel, 1994). In recent years there has been some application of these methods to treatment of language disorders, although it is difficult to achieve truly errorless training in aphasia. Results have been somewhat mixed. Maher et al. (2002) compared errorless and errorful approaches to treating sentence production disorders and found both approaches to be comparably effective. Fillingham, Hodgson, Sage, and Lambon-Ralph (2003) applied the technique to therapy for word-finding disorders and have found errorless and errorful learning to be equally effective. A recent study of anomia treatment technique examined the efficacy of an approach called spaced retrieval (SR) which uses errorless learning procedures to facilitate recall of a target name, but gradually increases the time between the facilitation and recall of the word (Fridriksson, Holland, Beeson, & Morrow, 2005). This technique was compared directly to a more traditional cueing hierarchy (as described earlier). Results indicate that the spaced retrieval technique fared better than the cueing hierarchy approach with respect to acquisition and maintenance of improvement. This training task has two critical components, each of which could have contributed to the improved naming: errorless learning and increased interval between target and recall. It is difficult to determine from these data the extent to which each component contributed to the improved naming.

These few studies indicate that we still have much to learn about the contexts in which errorful vs. errorless learning approaches would be most effective. It is possible that errorless learning is most effective if it is combined with a technique such as spaced retrieval, which encourages the subject to hold information in STM. We may also find differences in effectiveness of errorless learning depending on the kind of material that is being learned. It may be that restoration of phonological abilities will benefit from errorless learning, as the retrieval of sequences of phonemes and their articulation is in part a motor skill that benefits from intense practice. Restoration of lexical-semantic processing abilities, on the other hand, may require more "errorful" learning approaches, as in semantic feature analysis treatments (e.g., Boyle, 2004). This approach, as noted earlier, encourages the learner to generate semantic associations to a concept, which in turn presumably stimulates deeper processing and discrimination of many features of concepts.

Another area of research that focuses on effects of the dynamics of treatment methods includes recent studies of the efficacy of a "constraint-induced" therapy (CIT, Pulvermüller et al., 2001; Taub, 2002). This method was first used to treat movement disorders (Taub, Uswatte, & Pidikiti, 1999) and required that use of the good limb be restrained to force the individual to attempt movement with the impaired limb. Applied to language therapy in aphasia, the treatment environment is organised to encourage maximal use of verbal communication and minimal use of nonverbal communication. This approach also emphasises intensity of practice, particularly of speech/ language acts that are especially difficult for the individual. Constraint-induced aphasia therapy has met with some success (Pulvermüller et al., 2001) and is currently an active area of investigation.

The nature of processing dynamics is another area of research in which attention is focused on the "how" of language processing. Some models postulate that word retrieval involves a problem with refractoriness of activation (Warrington & Cipolotti, 1996): semantic relatedness between an intended utterance and its lexical neighbours causes interference in retrieval that increases with multiple exposures to a target word. Others suggest that the problem is one of increased inhibition (e.g., Schwartz & Hodgson, 2002). Still others emphasise the role of a short-term buffer and the possibility that word retrieval impairments are affected by limited capacity of this buffer (R. Martin et al., 1999). Several recent studies have explored treatment approaches that focus on improving auditory-verbal short-term memory, which in turn will improve comprehension and production of words and/or sentences (Francis, Clark, & Humphreys, 2003; Majerus, van der Kaa, Renard, Vander Linden, & Poncelet, 2005). These approaches are based on models that assume common activation processes supporting single-word and multiple-word processing tasks (e.g., Martin & Gupta, 2004) or models that view verbal STM as separate from language processing (Vallar & Baddeley, 1984).

What these recent studies indicate is that our focus in treatment research is beginning to shift from determining the content of therapy to under-standing the dynamics of the treatment process. This shift has been facili-tated by the availability of computer-instantiated connectionist cognitive models that can generate and test predictions about dynamics of processing involved in lexical access.

## Connectionist models and treatment

What do connectionist models of language and other cognitive processes have to offer to treatment research? To answer this, it might help to think of the language system as a computational device. Language impairments resulting from stroke reflect impaired computational abilities. Direct stimu-lation therapy to improve language ability involves stimulation of these damaged computational abilities. It is essential that our models of treat-ment generate and test hypotheses about the properties of language computation. Connectionist models have the potential to do this precisely because they are computationally instantiated. As discussed in Chapter 1, connectionist models attempt to define the parameters of the information flow within the language system, and in so doing, define the dynamics of computational operations of language processing. Although this application of cognitive models to issues relevant to treatment is very much in its infancy, computational connectionist models have already been used to investigate many aspects of language processing, including theories about mechanisms of lexical access (Dell, 1986; Harley, 1984; Levelt et al., 1999; McNellis & Blumstein, 2001; Plaut & Booth, 2000; Rapp & Goldrick, 2000; Ruml & Caramazza, 2000), word recognition (McLeod, Plaut, & Shallice, 2001), serial order mechanisms in word production (Vousden et al., 2000), and more recently, articulatory mechanisms in humans (Kello & Plaut, 2004).

Computational models have been contributed to our current understanding of the nature of impairments to lexical access (e.g., Dell et al., 1997; Gotts & Plaut, 2002; Miikkulainen, 1997) and impairments of semantic memory (e.g., Lambon-Ralph, McClelland, Patterson, Galton, & Hodges, 2001). They have been used in several studies to investigate possible mechanisms underlying recovery of language function after brain damage (Martin et al., 1994; Martin et al., 1996; Plaut, 1996; Schwartz & Brecher, 2000). In the domain of treatment, computational connectionist models have generated hypotheses about language learning (Plaut & Kello, 1999) and the role of short-term memory processes in word learning (Gupta & MacWhinney, 1997). Additionally, some researchers are beginning to use computer models to examine processes exploited in treatment tasks such as priming (Plaut & Booth, 2000) and others have generated predictions about interfering and facilitating effects of priming with semantically or phonologically related words on lexical access (Martin, Fink, Laine, & Ayala, 2004b). Below we discuss two recent studies that illustrate how such models can inform therapy.

### How can generalization of learning be maximised?

A particularly important study of relevance to treatment of anomia was reported by Plaut in 1996. He used a connectionist model to examine relearning of reading after damage to different aspects of the reading process, and demonstrated that re-learning is strongly influenced by the regularity of structure in mapping one representation onto another. In the computational network he used, the mapping between orthography and semantics was determined by the semantic organisation of the words. This suggested that if a set of words-to-be-trained was representative of the semantic structure of the entire set of words, generalisation to untrained words in the set could be expected. Plaut proposed that the typicality of a concept, i.e., its proximity to the central tendency of its category, is a variable that would affect the estimate of the semantic structure. His experiments yielded two important findings relevant to anomia rehabilitation. First, he found that rates of relearning and degree of generalisation vary depending on the location of the lesion in the model (whether it impairs semantic or phonological processes). Second, and most important to the question of generalisation, Plaut observed that training both atypical and typical members of a category produced far more generalisation to untrained items than training only typical members. Plaut proposed that this effect occurred because atypical members of a category provide more information about the structure and central tendencies of a category than do more typical members. Plaut's claim and the results of his simulation might at first appear to be counterintuitive, as it is common to use typical and familiar objects of a category in therapy programmes for word retrieval. The insights from Plaut's model are an example of how computational models can suggest and justify approaches to learning that might go against conventional wisdom.

Plaut's account of the typicality effects on generalisation of training to untrained items was later tested empirically by Kiran and Thompson (2003). They termed Plaut's finding the "semantic complexity" account, and predicted that training individuals with word retrieval problems on a set of atypical and typical exemplars in a category should result in more generalisation than training on items in a category that represent the most typical features of that category. They were able to test this hypothesis with four individuals with aphasia. This was a very carefully controlled study and the authors used only categories in which a sufficient number of typical and atypical members could be identified. This resulted in two categories, birds and vegetables, to be used in training. The results of their study supported the hypothesis that training atypical and typical members of a category leads to more generalisation than training only on typical items. Thus, in principle, this computational prediction appears to provide useful advice on how to maximise effects of training in individuals who are relearning after brain damage. It will be important in future studies to replicate this effect using other categories, and also to determine if this effect is present in modalities other than object naming.

### Effects of priming on recovery of word retrieval ability

Dell and O'Seaghdha's interactive activation model has been used recently as a framework for a series of treatment studies using repetition priming as the treatment method (Laine & Martin, 1996; Martin, Fink, & Laine, 2004a; Martin et al., 2004b; Renvall Laine, Laakso, & Martin, 2003; Renvall, Laine, & Martin, 2005). Two predictions of this model have been tested in several treatment studies using contextual priming as the treatment technique. Contextual priming uses repetition priming of words in combination with a context defined by the relationships of the words being primed to each other (semantically, phonologically, or unrelated). The interactive activation model predicts that in the case of impairment to lexical-semantic processes, repetition priming should be less effective than in the case of impairment to phonological processes (Martin & Ayala, 2004). This is because repetition can proceed without accessing semantic representations, and consequently will not stimulate these processes effectively (e.g., good repetition and poor comprehension in transcortical sensory aphasia). To date, this prediction has been confirmed in the case studies of Laine, Martin, and colleagues noted above. That is, individuals with relatively intact semantic processing appear to benefit more from repetition priming that engages semantic representations than individuals with semantic impairment, even when the latter group have relatively stable phonological processing skills. More cases studies of individuals with primarily semantic or phonological impairment are needed to confirm this hypothesis.

A second prediction of the interactive activation model was tested in a short-term facilitation study, using the contextual priming technique. Based on assumptions of this model, Martin et al. (2004b) hypothesised that the massive repetition priming would result in immediate interference with naming, but short-term facilitation. Martin et al. examined the immediate and short-term effects of contextual priming on the naming performance of 11 subjects with aphasia-related word retrieval deficits. These predictions were borne out in two measures of priming effects obtained immediately following priming trials and one measure of short-term effects obtained 5 minutes after the end of the priming session. For all but one subject, there was consistent evidence of immediate interference. Compared to the unrelated context, there were higher rates of intrusions from within the training set (contextual errors) and lower rates of correct responses in the related contexts. In contrast, the post-priming naming test administered 5 minutes after the end of the session indicated facilitation for all participants in at least one context condition. The clinical and theoretical implications of this finding are significant. The shift from interference to facilitation indicates a need to time the post-test to assess learning in both clinical and research contexts. Additionally, and in the context of the model, the two effects may likely reflect short-term priming activation (interference) and changes in connection weights reflecting short-term learning (facilitation).

## THE FUTURE

The treatment studies described here represent the beginning of a new wave of treatment research that focuses on how our treatment methods impact learning. This area of research is moving forward because of our ability to model dynamic aspects of information processing and information learning in normal and damaged brains. Additionally, our understanding of neuroplasticity has increased in recent years. Advances in this research domain indicate that the brain is more "plastic" than once thought and can respond to stimulation in real ways that promote recovery of behavioural function.

Recent advances in cerebral perfusion research indicate that language function can be affected when insufficient blood flow (hypoperfusion) is reaching critical neural tissue (e.g., Hillis et al., 2001). An additional exciting advance in this area of study is the finding that in some cases, language function can be restored by reperfusing neural tissue that is hypoperfused (Hillis et al., 2002a). These advances will guide clinical research of issues about timing of intervention, effects of treatment duration, and treatment intensity. Related to this is the current interest in pharmacological treatments to accompany behavioural therapies. Small (2004) provides an excellent review of direct and indirect mechanisms of pharmaceutical treatments on neural circuitry and the implications of this for aphasia therapy (see also Hillis & Heidler, 2005). At present, pharmacotherapy appears to be most effective in combination with behavioural therapy. But this area of research is in its early stages, and so we still have much to learn about the potential benefits of biological interventions.

In conclusion, we can say that we now have the tools to answer questions introduced by Luria and others when aphasia rehabilitation was first being practised. At that time, philosophies about neural changes accompanying recovery were proposed. Today, we can observe how these changes actually do occur at the neural level using perfusion techniques and observing changes related to pharmaceutical treatments. Additionally, we can use computational models of neural function and cognition to predict patterns of change at the neural and behavioural level.

## CHAPTER SUMMARY

In this chapter we have provided a critical evaluation of the cognitive model-based approach to treatment of naming disorders, the success of efforts to date, and the potential of connectionist models to address questions about the dynamics of treatment. Research on impairment-based treatment approaches has proceeded through several phases. An early phase devised treatment approaches based on intuitions and philosophies of how recovery might take place. With the introduction of cognitive models of language, anomia treatment benefited from more precise means of diagnosing what to treat in therapy. With the advent of computational models of cognition and advances in neural sciences, the field of aphasia rehabilitation research is now moving towards an understanding of how treatment methods interact with and impact neural structures and behavioural function.

# 6   Conclusions and future directions

In this final chapter we wrap up the book by providing some thoughts on where we stand now in anomia research and where to go next. There is no question that our knowledge on the neurocognitive aspects of naming and its disorders has expanded strongly during the last decades. The research field continues to thrive, as attested by various healthy controversies concerning, for example, the dynamics of word production, the structure of semantic memory, and the choice of anomia treatment methods. Addressing issues such as these should help to move the field forward, providing deeper understanding of lexical production mechanisms, their disorders, diagnosis, and effective treatment.

Contemporary models of naming inform us that during the fleeting moment (often less than a second) it takes for a normal adult to name aloud a familiar object or event, target-related information is retrieved from long-term memory in an orderly fashion. What needs to be retrieved or computed during a split second are different mental representations of the target: its essential sensory qualities (characteristic visual pattern if the target is perceived via the visual modality), meaning, phonological output form, corresponding syllabic and metric structure, and the phonetic-articulatory program needed for oral output. The retrieval processes are complicated by the fact that even in normal naming, much more is activated than is being produced. In other words, naming involves selection amongst competing lexical candidates. Moreover, there is evidence for interplay between semantic and phonological levels of word production, further emphasising the dynamic and probabilistic nature of the process.

The main stages of naming also find their correspondences in left hemisphere damaged patients suffering from word production difficulties, as have been detailed by cognitive neuropsychological analyses of anomic patients. Thus it is possible to differentiate lexical output deficits caused by lexical-semantic, lexical-phonological, phoneme assembly, and phonetic disorders. This distinction is rather coarse but useful for several purposes, including planning for treatment. In addition to dissociations along processing stages, naming deficits can entail more or less selective disruption of semantic or grammatical categories of words. The nature of these deficits is controversial, and it is thus difficult to draw definite conclusions about underlying organisation of semantic-syntactic information in the human brain.

With regard to the neural correlates of naming difficulties, lesion studies, cortical stimulation experiments, and functional neuroimaging research implicate an anatomically widespread network subserving word production. In most individuals this network is predominantly left lateralised. It encompasses both posterior and anterior brain structures and critical white matter tracts connecting these areas, with some of its key components being related to left temporal lobe function. Plasticity within this network is implied by spontaneous recovery of anomia and the treatment effects obtained in anomic patients. However, the dynamics that guide this plasticity are not yet well known.

## TOWARDS A MORE DYNAMIC VIEW ON WORD PRODUCTION AND ANOMIA: THE PROMISE OF COMPUTATIONAL SIMULATIONS

The cognitive neuropsychological approach has greatly influenced our current understanding of the naming process and how it can be impaired. It has provided principled ways to analyse and interpret patients' naming disorders. The cognitive neuropsychological accounts of anomia have mainly been at the functional, "boxes-and-arrows" level of description. And yet, as with studies of normal naming, progress in understanding anomia requires more than just labelling the hypothetical "box" or an "arrow" that is lesioned. For example, we have noted that the paradox of semantically intact anomic patients producing semantic naming errors requires specification of the dynamics of particular aspects of naming, especially the interplay between semantic and phonological levels during lexical selection. Thus for anomia research as well as for the study of normal naming, theoretical progress is dependent on advances in computational modelling. Computational models of naming and anomia allow, and therefore challenge us to provide, empirical data reflecting the dynamic aspects of naming. Such data provide the opportunity to test theoretically motivated predictions via computer simulations of the data.

As noted in Chapter 5, modelling work has also started to address the complex issue of anomia therapy where the inadequacies of static models of naming are most glaring, but this line of research is still at its beginning stages. Further refinement of computational models of naming and anomia is bound to be a continuing process. After all, we can only falsify models, not prove that they will hold for ever.

## NAMING, ANOMIA, AND BRAIN FUNCTION: GETTING DEEPER

In the last decade there has been a rebirth of interest in how cognitive functions such as language processing are implemented in the brain. This re-awakening was instigated by advances in functional neuroimaging, which have allowed researchers to combine behavioural tests of language and other cognitive abilities with imaging studies of the brain's activities during such tests. This "marriage" of the behavioural and the neurological is in some respects an updating of efforts in the 19th century to link behaviour and structure, but goes beyond this and asks additional questions about how the brain recovers from brain damage and how it responds to training—i.e., how it relearns functions.

At present, a large array of brain–behaviour research methods is available, spanning from the traditional lesion research to functional neuroimaging and cortical stimulation techniques. As we have seen, the results they provide on the neural basis of word production are overlapping, but only partially. A number of factors related to different stimuli, experimental designs, subjects, and method-specific features may explain this variation. Multimethod approaches to the neural correlates of naming and its disorders are expected to become more common, as any single technique has its pros and cons. With regard to drawing causal inferences, the transcranial magnetic stimulation technique will be a particularly interesting complement to PET and fMRI, as in principle it enables systematic spatial (location on the scalp) and temporal (time point in the naming chain) manipulation of a temporary disruption of a cognitive process.

When discussing methods to study brain–behaviour relationships, one should keep in mind that the study designs are driven by cognitive research. It provides theoretical frameworks for the lesion, cortical stimulation, and functional neuroimaging studies on naming and anomia. Thus the adequacy of an imaging study is, among other things, strongly dependent on the relevance of the cognitive architecture of naming it has adopted. Does the theoretical model succeed in identifying the "natural building blocks" of naming? For example, if we assume that semantic and phonological retrieval interacts during word production, the commonly used basic subtraction technique (activation caused by a control condition is subtracted from the activation caused by an experimental condition) in PET and fMRI studies cannot provide a fully adequate isolation of the brain structures related to these processing stages. Instead, interactive effects should be searched for.

The brain correlates of naming we discussed in Chapter 3 represent a macrolevel description. The cortical mantle has an intricate layered structure with cortical columns, but the spatial resolution of most of the present imaging methods is insufficient to reach this level. Thus our data typically represent summative action of a large number of sub-units, possibly showing some functional specialisation that we are unable to observe due to insufficient spatial (and temporal) resolution. Moreover, memory and learning are strongly linked to synaptic activity that is regulated by a large number of neurotransmitters, but we are not yet able to record on-line regional cortical neurotransmitter activity during cognitive performance such as naming (but see Aalto, Brück, Laine, Någren, & Rinne, 2005). Finally, the strong interactivity of the central nervous system calls for a shift of focus from functional specialisation of individual brain regions to the concerted activity of anatomically widespread functional networks. These points simply serve to highlight the fact that despite great advances in functional neuroimaging research, there is still a long way to go.

## WORD PRODUCTION IN CONTEXT

As language is a complex interpersonal communication system that builds on syntactically structured connected speech, and also includes extra-linguistic dimensions such as gestures, one could question the relevance of the study of single word production and its disorders that is the focus of this book. While connected speech also unfolds sequentially and requires the retrieval of single lexical items and their insertion into the sentence frame, it is clear that word production in context differs from naming of isolated words in many ways. Word retrieval in connected speech is influenced by communicative, conceptual, and linguistic contexts, as evidenced by slips of the tongue and experimental priming research. Working memory demands are also considerably higher in conversation than in single word production. Moreover, in conversation the speaker has many more possibilities for alternative means of linguistic expression than, for example, in a picture-naming task.

Given these differences, it is not surprising that the few studies that have looked at the correlation between word retrieval in confrontation naming and in conversational speech have provided conflicting results (e.g., Mayer & Murray, 2003). What are the implications for the diagnosis and treatment of anomia? Ideally, one should evaluate patients' word-finding abilities with single word production tasks and narrative production tasks, and in conversational speech. Evaluation of single word production reveals crucial information on the underlying impairment in the language production system, and helps in detecting even mild word-finding deficits that may go unnoticed in ordinary conversation, which provides many ways to circumlocute difficult items, such as low-frequency words. Narrative production (e.g., describing the chain of events in a cartoon) provides a more natural yet controlled situation to assess patients' speech production. Examination of lexical retrieval in conversation (including the use of non-linguistic means of communication as well as strategies used to overcome communication problems caused by word-finding deficits) is important in characterising patients' communicative ability in a context that is held as most important by aphasic patients and their families. Unfortunately, this aspect is difficult to assess in detail: there is no consensus as to which lexical retrieval measures should be used, conversational analysis takes considerable time and effort, and the results may be context dependent (e.g., conversations with a physician vs. with a spouse may be very different). Clearly more research is needed to highlight the complexities of lexical retrieval in conversation. At any rate, the clinician may attempt a more impressionistic evaluation of patients' communicative ability and strategies used in conversation.

## HELPING THE ANOMIC PATIENT

The positive news for a clinician treating anomic patients is that there is a strong research interest in the area. Even though the accumulation of evidence is somewhat slow due to the case study approach adopted in most anomia treatment studies, a wide variety of possible treatment methods is available. The disturbing fact is that there continues to be a gap between the diagnosis of anomia and the choice of treatment methods. In other words, identifying a patient's underlying deficit, for instance at the interface between meaning and word form retrieval, does not tell us which kind of treatment methods will or will not be benefial to alleviate anomia. This is not only problematic for a clinician who may need to proceed with trial and error when designing a treatment plan for a particular patient, but it also indicates that at the theoretical level, there is more to learn about the dynamics of normal and impaired naming.

Models of naming should eventually also account for change, i.e., learning, forgetting, and re-learning the meaning and phonology of lexical items. It seems evident that multiple memory and learning mechanisms from low-level priming and working memory up to conscious learning strategies are involved in word learning. However, there are many questions that remain open. Human word learning is a very impressive capacity, but is it based on content-specific or more general learning mechanisms? To what extent does the learning of new words rely on the same mechanisms as the re-learning of forgotten or (due to brain damage) hard-to-name items? Systematic studies of these issues will hopefully help in closing the gap between anomia diagnosis and choice of treatment. In the meantime, in clinical practice one should employ tailor-made treatment programmes that take into account diagnostic results, communicative needs of the patient, and practical limitations (time and resources available). Creativity and a trial-and-error approach is often called for, and it is not a bad idea to document and develop one's own clinical work by incorporating features of systematic single case intervention designs in everyday work.

# References

Aalto, S., Brück, A., Laine, M., Någren, K., & Rinne, J.O. (2005). Frontal and temporal dopamine release during working memory and attention tasks in healthy humans—a PET study using high-affinity dopamine D2 receptor ligand [$^{11}$C]FLB 457. *Journal of Neuroscience, 25*, 2471–2477.

Ackermann, H., Mathiak, K., & Ivry, R.B. (2004). Temporal organization of "internal speech" as a basis for cerebellar modulation of cognitive functions. *Behavioral and Cognitive Neuroscience Reviews, 3*, 14–22.

Adolphs, R., Damasio, H., Tranel, D., Cooper, G., & Damasio, A.R. (2000). A role for somatosensory cortices in the visual recognition of emotion as revealed by three-dimensional lesion mapping. *Journal of Neuroscience, 20*, 2683–2690.

Alario, F-X., Schiller, N.O., Domoto-Reilly, K., & Caramazza, A. (2003). The role of phonological and orthographic information in lexical selection. *Brain and Language, 84*, 372–398.

Alexander, M.P. (2000). Aphasia I: Clinical and anatomic issues. In M.J. Farah & T.E. Feinberg (Eds.), *Patient-based approaches to cognitive neuroscience* (pp. 165–181). Cambridge, MA: MIT Press.

Almkvist O., Bäckman L., Basun, H., & Wahlund, L-O. (1993). Patterns of neuropsychological performance in Alzheimer's disease and vascular dementia. *Cortex, 29*, 661–673.

Antonucci, S.M., Beeson, P.M., & Rapcsak, S.Z. (2004). Anomia in patients with left inferior temporal lobe lesions. *Aphasiology, 18*, 543–554.

Ardila, A., & Rosselli, M. (1989). Neuropsychological characteristics of normal aging. *Developmental Neuropsychology, 5*, 307–320.

Au, R., Joung, P., Nicholas, M., Kass, R., Obler, L.K., & Albert, M.L. (1995). Naming ability across the lifespan. *Aging and Cognition, 2*, 300–311.

Baars, B.J., Motley, M.T., & MacKay, D.G. (1975). Output editing for lexical status in artificially elicited slips of the tongue. *Journal of Verbal Learning and Verbal Behavior, 14*, 382–391.

Baayen, R.H. (1994). Productivity in language production. *Language and Cognitive Processes, 9*, 447–469.

Bachoud-Lévi, A-C., & Dupoux, E., (2003). An influence of syntactic and semantic variables on word form retrieval. *Cognitive Neuropsychology, 20*, 163–188.

Badecker, W. (2001). Lexical composition and the production of compounds: Evidence from errors in naming. *Language and Cognitive Processes, 16*, 337–366.

Ballard, K.J., Granier, J.P., & Robin, D.A. (2000) Understanding the nature of apraxia of speech: Theory, analysis, and treatment. *Aphasiology, 14*, 969–995.

Basso, A. (1993). Therapy for aphasia in Italy. In A.L. Holland & M.M. Forbes (Eds.), *Aphasia treatment: World perspectives* (pp. 1–24). San Diego: Singular Publishing Group.

Basso, A., & Marangolo, P. (2000). Cognitive neuropsychological rehabilitation: The emperor's new clothes? *Neuropsychological Rehabilitation, 10,* 219–229.

Baum, S., & Leonard, C. (1999). Automatic versus strategic effects of phonology and orthography on lexical access in brain damaged patients as a function of interstimulus interval. *Cortex, 35,* 647–660.

Baxter, D.M., & Warrington, E.K. (1985). Category specific phonological dysgraphia. *Neuropsychologia, 23,* 653–666.

Baynes, K. (1990). Right hemisphere language and reading: Highways or byways of the brain? *Journal of Cognitive Neuroscience, 2,* 159–179.

Béland, R., & Lecours, A.R. (1990). The MT-86 Beta Aphasia Battery: A subset of normative data in relation to age and level of school education. *Aphasiology, 4,* 439–462.

Benson, D.F. (1979). Neurologic correlates of anomia. In H. Whitaker & H.A. Whitaker (Eds.), *Studies in neurolinguistics, vol. 4* (pp. 293–328). New York: Academic Press.

Bergego, C., Deloche, G., Pradat-Diehl, P., Robineau, F., & Lauriot-Prevost, M.C. (1993). Visual recognition in right brain-damaged patients: Evidence from a tachistoscopic confrontation naming task. *Brain and Language, 44,* 181–190.

Berndt, R.S. (1987). Symptom co-occurrence and dissociation in the interpretation of agrammatism. In M. Coltheart, G. Sartori, & R. Job (Eds.), *The Cognitive Neuropsychology of Language* (pp. 221–233). Hove, UK: Lawrence Erlbaum Associates Ltd.

Berndt, R.S., Haendiges, A.N., Burton, M.W., & Mitchum, C.C. (2002). Grammatical class and imageability in aphasic word production: Their effects are independent. *Journal of Neurolinguistics, 15,* 353–371.

Best, W., Howard, D., Bruce, C., & Gatehouse, C. (1997). Cueing the words: A single case study of treatments for anomia. *Neuropsychological Rehabilitation, 7,* 105–141.

Bird, H., Howard, D., & Franklin, S. (2000). Why is a verb like an inanimate object. Grammatical category and semantic category deficits. *Brain and Language, 72,* 246–509.

Bird, H., Howard, D., & Franklin, S. (2003). Verbs and nouns: The importance of being imageable. *Journal of Neurolinguistics, 16,* 113–149.

Black, M., & Chiat, S. (2003). Noun–verb dissociations: A multi-faceted phenomenon. *Journal of Neurolinguistics, 16,* 231–250.

Blank, S.C., Scott, S.K., Murphy, K., Warburton, E., & Wise, R.J.S. (2002). Speech production: Wernicke, Broca and beyond. *Brain, 125,* 1829–1838.

Blanken, G. (1990). Formal paraphasias: A single case study. *Brain and Language, 38,* 534–554.

Blanken, G. (1998). Lexicalisation in speech production: Evidence from form-related word substitutions in aphasia. *Cognitive Neuropsychology, 15,* 321–360.

Blanken, G. (2000). The production of nominal compounds in aphasia. *Brain and Language, 74,* 84–102.

Boles, L. (1997). A comparison of naming errors in individuals with mild naming impairment following post-stroke aphasia, Alzheimer's disease, and traumatic brain injury. *Aphasiology, 11,* 1043–1056.

Bouillaud, J-B. (1825). Recherches cliniques propres à démontrer que la perte de la parole correspond à la lésion des lobules antérieurs du cervau et à confirmer l'opinion de M. Gall, sur le siège de l'organe du langage articulé. *Archives Générales de Médecine, 8*, 25–43.

Bowles, N.L., Obler, L.K., & Albert, M.L. (1987). Naming errors in healthy aging and dementia of the Alzheimer type. *Cortex, 23*, 519–524.

Boyle, M. (2004). Semantic feature analysis treatment for anomia in two fluent aphasia syndromes. *American Journal of Speech-Language Pathology, 13*, 236–249.

Boyle, M., & Coehlo, C.A. (1995). Application of semantic feature analysis as a treatment for aphasic dysnomia. *American Journal of Speech-Language Pathology, 4*, 94–98.

Brédart, S., & Valentine, T. (1992). From Monroe to Moreau: An analysis of face naming errors. *Cognition, 45*, 187–223.

Breedin, S.D., Saffran, E.M., & Coslett, H. (1994). Reversal of the concreteness effect in a patient with semantic dementia. *Cognitive Neuropsychology, 11*, 617–660.

Broca, P. (1865). Du siège de la faculté du langage articulé. *Bulletin de la Société d'Anthropologie, 6*, 337.

Brown, R. (1970). Psychology and reading: Commentary on chapters 5 to 10. In H. Levin & J.P. Williams (Eds.), *Basic studies on reading* (pp. 164–187). New York: Basic Books.

Brown, R., & McNeill, D. (1966). The "tip of the tongue" phenomenon. *Journal of Verbal Learning and Verbal Behavior, 5*, 325–337.

Bruce, C., & Howard, D. (1987). Computer-generated phonemic cues: An effective aid for naming in aphasia. *British Journal of Disorders of Communication, 22*, 191–202.

Buckingham, H.W. (1986). The scan-copier mechanism and the positional level of language production: Evidence from phonemic paraphasia. *Cognitive Science, 10*, 195–217.

Buckingham, H.W. (1998). Explanations for the concept of apraxia of speech. In M.T. Sarno (Ed.), *Acquired aphasia. Third edition* (pp. 269–307). San Diego, CA: Academic Press.

Burke, D., MacKay, D.G., Worthley, J.S., & Wade, E. (1991). On the tip-of-the-tongue: What causes word finding failures in young and older adults? *Journal of Memory and Language, 30*, 237–246.

Burnstine, T.H., Lesser, R.P., Hart, J. Jr., Uematsu, S., Zinreich, S.J., Krauss, G.L. et al. (1990). Characterization of the basal temporal language area in patients with left temporal lobe epilepsy. *Neurology, 40*, 966–970.

Butfield, E., & Zangwill, O.L. (1946). Re-education in aphasia: A review of 70 cases. *Journal of Neurology, Neurosurgery and Psychiatry, 9*, 75–79.

Butters, N., Granholm, E., Salmon, D.P., Grant, I., & Wolfe, J. (1987). Episodic and semantic memory: A comparison of amnesic and demented patients. *Journal of Clinical and Experimental Neuropsychology, 9*, 479–497.

Butterworth, B. (1975). Hesitation and semantic planning in speech. *Journal of Psycholinguistic Research, 4*, 75–87.

Butterworth, B. (1979). Hesitation and the production of neologisms in jargon aphasia. *Brain and Language, 8*, 133–161.

Butterworth, B. (1982). Speech errors: Old data in search of new theories. In A. Cutler (Ed.), *Slips of the tongue and language production* (pp. 73–108). Amsterdam: Mouton.

Butterworth, B. (1989). Lexical access in speech production. In W. Marslen-Wilson (Ed.), *Lexical representation and process* (pp. 108–135). Cambridge, MA: MIT Press.

Butterworth, B. (1992). Disorders of phonological encoding. *Cognition, 42,* 261–286.

Byng, S. (1993). Hypothesis testing and aphasia therapy. In A.L. Holland & M.M. Forbes (Eds.), *Aphasia treatment: World perspectives* (pp. 115–130). San Diego, CA: Singular Publishing Group.

Byng, S., & Duchan, J. (2005). Social model philosophies and principles: Their applications to therapies for aphasia. *Aphasiology, 19,* 906–922.

Cao, Y., Vikingstad, E.M., George, K.P., Johnson, A.F., & Welch, K.M.A. (1999). Cortical language activation in stroke patients recovering from aphasia with functional MRI. *Stroke, 30,* 2331–2340.

Capitani, E., Laiacona, M., Mahon, B., & Caramazza, A. (2003). What are the facts of category-specific deficits? A critical review of the clinical evidence. *Cognitive Neuropsychology, 20,* 213–261.

Caplan, D. (1992). *Language: Structure, processing and disorders.* Cambridge, MA: MIT Press.

Caplan, D., Kellar, L., & Locke, S. (1972). Inflection of neologisms in aphasia. *Brain, 95,* 169–172.

Caramazza, A., & Hillis, A.E. (1990). Where do semantic errors come from? *Cortex, 26,* 95–122.

Caramazza, A., & Hillis, A. (1991). Lexical organisation of nouns and verbs in the brain. *Nature, 349,* 788–790.

Caramazza, A., Hillis, A.E., Rapp, B.C., & Romani, C. (1990). The multiple semantics hypothesis: Multiple confusions? *Cognitive Neuropsychology, 7,* 161–189.

Caramazza, A., & Shelton, J.R. (1998). Domain-specific knowledge systems in the brain: The animate–inanimate distinction. *Journal of Cognitive Neuroscience, 10,* 1–34.

Chertkow, H., Bub, D., Bergman, H., Bruemmer, A., Merling, A., & Rothfleisch, J. (1994). Increased semantic priming in patients with dementia of the Alzheimer's type. *Journal of Clinical and Experimental Neuropsychology, 16,* 608–622.

Chertkow, H., Bub, D., & Caplan, D. (1992). Constraining theories of semantic memory: Evidence from dementia. *Cognitive Neuropsychology, 9,* 327–365.

Chertkow, H., Bub, D., & Seidenberg, M. (1989). Priming and semantic memory loss in Alzheimer's disease. *Brain and Language, 36,* 420–446.

Chiarello, C. (1991). Interpretation of word meanings by the cerebral hemispheres: One is not enough. In P. Schwanenflugel (Ed.), *The psychology of word meanings* (pp. 251–278). Hillsdale, NJ: Lawrence Erlbaum Associates Inc.

Code, C., & Müller, D. (1995). *Treatment of aphasia: From theory to practice.* London: Whurr Publishers.

Cohen, L., Bolgert, F., Timsit, S., & Chermann, J.F. (1994). Anomia for proper names following left thalamic infarct. *Journal of Neurology Neurosurgery and Psychiatry, 57,* 1283–1284.

Cole-Virtue, J., & Nickels, L. (2004) Spoken word to picture matching from PALPA: A critique and some new matched sets. *Aphasiology, 18,* 77–102.

Coltheart, M., Patterson, K., & Marshall, J.C. (1980) *Deep dyslexia.* London: Routledge & Kegan Paul.

Connor, L.T., Spiro III, A., Obler, L.K., & Albert, M.L. (2004). Change in object naming ability during adulthood. *The Journals of Gerontology Series B: Psychological Sciences and Social Sciences, 59,* 203–209.

Coppens, P., Hungerford, S., Yamaguchi, S., & Yamadori, A. (2002). Crossed aphasia: An analysis of the symptoms, their frequency, and a comparison with left-hemisphere symptomatology. *Brain and Language, 83,* 425–463.

Cornelissen, K., Laine, M., Tarkiainen, A., Järvensivu, T., Martin, N., & Salmelin, R. (2003). Adult brain plasticity elicited by anomia treatment. *Journal of Cognitive Neuroscience, 15,* 444–461.

Coughlan, A.K., & Warrington, E.K. (1978). Word-comprehension and word-retrieval in patients with localized cerebral lesions. *Brain, 101,* 163–185.

Cummings, J.L. (1995). Dementia: The failing brain. *Lancet, 345,* 1481–1484.

Dalby, P.R., & Obrzut, J.E. (1991). Epidemiologic characteristics and sequelae of closed head injured children and adolescents: A review. *Developmental Neuropsychology, 7,* 35–68.

Damasio, H., & Damasio, A.R. (1980). The anatomical basis of conduction aphasia. *Brain, 103,* 337–350.

Damasio, H., Grabowski, T.J., Tranel, D., Hichwa, R.D., & Damasio, A.R. (1996). A neural basis for lexical retrieval. *Nature, 380,* 499–505.

Damasio, A.R., & Tranel, D. (1993). Nouns and verbs are retrieved with differently distributed neural systems. *Proceedings of the National Academy of Sciences, 90,* 4957–4960.

Damasio, H., Tranel, D., Grabowski, T., Adolphs, R., & Damasio, A. (2004). Neural systems behind word and concept retrieval. *Cognition, 92,* 179–229.

Daniele, A., Giustolisi, L., Silveri, M.C., Colosimo, C., & Gainotti, G. (1994). Evidence for a possible neuroanatomical basis for lexical processing of nouns and verbs. *Neuropsychologia, 32,* 1325–1341.

Davis, A., & Pring, T. (1991). Therapy for word finding deficits: More on the effects of semantic and phonological approaches to treatment with dysphasic patients. *Neuropsychological Rehabilitation, 1,* 135–145.

Dell, G.S. (1986). A spreading activation theory of retrieval in language production. *Psychological Review, 93,* 283–321.

Dell, G.S., Lawler, E.N., Harris, H.D., & Gordon, J.K. (2004). Models of errors of omission in aphasic naming. *Cognitive Neuropsychology, 21,* 125–146.

Dell, G.S., & O'Seaghdha, P.G. (1992). Stages in lexical access in language production. *Cognition, 42,* 287–314.

Dell, G.S., & Reich, P.A. (1981). Stages in sentence production: An analysis of speech error data. *Journal of Verbal Learning and Verbal Behavior, 20,* 611–629.

Dell, G.S., Schwartz M.F., Martin N., Saffran E.M., & Gagnon, D.A. (1997). Lexical access in aphasic and non-aphasic speakers. *Psychological Review, 104,* 801–838.

Dell, G.S., Schwartz, M.F., Martin, N., Saffran, E.M., & Gagnon, D.A. (2000). The role of computational models in neuropsychological investigations of language: Reply to Ruml and Caramazza. *Psychological Review, 107,* 635–645.

Denes, G., & Dalla Barba, G. (1998). G.B. Vico, precursor of cognitive neuro-psychology? The first reported case of noun–verb dissociation following brain damage. *Brain and Language, 62,* 29–33.

Doesborgh, S.J.C., van de Standt-Koenderman, M.W.M.E., Dippel, D.W.J., van Harskamp, F., Koudstaal, P.J., & Visch-Brink, E.G. (2004). Cues on request: The efficicacy of Multicue, a computer program for wordfinding therapy. *Aphasiology, 18*, 213–222.

Drew, R.L., & Thompson, C.K. (1999). Model-based semantic treatment for naming deficits in aphasia. *Journal of Speech, Language, and Hearing Research, 42*, 972–989.

Dronkers, N.F. (1996). A new brain region for coordinating speech articulation. *Nature, 384*, 159–161.

Druks, J. (2002). Verbs and nouns—a review of the literature. *Journal of Neurolinguistics, 15*, 289–315.

Druks, J., & Froud, K. (2002). The syntax of single words: Evidence from a patient with a selective function word reading deficit. *Cognitive Neuropsychology, 19*, 207–244.

Druks, J., & Masterson, J. (2000) *Object and action naming battery*. Hove, UK: Psychology Press.

Duffau, H., Capelle, L., Sichez, N., Denvil, D., Lopes, M., Sichez, J.P. et al. (2002). Intraoperative mapping of the subcortical language pathways using direct electrical stimulations: An anatomo-functional study. *Brain, 125*, 199–214.

Dunn, L.M., & Dunn, L.M. (1997). *Peabody picture vocabulary test* (3rd ed.). Circle Pines, MN: American Guidance Service.

Eikmeyer, H-J., Schade, U., Kupietz, M., & Laubenstein, U. (1999). A connectionist view of language production. In R. Klabunde & C. von Stutterheim (Eds.), *Representations and processes in language production* (pp. 205–236). Wiesbaden: Deutscher Universitäts-Verlag.

Ellis, A.E. (1987). Intimations of modularity or the modularity of mind: Doing cognitive neuropsychology without syndromes. In M. Coltheart, G. Sartori, & R. Job (Eds.), *The cognitive neuropsychology of language*. London: Lawrence Erlbaum Associates Ltd.

Ellis, A.E., Franklin, S., & Crerar, A. (1994). Cognitive neuropsychology and the remediation of disorders of spoken language. In M.J. Riddoch & G.W. Humphreys (Eds.), *Cognitive neuropsychology and cognitive rehabilitation* (pp. 287–315). Hove, UK: Lawrence Erlbaum Associates Ltd.

Ellis, A.W., & Young, A.W. (1988). *Human cognitive neuropsychology*. Hove, UK: Lawrence Erlbaum Associates Ltd.

Farah, M.J. (2004). *Visual agnosia. Second edition*. Cambridge, MA: MIT Press.

Farmer, A. (1990). Performance of normal males on the Boston Naming Test and the word test. *Aphasiology, 4*, 293–296.

Faust, M.E., Balota, D.A., & Multhaup, K.S. (2004). Phonological retrieval blocking in aging and Alzheimer's disease. *Neuropsychology, 18*, 526–536.

Felton, R.H., Naylor, C.E., & Wood, F.B. (1990). Neuropsychological profile of adult dyslexics. *Brain and Language, 39*, 485–497.

Ferro, J., Cantinho, M., Guilhermina, B., & Elia, J.N. (1991). Transient crossed aphasia: A case study with SPECT. *Behavioural Neurology, 4*, 75–79.

Fillenbaum, G.G., Huber, M., & Taussig, I.M. (1997). Performance of elderly White and African American community residents on the abbreviated CERAD Boston Naming Test. *Journal of Clinical and Experimental Neuropsychology, 19*, 204–210.

Fillingham, J., Hodgson, C., Sage, K., & Lambon Ralph, M.A. (2003). The application of errorless learning to aphasic disorders: A review of the theory and practice. *Neuropsychological Rehabilitation, 13*(3), 337–363.

Fink, R.B., Brecher, A.R., Montgomery, M., & Schwartz, M.F. (2001). *MossTalk Words* [computer software manual]. Philadelphia: Albert Einstein Healthcare Network.

Fink, R.B., Brecher, A., Schwartz, M.F., & Robey, R.R. (2002). A computer implemented protocol for treatment of naming disorders: Evaluation of clinician-guided and partially self-guided instruction. *Aphasiology, 16*, 1061–1086.

Flicker, C., Ferris, S., Crook, T., & Bartus, R. (1987). Implications of memory and language dysfunction in the naming deficit of senile dementia. *Brain and Language, 31*, 187–200.

Foundas, A., Daniels, S.K., & Vasterling, J.J. (1998). Anomia: Case studies with lesion localisation. *Neurocase, 4*, 35–43.

Foygel, D., & Dell, G.S. (2000). Models of impaired lexical access in speech production. *Journal of Memory and Language, 43*, 182–216.

Frackowiak, R.S.J., Friston, K.J., Frith, C.D., Dolan, R.J., Price, C.J., Zeki, S. et al. (2003). *Human brain function. Second edition.* San Diego, CA: Elsevier Academic Press.

Francis, D.R., Clark, N., & Humphreys, G.W. (2003). The treatment of an auditory working memory deficit and the implications for sentence comprehension abilities in mild "receptive" aphasia. *Aphasiology, 17*, 723–750.

Freed, D.B., Celery, K., & Marshall, R.C. (2004). A comparison of personalized and phonological cueing on the long-term naming accuracy by subjects with aphasia. *Aphasiology, 18*, 674–686.

Fridriksson, J., Holland, A.L., Beeson, P., & Morrow, L. (2005). Spaced retrieval treatment of anomia. *Aphasiology, 19*, 99–109.

Fromkin, V.A. (1971). The non-anomalous nature of anomalous utterances. *Language, 47*, 27–52.

Funnell, E. (2002). Semantic memory. In A.E. Hillis (Ed.), *The handbook of adult language disorders* (pp. 185–205). Hove, UK: Psychology Press.

Gainotti, G. (2000). What the locus of brain lesion tells us about the nature of the cognitive defect underlying category-specific disorders: A review. *Cortex, 36*, 539–559.

Galton, C.J., Patterson, K., Graham, K., Lambon Ralph, M.A., Williams, G., Antoun, N. et al. (2001). Differing patterns of temporal atrophy in Alzheimer's disease and semantic dementia. *Neurology, 57*, 216–225.

Garnham, A., Shillcock, R.C., Brown, G.D.A., Mill A.I.D., & Cutler, A. (1982). Slips of the tongue in the London–Lund corpus of spontaneous conversation. In A. Cutler (Ed.), *Slips of the tongue and language production* (pp. 251–263). Amsterdam: Mouton.

Garrard, P., Patterson, K., Watson, P.C., & Hodges, J.R. (1998). Category specific semantic loss in dementia of Alzheimer's type. Functional–anatomical correlations from cross-sectional analyses. *Brain, 121*, 633–646.

Garrett, M.F. (1975). The analysis of sentence production. In G.H. Bower (Ed.), *The psychology of learning and motivation. Vol. 9* (pp. 133–177). New York: Academic Press.

Garrett, M.F. (1976). Syntactic processes in sentence production. In R.J. Wales & E. Walker (Eds.), *New approaches to language mechanisms* (pp. 231–255). Amsterdam: North Holland.

Garrett, M.F. (1982). Production of speech: Observations from normal and pathological language use. In A. Ellis (Ed.), *Normality and pathology in cognitive functions* (pp. 19–76). London: Academic Press.

Gentileschi, V., Sperber, S., & Spinnler, H. (2001). Crossmodal agnosia for familiar people as a consequence of right infero-polar temporal atrophy. *Cognitive Neuropsychology, 18,* 439–463.

Georgieff, N., Dominey, P.F., Michel, F., Marie-Cardine, M., & Dalery, J. (1998). Anomia in major depressive state. *Psychiatry Research, 77,* 197–208.

Geschwind, N. (1965). Disconnexion syndromes in animals and man. *Brain, 88,* 237–294 and 585–644.

Goldman-Eisler, F. (1958). Speech production and the predictability of words in context. *Quarterly Journal of Experimental Psychology, 10,* 96–106.

Goldman-Eisler, F. (1968). *Psycholinguistics: Experiments in spontaneous speech.* London: Academic Press.

Goldstein, F.C., Green, J., Presley, R., & Green, R.C. (1992). Dysnomia in Alzheimer's disease: An evaluation of neurobehavioral subtypes. *Brain and Language, 43,* 308–322.

Goldstein, K. (1919). *Die Behandlung, Fürsorge und Begutachtung der Hirnverletzten.* Leipzig: Vogel.

Gonnerman, L.M., Andersen, E.S., Devlin, J.T., Kempler, D., & Seidenberg, M.S. (1997). Double dissociation of semantic categories in Alzheimer's disease. *Brain and Language, 57,* 254–279.

Goodglass, H. (1993). *Understanding aphasia.* New York: Academic Press.

Goodglass, H., & Kaplan, E. (1983). *The assessment of aphasia and related disorders. Second edition.* Philadelphia: Lea & Febiger.

Goodglass, H., Kaplan, E., & Barresi, B. (2001). *Boston diagnostic aphasia examination. Third edition.* Philadelphia: Lippincott Williams & Wilkins.

Goodglass, H., Klein, H., Carey, P., & Jones, K.J. (1966). Specific semantic word categories in aphasia. *Cortex, 2,* 74–89.

Gorno-Tempini, M.L., & Price, C.J. (2001). Identification of famous faces and buildings. A functional neuroimaging study of semantically unique items. *Brain, 124,* 2087–2097.

Gorno-Tempini, M-L., Wenman, R., Price, C., Rudge, P., & Cipolotti, L. (2001). Identification without naming: A functional neuroimaging study of an anomic patient. *Journal of Neurology Neurosurgery and Psychiatry, 70,* 397–400.

Gotts, S.J., & Plaut, D.C. (2002). The impact of synaptic depression following brain damage: A connectionist account of "access/refractory" and "degraded-store" semantic impairments. *Cognitive, Affective, & Behavioral Neuroscience, 2,* 187–213.

Goulet, P., Ska, B., & Kahn, H.J. (1994). Is there a decline in picture naming with increasing age? *Journal of Speech and Hearing Research, 37,* 629–644.

Grabowski, T.J., Damasio, H., Tranel, D., Cooper, G.E., Boles Ponto, L.L., Watkins, G.L. et al. (2003). Residual naming after damage to the left temporal pole: A PET activation study. *Neuroimage, 19,* 846–860.

Graham, K., Patterson, K., & Hodges, J.R. (1995). Progressive pure anomia: Insufficient activation of phonology by meaning. *Neurocase, 1,* 25–38.

Graham, K.S., Becker, J.T., & Hodges, J.R. (1997). On the relationship between knowledge and memory for pictures: Evidence from the study of patients with semantic dementia and Alzheimer's disease. *Journal of the International Neuropsychological Society, 3,* 534–544.

Graham, K.S., Patterson, K., Pratt, K., & Hodges, J.R. (2001). Can repeated exposure to "forgotten" vocabulary help alleviate word-finding difficulties in semantic dementia? An illustrative case study. *Neuropsychological Rehabilitation, 3,* 429–454.

Grandmaison, E., & Simard, M. (2003). A critical review of memory stimulation programs in Alzheimer's disease. *Journal of Neuropsychiatry and Clinical Neurosciences, 15,* 130–144.

Greenwald, M.L., Raymer, A.M., Richardson, M.E., & Rothi, L.J.G. (1995). Contrasting treatments for severe impairments of picture naming. *Neuropsychological Rehabilitation, 5,* 17–49.

Grober, E., Buschke, H., Kawas, C., & Fuld, P. (1985). Impaired ranking of semantic attributes in dementia. *Brain and Language, 26,* 276–286.

Gupta, P., & MacWhinney, B. (1997). Vocabulary acquisition and verbal short-term memory: Computational and neural bases. *Brain and Language, 59,* 267–333.

Hadar, U., Ticehurst, S., & Wade, J.P. (1991). Crossed anomic aphasia: Mild naming deficits following right brain damage in a dextral patient. *Cortex, 27,* 459–468.

Hanley, J.R., & Kay, J. (1998). Proper name anomia and anomia for the names of people: Functionally dissociable impairments? *Cortex, 34,* 155–158.

Harley, T.A. (1984). A critique of top-down independent levels models of speech production: Evidence from non-plan internal speech errors. *Cognitive Science, 8,* 191–219.

Harley, T.A. (1990). Environmental contamination of normal speech. *Applied Psycholinguistics, 11,* 45–72.

Harley, T.A. (1995). Connectionist models of anomia: A reply to Nickels. *Language and Cognitive Processes, 10,* 47–58.

Harley, T.A., & MacAndrew, S.B.G. (1992). Modelling paraphasias in normal and aphasic speech. *Proceedings of the 14th annual conference of the Cognitive Science Society* (pp. 378–383). Hillsdale, NJ: Lawrence Erlbaum Associates Inc.

Harrington, A. (1987) *Medicine, mind, and the double brain.* Princeton, NJ: Princeton University Press.

Harris, D.M., & Kay, J. (1995). I recognise your face, but I can't remember your name: Is it because names are unique?, *British Journal of Psychology 86,* 345–358.

Hart, J. Jr., Berndt, R.S., & Caramazza, A. (1985). Category-specific naming deficit following cerebral infarction. *Nature, 316,* 439–440.

Hartley, L.L., & Jensen, P.J. (1991). Narrative and procedural discourse after closed head injury. *Brain Injury, 5,* 267–285.

Haxby, J.V., Hoffman, E.A., & Gobbini, M.I. (2000). The distributed human neural system for face perception. *Trends in Cognitive Sciences, 4,* 223–233.

Henderson, L.W., Frank, E.M., Pigatt, T., Abramson, R.K., & Houston, M. (1998). Race, gender and educational level effects on Boston Naming Test scores. *Aphasiology, 12,* 901–911.

Hermann, B.P., Perrine, K., Chelune, G.J., Barr, W., Loring, D.W., Strauss, E. et al. (1999). Visual confrontation naming following left anterior temporal lobectomy: A comparison of surgical approaches. *Neuropsychology, 13,* 3–9.

Hickok, G., & Poeppel, D. (2004). Dorsal and ventral streams: A framework for understanding aspects of the functional anatomy of language. *Cognition, 92*, 67–99.

Hillis, A.E. (1991). Effects of separate treatments for distinct impairments within the naming process. In T. Prescott (Ed.), *Clinical aphasiology. Vol. 19* (pp. 255–265). Austin, TX: Pro-Ed.

Hillis, A.E. (1993). The role of models of language processing in rehabilitation of language impairments. *Aphasiology, 7*, 5–26.

Hillis, A.E. (1998). Treatment of naming disorders: New issues regarding old therapies. *Journal of International Neurolopsychological Society, 4*, 648–660.

Hillis, A.E., & Heidler, J. (2005). Contributions and limitations of the "Cognitive Neuropsychological Approach" to treatment: Illustrations from studies of reading and spelling therapy. *Aphasiology, 19*, 985–993.

Hillis, A.E., Kane, A., Tuffiash, E. Ulatowski, J.A., Barker, P.B., Beauchamp, N.J. et al. (2002a). Reperfusion of specific brain regions by raising blood pressure restores selective language functions in acute stroke. *Brain and Language, 79*, 495–510.

Hillis, A.E., Rapp, B.C., & Caramazza, A. (1999). When a rose is a rose in speech but a tulip in writing. *Cortex, 35*, 337–356.

Hillis, A.E., Rapp, B.C., Romani, C., & Caramazza, A. (1990). Selective impairment of semantics in lexical processing. *Cognitive Neuropsychology, 7*, 191–243.

Hillis, A.E., Wityk, R.J., Tuffiash, E., Beauchamp, N.J., Jacobs M.A., Barker, P.B. et al. (2001). Hypoperfusion in Wernicke's aphasia predicts severity of semantic deficit in acute stroke. *Annals of Neurology, 50*, 561–566.

Hillis, A.E., Wityk, R.J., Barker, P.B., Beauchamp, N.J., Gailloud, P., Murphy, K. et al. (2002b). Subcortical aphasia and neglect in acute stroke: The role of cortical hypoperfusion. *Brain, 125*, 1094–1104.

Hillis, A.E., Work, M., Barker, P.B., Jacobs, M.A., Breese, E.L., & Maurer, K. (2004). Re-examining the brain regions crucial for orchestrating speech articulation. *Brain, 127*, 1479–1487.

Hinton, G., & Shallice, T. (1991). Lesioning an attractor network: Investigations of acquired dyslexia. *Psychological Review, 98*, 74–95.

Hittmair-Delazer, M., Andree, B., Semenza, C., De Bleser, R., & Benke, T. (1994). Naming by German compounds. *Journal of Neurolinguistics, 8*, 27–41.

Hodges, J.R., Patterson, K., Oxbury, S. & Funnell, E. (1992a). Semantic dementia. Progressive fluent aphasia with temporal lobe atrophy. *Brain, 115*, 1783–1806.

Hodges, J.R., Patterson, K., Ward, R., Garrard, P., Bak, T., Perry, R. et al. (1999). The differentiation of semantic dementia and frontal lobe dementia (temporal and frontal variants of frontotemporal dementia) from early Alzheimer's disease. *Neuropsychology, 13*, 31–40.

Hodges, J.R., Salmon, D.P., & Butters, N. (1992b). Semantic memory impairment in Alzheimer's disease: Failure of access or degraded knowledge? *Neuropsychologia, 30*, 301–314.

Holland, A.L. (1991). Pragmatic aspects of intervention in aphasia. *Journal of Neurolinguistics, 6*, 197–211.

Holland, A.L., & Hinckley, J.J. (2002). Assessment and treatment of pragmatic aspects of communication in aphasia. In A.E. Hillis (Ed.), *The handbook of adult language disorders* (pp. 413–427). New York: Psychology Press.

Hopper, T. (2004, May). *Learning by individuals with dementia: The effects of spaced retrieval training.* Paper presented at the Clinical Aphasiology Conference, Park City, Utah.

Horton, S., & Byng, S. (2002). "Semantic therapy" in day-to-day clinical practice: Perspectives on diagnosis and therapy related to semantic impairments in aphasia. In A.E. Hillis (Ed.), *The handbook of adult language disorders* (pp. 229–249). New York: Psychology Press.

Howard, D., & Franklin, S. (1988). *Missing the meaning? A cognitive neuropsychological study of processing words by an aphasic patient.* Cambridge, MA: MIT Press.

Howard, D., & Hatfield, F.M. (1987). *Aphasia therapy: Historical and contemporary issues.* Hove, UK: Lawrence Erlbaum Associates Ltd.

Howard, D., & Orchard-Lisle, V.M. (1984). On the origin of semantic errors in naming: Evidence from the case of a global dysphasic. *Cognitive Neuropsychology, 1,* 163–190.

Howard, D., & Patterson, K.E. (1992). *The Pyramids and Palm Trees Test.* Bury St. Edmonds, UK: Thames Valley Test Company.

Howard, D., & Patterson, K. (1994). Models of therapy. In X. Seron & G. Deloche (Eds.), *Cognitive approaches in neuropsychological rehabilitation* (pp. 39–64). Hillsdale, NJ: Lawrence Erlbaum Associates Inc.

Howard, D., Patterson, K., Franklin, S., Orchard-Lisle, V., & Morton, J. (1985a). The facilitation of picture naming in aphasia. *Cognitive Neuropsychology, 2,* 49–80.

Howard, D., Patterson, K., Franklin, S., Orchard-Lisle, V., & Morton, J. (1985b). Treatment of word retrieval deficits in aphasia. *Brain, 108,* 817–829.

Huber, W., Springer, L., & Willmes, K. (1993). Approaches to aphasia therapy in Aachen. In A.L. Holland & M.M. Forbes (Eds.), *Aphasia treatment: World perspectives* (pp. 5–86). San Diego, CA: Singular Publishing.

Ilmberger, J., Rau, S., Noachtar, S., Arnold, S., & Winkler, P. (2002). Naming tools and animals: Asymmetries observed during direct electrical cortical stimulation. *Neuropsychologia, 40,* 695–700.

Indefrey, P., & Levelt, W.J.M. (2000). The neural correlates of language production. In M. Gazzaniga (Ed.), *The new cognitive neurosciences. Second edition* (pp. 845–865). Cambridge, MA: MIT Press.

Indefrey, P., & Levelt, W.J.M. (2004). The spatial and temporal signatures of word production components. *Cognition, 92,* 101–144.

Jacobs, D.H., Shuren J., Bowers, D., & Heilman, K.M. (1995). Anomia in a patient with a basal forebrain lesion. *Neuropsychiatry, Neuropsychology, and Behavioral Neurology, 8,* 200–207.

Jansma, B.M., Rodríguez-Fornells, A., Moeller, J., & Muente, T.F. (2004). Electrophysiological studies of speech production. In T. Pechmann & C. Habel (Eds.), *Multidisciplinary approaches to language production* (pp. 361–396). Berlin: Mouton de Gruyter.

Jefferies, E., & Lambon-Ralph, M. (2005). Non-verbal semantic impairment in stroke aphasia: A comparison with semantic dementia. *Brain and Language, 95,* 45–46.

Joanisse, M., & Seidenberg, M.S. (1999). Impairments in verb morphology following brain injury: A connectionist model. *Proceedings of the National Academy of Sciences (USA), 96,* 7592–7597.

Johnson-Frey, S.H. (2004). The neural bases of complex tool use in humans. *Trends in Cognitive Sciences, 8,* 71–78.

Jones, H.G.V., & Langford, S. (1987). Phonological blocking in the tip-of-the-tongue state. *Cognition, 26,* 115–122.

Kaplan, E., Goodglass, H., & Weintraub, S. (1983). *Boston naming test.* Philadelphia: Lea & Febiger.

Kapur, N., Friston, K.J., Young, A., Frith, C.D., & Frackowiak, R.S. (1995). Activation of human hippocampal formation during memory for faces: A PET study. *Cortex, 31,* 99–108.

Kay, J., & Ellis, A. (1987). A cognitive neuropsychological case study of anomia. Implications for psychological models of word retrieval. *Brain, 110,* 613–629.

Kay, J., & Hanley, J.R. (1999). Person-specific knowledge and knowledge of biological categories. *Cognitive Neuropsychology, 16,* 171–180.

Kay, J., Lesser, R., & Coltheart, M. (1992). *PALPA: Psycholinguistic assessments of language processing in aphasia.* Hove, UK: Lawrence Erlbaum Associates Ltd.

Kello, C.T., & Plaut, D.C. (2004). A neural network model of the articulatory-acoustic forward mapping trained on recordings of articulatory parameters. *Journal of the Acoustical Society of America, 116,* 2354–2364.

Kemmerer, D., & Tranel, D. (2000). Verb retrieval in brain-damaged subjects: 2. Analysis of errors. *Brain and Language, 73,* 393–420.

Kempen, G., & Huijbers, P. (1983). The lexicalization process in sentence production and naming: Indirect election of words. *Cognition, 14,* 185–209.

Kerr, C. (1995). Dysnomia following traumatic brain injury: An information-processing approach to assessment. *Brain Injury, 9,* 777–796.

Kertesz, A. (1982). *Western aphasia battery.* New York: Grune & Stratton.

Kertesz, A., Hudson, A.L., Mackenzie, I.R.A., & Munoz, D.G. (1994). The pathology and nosology of primary progressive aphasia. *Neurology, 44,* 2065–2072.

Kertesz, A., Sheppard, A., & MacKenzie, R. (1982). Localization in transcortical sensory aphasia. *Archives of Neurology, 39,* 475–478.

Kiran, S., & Thompson, C.K. (2003). The role of semantic complexity in treatment of naming deficits: Training semantic categories in fluent aphasia by controlling exemplar typicality. *Journal of Speech, Language and Hearing Research, 46,* 608–622.

Kirshner, H.S., Webb, W.G., & Kelly, M.P. (1984). The naming disorder of dementia. *Neuropsychologia, 22,* 23–30.

Knopman, D.S., Selbes, O.A., Niccum, N., & Rubens, A.B. (1984). Recovery of naming in aphasia: Relationship to fluency, comprehension and CT findings. *Neurology, 34,* 1461–1470.

Knott, R., Patterson, K., & Hodges, J.R. (1997). Lexical and semantic binding effects in short-term memory: Evidence from semantic dementia. *Cognitive Neuropsychology, 14,* 1165–1216.

Kohn, S.E. (1984). The nature of the phonological disorder in conduction aphasia. *Brain and Language, 23,* 97–115.

Kohnert, K., Hernandez, A., & Bates, E. (1998). Bilingual performance on the Boston Naming Test: Preliminary norms in Spanish and English. *Brain and Language, 65,* 422–440.

Kohonen, T. (2001). *Self-organizing maps.* Berlin: Springer-Verlag.

LaBarge, E., Edwards, D., & Knesevich, J.W.M. (1986). Performance of normal elderly on the Boston Naming Test. *Brain and Language, 27,* 380–384.

Laine, M., Kujala, P., Niemi, J., & Uusipaikka, E. (1992). On the nature of naming difficulties in aphasia. *Cortex*, *28*, 537–554.

Laine, M., & Martin, N. (1996). Lexical retrieval deficit in picture naming: Implications for word production models. *Brain and Language*, *53*, 283–314.

Laine, M., Niemi, J., Koivuselkä-Sallinen, P., & Hyönä, J. (1995). Morphological processing of polymorphemic nouns in a highly inflecting language. *Cognitive Neuropsychology*, *12*, 457–502.

Laine, M., Tikkala, A., & Juhola, M. (1998). Modelling anomia by the discrete two-stage word production architecture. *Journal of Neurolinguistics*, *10*, 139–158.

Laine, M., Vuorinen, E., & Rinne, J.O. (1997). Picture naming deficits in vascular dementia and Alzheimer's disease. *Journal of Clinical and Experimental Neuropsychology*, *19*, 126–140.

Lambon Ralph, M.A., Graham, K.S., Patterson, K., & Hodges, J.R. (1999). Is a picture worth a thousand words? Evidence from concept definitions by patients with semantic dementia. *Brain and Language*, *70*, 309–335.

Lambon Ralph, M.A., McClelland, J.L., Patterson, K., Galton, C.J., & Hodges, J.R. (2001). No right to speak? The relationship between object naming and semantic impairment: Neuropsychological evidence and a computational model. *Journal of Cognitive Neuroscience*, *13*, 341–356.

Lambon Ralph, M.A., Patterson, K., Garrard, P., & Hodges, J.R. (2003). Semantic dementia with category specificity: A comparative case-series study. *Cognitive Neuropsychology*, *20*, 307–326.

Lambon Ralph, M.A., Sage, K., & Roberts, J. (2000). Classical anomia: A neuro-psychological perspective on speech production. *Neuropsychologia*, *38*, 186–202.

Larner, A.J., Robinson, G., Kartsounis, L.D., Rakshi, J.S., Muqit, M.M.K., Wise, R.J.S. et al. (2004). Clinical–anatomical correlation in a selective phonemic speech production impairment. *Journal of the Neurological Sciences*, *219*, 23–29.

Larrabee, G., Holliman, J., Doreen, G., & Zachariah, S.J.N. (1991). Reversed laterality and crossed aphasia: A case study. *Neuropsychology*, *5*, 67–79.

Lecours, A.R., & Lhermitte, F. (1976). The "pure form" of the phonetic dis-integration syndrome (pure anarthria): Anatomico-clinical report of a historical case. *Brain and Language*, *3*, 88–113.

LeDorze, G., Boulay, N., Gaudreau, J., & Brassard, C. (1994). The contrasting effects of a semantic vs. a formal-semantic technique for the facilitation of naming in a case of anomia. *Aphasiology*, *8*, 127–141.

LeDorze, G., & Durocher, J. (1992). The effects of age, educational level, and stimulus length on naming in normal subjects. *Journal of Speech Language Pathology and Audiology*, *16*, 21–29.

Levelt, W.J.M. (1983). Monitoring and self-repair in speech. *Cognition*, *14*, 41–104.

Levelt, W.J.M. (1989). *Speaking: From intention to articulation*. Cambridge, MA: MIT Press.

Levelt, W.J.M. (1992). Accessing words in speech production: Stages, processes and representations. *Cognition*, *42*, 1–22.

Levelt, W.J.M., Praamstra, P., Meyer, A.S., Helenius, P., & Salmelin, R. (1998). An MEG study of picture naming. *Journal of Cognitive Neuroscience*, *10*, 553–567.

Levelt, W.J.M., Roelofs, A., & Meyer, A.S. (1999). A theory of lexical access in speech production. *Behavioral and Brain Sciences*, *22*, 1–38.

Levelt, W.J.M., Schriefers, H., Vorberg, D., Meyer, A.S., Pechmann, T., & Havinga, J. (1991). The time course of lexical access in speech production: A study of picture naming. *Psychological Review, 98*, 122–142.

Levelt, W.J.M., & Wheeldon, L.R. (1994). Do speakers have access to a mental syllabary? *Cognition, 50*, 239–269.

Levin, H.S., Grossman, R.G., Sarwar, M., & Meyers, C.A. (1981). Linguistic recovery after closed head injury. *Brain and Language, 12*, 360–374.

Lichtheim, O. (1885). On aphasia. *Brain, 7*, 443–484.

Lordat, J. (1843). Analyse de la parole pour servir à la théorie de divers cas d'alalie et de paralalie (de mutisme et d'imperfection de parler) que les neurologistes ont mal connus. *Journal de la Société Pratique de Montpellier, 7*, 333 & 417.

Lowell, S., Beeson, P.M., & Holland, A.L. (1995). The efficacy of a semantic cueing procedure on naming performance of adults with aphasia. *American Journal of Speech-Language Pathology, 4*, 109–114.

Lucchelli, F., & De Renzi, E. (1992). Proper name anomia. *Cortex, 28*, 221–230.

Lüders, H., Lesser, R.P., Hahn, J., Dinner, D.S., Morris, H., Resor, S. et al. (1986). Basal temporal language area demonstrated by electrical stimulation. *Neurology, 36*, 505–510.

Lüders, H., Lesser, R.P., Hahn, J., Dinner, D.S., Morris, H.H., Wyllie, E. et al. (1991). Basal temporal language area. *Brain, 114*, 743–754.

Luria, A.R. (1969). *Restoration of function after brain injury*. New York: Macmillan.

Luzzatti, C., Mondini, S., & Semenza, C. (2001). Lexical representation and processing of morphologically complex words: Evidence from the reading performance of an Italian agrammatic patient. *Brain and Language, 79*, 345–359.

Lyons, F., Hanley, J.R., & Kay, J. (2002). Anomia for common names with preserved retrieval of names of people. *Cortex, 38*, 23–35.

MacKay, A., Connor, L.T., & Storandt, M. (2005). Dementia does not explain correlation between age and scores on Boston Naming Test. *Archives of Clinical Neuropsychology, 20*, 129–133.

Maess, B., Friederici, A.D., Damian, M., Meyer, A.S., & Levelt, W.J.M. (2002). Semantic category interference in overt picture naming: Sharpening current density localization by PCA. *Journal of Cognitive Neuroscience, 14*, 455–462.

Maher, L., Singletary, F., Swearingen, M.C., Moore, A., Wierenga, C., Crosson, B. et al. (2002). An errorless learning approach to sentence generation in aphasia. *Proceedings. Rehabilitation research for the 21st century: The new challenges* (p. 138). Washington, DC: Department of Veterans Affairs.

Majerus, S., van der Kaa, M-A., Renard, C., Van der Linden, M., & Poncelet, M. (2005). Treating verbal short-term memory deficits by increasing duration of temporary phonological representations: A case study. *Brain and Language, 95*, 174–175.

Marshall, J., Pound, C., White-Thomson, M., & Pring, T. (1990). The use of picture/word matching tasks to assist word retrieval in aphasic patients. *Aphasiology, 4*, 167–184.

Marshall, R.C., Freed, D.B., & Karow, C.M. (2001). Learning the subordinate category names by aphasic subjects: A comparison of deep and surface-level training methods. *Aphasiology, 15*, 585–598.

Martin, A., & Chao, L.L. (2001). Semantic memory and the brain: Structure and processes. *Current Opinion in Neurobiology, 11*, 194–201.

Martin, A., & Fedio, P. (1983). Word production and comprehension in Alzheimer's disease: The breakdown in semantic knowledge. *Brain and Language, 19,* 124–141.

Martin, N. (2005). Verbal and nonverbal semantic impairment in aphasia: An activation deficit hypothesis. *Brain and Language, 95,* 251–252.

Martin, N., & Ayala, J. (2004). Measurements of auditory-verbal STM in aphasia: Effects of task, item and word processing impairment. *Brain and Language, 89,* 464–483.

Martin, N., & Dell, G.S. (2004). Perseverations and anticipations in aphasia: Primed intrusions from the past and future. *Seminars in Speech and Language Pathology, 25,* 349–362.

Martin, N., Dell, G.S., Saffran, E.M., & Schwartz, M.F. (1994). Origins of paraphasias in deep dysphasia: Testing the consequences of a decay impairment to an interactive spreading activation model of language. *Brain and Language, 47,* 609–660.

Martin, N., Fink, R., & Laine, M. (2004a). Treatment of word retrieval with contextual priming. *Aphasiology, 18,* 457–471.

Martin, N., Fink, R., Laine, M., & Ayala, J. (2004b). Immediate and short-term effects of contextual priming on word retrieval. *Aphasiology, 18,* 867–898.

Martin, N., & Gupta, P. (2004). Exploring the relationship between word processing and verbal STM: Evidence from associations and dissociations. *Cognitive Neuropsychology, 21,* 213–228.

Martin, N., Laine, M., & Harley, T.A. (2002). How can connectionist cognitive models of language inform models of language rehabilitation? In A.E. Hillis (Ed.), *The handbook of adult language disorders* (pp. 375–396). Hove, UK: Psychology Press.

Martin, N., & Saffran, E.M. (1992). A computational account of deep dysphasia: Evidence from a single case study. *Brain and Language, 43,* 240–274.

Martin, N., & Saffran, E.M. (1997). Language and auditory-verbal short-term memory impairments: Evidence for common underlying processes. *Cognitive Neuropsychology, 14,* 641–682.

Martin, N., & Saffran, E.M. (2002). The relationship of input and output phonology in single word processing: Evidence from aphasia. *Aphasiology, 16,* 107–150.

Martin, N., Saffran, E.M., & Dell, G.S. (1996). Recovery in deep dysphasia: Evidence for a relation between auditory-verbal STM capacity and lexical errors in repetition. *Brain and Language, 52,* 83–113.

Martin, N., Weisberg, R.W., & Saffran, E.M. (1989). Variables influencing the occurrence of naming errors: Implications for models of lexical retrieval. *Journal of Memory and Language, 28,* 462–485.

Martin, R.C., Lesch, M., & Bartha, M.C. (1999). Independence of input and output phonology in word processing and short-term memory. *Journal of Memory and Language, 40,* 1–27.

Mayer, J.F., & Murray, L.L. (2003). Functional measures of naming in aphasia: Word retrieval in confrontation naming versus connected speech. *Aphasiology, 17,* 481–497.

McCarthy, R., & Warrington, E.K. (1985). Category specificity in an agrammatic patient: The relative impairment of verb retrieval and comprehension. *Neuropsychologia, 23,* 709–727.

McCarthy, R.A., & Warrington, E.K. (1988). Evidence for modality-specific meaning systems in the brain. *Nature, 334*, 428–430.

McClelland, J.L., & Rumelhart, D.E. (1988). *Explorations in parallel distributed processing*. Cambridge, MA: MIT Press.

McKenna, P. (1998). *The category-specific names test*. Hove, UK: Psychology Press.

McKenna, P., & Parry, R. (1994). Category specificity in the naming of natural and man-made objects: Normative data from adults and children. *Neuropsychological Rehabilitation, 4*, 225–281.

McKenna, P., & Warrington, E.K. (1978). Category-specific naming preservation: A single case study. *Journal of Neurology, Neurosurgery, and Psychiatry, 41*, 571–574.

McKenna, P., & Warrington, E.K. (1980). Testing for nominal dysphasia. *Journal of Neurology, Neurosurgery, and Psychiatry, 43*, 781–788.

McKenna, P., & Warrington, E.K. (1983). *Graded naming test manual*. Windsor, UK: NFER-Nelson.

McLeod, P., Plaut, D., & Shallice, T. (2001). Connectionist modelling of word recognition. *Synthese, 129*, 173–183.

McNeil, M.R., Doyle, P.J., Fossett, T.R.D., Park, G.H., & Goda, A.J. (2001). Reliability and concurrent validity of the information unit scoring metric for the story retelling procedure. *Aphasiology, 15*, 991–1006.

McNeil, M.R., Robin, D.A., & Schmidt, R.A. (1997). Apraxia of speech: Definition, differentiation, and treatment. In M.R. McNeil (Ed.), *Clinical management of sensorimotor speech disorders* (pp. 31–344). New York: Thieme.

McNellis, M.G., & Blumstein, S. (2001). Self-organizing dynamics of lexical access in normals and aphasics. *Journal of Cognitive Neuroscience, 13*, 151–170.

Meyer, A.S., & Bock, K. (1992). The tip-of-the-tongue phenomenon: Blocking or partial activation? *Memory and Cognition, 20*, 715–726.

Miceli, G., Amitrano, A., Capasso, R., & Caramazza, A. (1996). The treatment of anomia resulting from output lexical damage: Analysis of two cases. *Brain and Language, 52*, 150–174.

Miceli, G., Capasso, R., Daniele, A., Esposito, T., Magarelli, M., & Tomaiuolo, F. (2000). Selective deficit for people's names following left temporal damage: An impairment of domain-specific conceptual knowledge. *Cognitive Neuropsychology, 17*, 489–516.

Miceli, G., & Caramazza, A. (1988). Dissociation of inflectional and derivational morphology. *Brain and Language, 35*, 24–65.

Miceli, G., Mazzucchi, A., Menn, L., & Goodglass, H. (1983). Contrasting cases of Italian agrammatic aphasia without comprehension disorder. *Brain and Language, 19*, 65–97.

Miceli, G., Silveri, M.C., Nocentini, U., & Caramazza, A. (1988). Patterns of dissociation in comprehension and production of nouns and verbs. *Aphasiology, 2*, 251–258.

Miceli, G., Silveri, M.C., Villa, G., & Caramazza, A. (1984). On the basis for the agrammatic's difficulty in producing main verbs. *Cortex, 20*, 207–220.

Miikkulainen, R. (1997). Dyslexic and category-specific aphasic impairments in a self-organizing feature map model of the lexicon. *Brain and Language, 59*, 334–366.

Milberg, W., Blumstein, S., & Dworetzky, B. (1988). Phonological processing and lexical accesss in aphasia. *Brain and Language, 34*, 279–293.

Milberg, W., Blumstein, S., Katz, D., Gershberg, F., & Brown, T. (1995). Semantic facilitation in aphasia: Effects of time and expectancy. *Journal of Cognitive Neuroscience, 7,* 33–50.

Miller, N., Willmes, K., & De Bleser, R. (2000). The psychometric properties of the English language version of the Aachen Aphasia Test (EAAT). *Aphasiology, 14,* 683–722.

Mills, C.K., & McConnell, J.W. (1895). The naming centre, with the report of a case indicating its location in the temporal lobe. *Journal of Nervous and Mental Disease, 22,* 1–7.

Miozzo, M. (2003). On the processing of regular and irregular forms of verbs and nouns: Evidence from neuropsychology. *Cognition, 87,* 101–127.

Miozzo, A., Soardi, M., & Cappa, S.F. (1994). Pure anomia with spared action naming due to a left temporal lesion. *Neuropsychologia, 32,* 1101–1109.

Monsell, S. (1987). On the relation between lexical input and output pathways for speech. In A. Allport, D. MacKay, W. Prinz, & E. Scheerer (Eds.), *Language perception and production: Relationships between listening, speaking, reading and writing* (pp. 273–312). London: Academic Press.

Morton, J. (1970). A functional model for human memory. In D.A. Norman (Ed.), *Models of human memory* (pp. 203–260). New York: Academic Press.

Morton, J., & Patterson, K. (1980). A new attempt at an interpretation or an old attempt at a new interpretation. In M. Coltheart, K. Patterson, & J.C. Marshall (Eds.), *Deep dyslexia* (pp. 91–118). London: Routledge & Kegan Paul.

Mummery, C.J., Patterson, K., Wise, R.J.S., Vandenbergh, R., Price, C.J., & Hodges, J.R. (1999). Disrupted temporal lobe connections in semantic dementia. *Brain, 122,* 61–73.

Murre, J.M.J., Graham, K.S., & Hodges, J.R. (2001). Semantic dementia: Relevance to connectionist models of long-term memory. *Brain, 124,* 647–675.

Murtha, S., Chertkow, H., Beauregard, M., & Evans, A. (1999). The neural substrate of picture naming. *Journal of Cognitive Neuroscience, 11,* 399–423.

Nadeau, S., & Crosson, B. (1997). Subcortical aphasia. *Brain and Language, 58,* 355–402.

Naeser, M.A., Palumbo, C.L., Helm-Estabrooks, N., Stiassny-Eder, D., & Albert, M.L. (1989). Severe nonfluency in aphasia. Role of the medial subcallosal fasciculus and other white matter pathways in recovery of spontaneous speech. *Brain, 112,* 1–38.

Neary, D. (1999). Overview of frontotemporal dementias and the consensus applied. *Dementia and Geriatric Cognitive Disorders, 10,* 6–9.

Nettleton, J., & Lesser, R. (1991). Therapy for naming difficulties in aphasia: Application of a cognitive neuropsychological model. *Journal of Neurolinguistics, 6,* 139–157.

Newcombe, F., Oldfield, R.C., Ratcliff, G.C., & Wingfield, A. (1971). Recognition and naming of object-drawings by men with focal brain wounds. *Journal of Neurology, Neurosurgery, and Psychiatry, 34,* 329–340.

Nicholas, L.E., Brookshire, R.H., MacLennan, D.L., Schumacher, J.G., & Porrazzo, S.A. (1989). The Boston Naming Test: Revised administration and scoring procedures and normative information for non-brain-damaged adults. In T.E. Prescott (Ed.), *Clinical aphasiology. Vol. 18* (pp. 103–115). Austin, TX: Pro-Ed.

Nicholas, M., Barth, C., Obler, L.K., Au, R., & Albert, M.L. (1997). Naming in normal aging and dementia of the Alzheimer's type. In H. Goodglass & A. Wingfield (Eds.), *Anomia. Neuroanatomical and cognitive correlates* (pp. 166–188). San Diego, CA: Academic Press.

Nickels, L. (1992). The autocue? Self-generated phonemic cues in the treatment of a disorder of reading and naming. *Cognitive Neuropsychology, 9,* 155–182.

Nickels, L. (1997). *Spoken word production and its breakdown in aphasia.* Hove, UK: Psychology Press.

Nickels, L., & Best, W. (1996a). Therapy for naming disorders (Part I): Principles, puzzles and progress. *Aphasiology, 10,* 21–47.

Nickels, L., & Best, W. (1996b). Therapy for naming disorders (Part II): Specifics, surprises, and suggestions. *Aphasiology, 10,* 109–136.

Nickels, L.A., & Howard, D. (1994). A frequent occurrence? Factors affecting the production of semantic errors in aphasic naming. *Cognitive Neuropsychology, 11,* 289–320.

Nickels, L.A., & Howard, D. (1995). Aphasic naming: What matters? *Neuropsychologia, 33,* 1281–1303.

Ober, B.A., Dronkers, N.F., Koss, E., Delis, D.C., & Friedland, R.P. (1986). Retrieval from semantic memory in Alzheimer-type dementia. *Journal of Clinical and Experimental Neuropsychology, 8,* 75–92.

Ochipa, C., Maher, L.M., & Raymer, A.M. (1998). One approach to the treatment of anomia. *ASHA Special Interest Division 2: Neurophysiology and Neurogenic Speech and Language Disorders, 15,* 18–23.

Ojemann, G.A. (1991). Cortical organization of language. *Journal of Neuroscience, 11,* 2281–2287.

Östberg, P. (2003). 18th century cases of noun–verb dissociation: The contribution of Carl Linnaeus. *Brain and Language, 84,* 448–450.

Pachalska, M. (1993). The concept of holistic rehabilitation of persons with aphasia. In A.L. Holland & M.M. Forbes (Eds.), *Aphasia treatment: World perspectives* (pp. 145–169). San Diego, CA: Singular Publishing.

Paivio, A. (1991). Dual coding theory: Retrospect and current status. *Canadian Journal of Psychology, 45,* 255–287.

Palumbo, C.L., Alexander, M.P., & Naeser, M.A. (1992). CT scan lesion cites associated with conduction aphasia. In S. Kohn (Ed.), *Conduction aphasia* (pp. 51–75). Hillsdale, NJ: Lawrence Erlbaum Associates Inc.

Paradis, M. (2001). Bilingual and polyglot aphasia. In R.S. Berndt (Ed.), *Handbook of neuropsychology. Second edition* (pp. 69–91). Oxford, UK: Elsevier Science.

Parnwell, E.C. (1977). *The Oxford English picture dictionary.* Coleford, UK: Forest Books.

Pascual-Leone, A., Gates, J.R., & Dhuna, A. (1991). Induction of speech arrest and counting errors with rapid-rate transcranial magnetic stimulation. *Neurology, 41,* 697–702.

Pashek, G.V., & Tompkins, C.A. (2002). Context and word class influences on lexical retrieval in aphasia. *Aphasiology, 16,* 261–286.

Pate, D.S., Saffran, E.M., & Martin, N. (1987). Specifying the nature of the production impairment in a conduction aphasic: A case study. *Language and Cognitive Processes, 2,* 43–84.

Patterson, K., Lambon Ralph, M.A., Hodges, J.R., & McClelland, J.L. (2001). Deficits in irregular past-tense verb morphology associated with degraded semantic knowledge. *Neuropsychologia, 39*, 709–724.

Perani, D., Cappa, S.F., Schnur, T., Tettamanti, M., Collina, S., Rosa, M.M. et al. (1999). The neural correlates of verb and noun processing: A PET study. *Brain, 122*, 2337–2344.

Perfect, T.J., & Hanley, J.R. (1992). The tip-of-the-tongue phenomenon: Do experimenter-presented interlopers have any effect? *Cognition, 45*, 55–75.

Peterson, S.E., & Savoy, P. (1998). Lexical selection and phonological encoding during language production: Evidence for cascaded processing. *Journal of Experimental Psychology: Learning, Memory and Cognition, 24*, 539–557.

Pinker, S. (1998). Words and rules. *Lingua, 106*, 219–242.

Plaut, D. (1996). Relearning after damage in connectionist networks: Toward a theory of rehabilitation. *Brain and Language, 52*, 25–82.

Plaut, D.C., & Booth, J.R. (2000). Individual and developmental differences in semantic priming: Empirical and computational support for a single-mechanism account of lexical processing. *Psychological Review, 107*, 786–823.

Plaut, D.C., & Kello, C.T. (1999). The emergence of phonology from the interplay of speech comprehension and production: A distributed connectionist approach. In B. MacWhinney (Ed.), *The emergence of language* (pp. 381–415). Mahwah, NJ: Lawrence Erlbaum Associates Inc.

Plaut, D.C., & Shallice, T. (1991). Effects of word abstractness in a connectionist model of deep dyslexia. *Proceedings of the 13th annual conference of the Cognitive Science Society* (pp. 73–78). Hillsdale, NJ: Lawrence Erlbaum Associates Inc.

Plaut, D., & Shallice, T. (1993a). Perseverative and semantic influences on visual object naming errors in optic aphasia: A connectionist account. *Journal of Cognitive Neuroscience, 5*, 89–117.

Plaut, D., & Shallice, T. (1993b). Deep dyslexia: A case study of connectionist neuropsychology. *Cognitive Neuropsychology, 10*, 377–500.

Powell, A.L., Cummings, J.L., Hill, M.A., & Benson, D.F. (1988). Speech and language alterations in multi-infarct dementia. *Neurology, 38*, 717–719.

Prins, R., & Bastiaanse, R. (2004) Analysing the spontaneous speech of aphasic speakers. *Aphasiology, 18*, 1075–1091. Psychonomic Society Archive of Norms, Stimuli, and Data (n.d.) Retrieved June 6, 2006 from http://www.psychonomic. org/archive.

Pulvermüller, F., Neininger, B., Elbert, T., Mohr, B., Rockstroh, B., Koebbel, P. et al. (2001). Constraint-induced therapy of chronic aphasia after stroke. *Stroke, 31*, 1621–1626.

Rapcsak, S.Z., Comer, J.F., & Rubens, A.B. (1993). Anomia for facial expressions: Neuropsychological mechanisms and anatomical correlates. *Brain and Language, 45*, 233–252.

Rapcsak, S.Z., Kaszniak, A.W., & Rubens, A.B. (1989). Anomia for facial expressions: Evidence for a category specific visual–verbal disconnection syndrome. *Neuropsychologia, 27*, 1031–1041.

Rapp, B.C., & Caramazza, A. (1993). On the distinction between deficits of access and deficits of storage: A question of theory. *Cognitive Neuropsychology, 10*, 113–141.

Rapp, B., & Caramazza, A. (1997). The modality specific organization of grammatical categories: Evidence from impaired spoken and written sentence production. *Brain and Language, 56,* 248–286.

Rapp, B., & Goldrick, M. (2000). Discreteness and interactivity in spoken word production. *Psychological Review, 107,* 406–499.

Raymer, A.M., Foundas, A.L., Maher, L.M., Greenwald, M.L., Morris, M., Rothi, L.J.G. et al. (1997a). Cognitive neuropsychological analysis and neuroanatomic correlates in a case of acute anomia. *Brain and Language, 58,* 137–156.

Raymer, A.M., Moberg, P.J., Crosson, B., Nadeau, S., & Gonzalez-Rothi, L.J. (1997b). Lexical-semantic deficits in two patients with dominant thalamic infarction. *Neuropsychologia, 35,* 211–219.

Raymer, A.M., Thompson, C.K., Jacobs, B., & Le Grand, H.R. (1993). Phonological treatment of naming deficits in aphasia: Model-based generalization analysis. *Aphasiology, 7,* 27–54.

Reilly, J., Martin, N., & Grossman, M. (2005). Verbal learning in semantic dementia: Is repetition priming a useful strategy? *Aphasiology, 19,* 329–339.

Renvall, K., Laine, M., Laakso, M., & Martin, N. (2003). Anomia treatment with contextual priming: A case study. *Aphasiology, 17,* 305–328.

Renvall, K., Laine, M., & Martin, N. (2005). Contextual priming in semantic anomia: A case study. *Brain and Language, 95,* 327–341.

Riddoch, M.J., & Humphreys, G.W. (1993). *The Birmingham object recognition battery.* Hove, UK: Lawrence Erlbaum Associates Ltd.

Riepe, M.W., Riss, S., Bittner, D., & Huber, R. (2004). Screening for cognitive impairment in patients with acute stroke. *Dementia and Geriatric Cognitive Disorders, 17,* 49–53.

Roach, A., Schwartz, M.F., Martin, N., Grewal, R.S., & Brecher, A. (1996). The Philadelphia Naming Test. *Clinical Aphasiology, 24,* 121–133.

Roberts, R.J., & Hamsher, K.D. (1984). Effects of minority status on facial recognition and naming performance. *Journal of Clinical Psychology, 40,* 539–545.

Robson, J., Marshall, J., Pring, T., & Chiat, S. (1998). Phonological naming therapy in jargonaphasia: Positive but paradoxical effects. *Journal of the International Neuropsychological Society, 4,* 675–686.

Rochford, G. (1971). A study of naming errors in dysphasia and in demented patients. *Neuropsychologia, 9,* 437–443.

Roelofs, A. (1992). A spreading activation theory of lemma retrieval in speaking. *Cognition, 42,* 107–142.

Romani, C., Olson, A., Semenza, C., & Granà, A. (2002). Patterns of phonological errors as a function of a phonological versus an articulatory locus of impairment. *Cortex, 38,* 541–567.

Ruml, W., & Caramazza, A. (2000). An evaluation of a computational model of lexical access: Comment on Dell et al. (1997). *Psychological Review, 107,* 609–634.

Saffran, E.M., Schwartz, M.F., Linebarger, M., Martin, N., & Bochetto, P. (1988). *Philadelphia comprehension battery* [unpublished test battery].

Saffran, E.M., Schwartz, M.F., & Marin, O.S.M. (1980). Evidence from aphasia: Isolating the components of a production model. In B. Butterworth (Ed.), *Language production: Vol. 1. Speech and talk* (pp. 221–241). London: Academic Press.

Salmelin, R., Hari, R., Lounasmaa, O., & Sams, M. (1994). Dynamics of brain activation during picture naming. *Nature, 368*, 463–465.

Salmon, D.P., Shimamura, A.P., Butters, N., & Smith, S. (1988). Lexical and semantic priming deficits in patients with Alzheimer's disease. *Journal of Clinical and Experimental Neuropsychology, 10*, 477–494.

Sasanuma, S. (1993). Aphasia treatment in Japan. In A.L. Holland & M.M. Forbes (Eds.), *Aphasia treatment: World perspectives* (pp. 175–198). San Diego, CA: Singular Publishing.

Schiff, H.B., Alexander, M.P., Naeser, M.A., & Galaburda, A.M. (1983). Aphemia: Clinical–anatomical correlations. *Archives of Neurology, 40*, 720–727.

Schirmer, A. (2004). Timing speech: A review of lesion and neuroimaging findings. *Cognitive Brain Research, 21*, 269–287.

Schriefers, H., Meyer, A.S., & Levelt, W.J.M. (1990). Exploring the time course of lexical access in production: Picture–word interference studies. *Journal of Memory and Language, 29*, 86–102.

Schuell, H. (1974). *Aphasia theory and therapy: Selected lectures and papers of Hildred Schuell*. Baltimore, MD: University Park Press.

Schwartz, M.F. (1987). Patterns of speech production deficit within and across aphasia syndromes: Application of a psycholinguistic model. In M. Coltheart, G. Sartori, & R. Job (Eds.), *The cognitive neuropsychology of language* (pp. 163–199). Hove, UK: Lawrence Erlbaum Associates Ltd.

Schwartz, M.F., & Brecher, A. (2000). A model-driven analysis of severity, response characteristics, and partial recovery in aphasic's picture naming. *Brain and Language, 73*, 62–91.

Schwartz, M.F., Dell, G.S., & Martin, N. (2004). Testing the interactive two-step model of lexical access: Part I. Picture naming. *Brain and Language, 91*, 71–72. [Abstract].

Schwartz, M.F., & Hodgson, C. (2002). A new multiword naming deficit: Evidence and interpretation. *Cognitive Neuropsychology, 19*, 263–288.

Schwartz, M.F., Marin, O.S.M., & Saffran, E. (1979). Dissociations of language function in dementia: A case study. *Brain and Language, 7*, 277–306.

Schwartz, M.F., Montgomery, M.W., Fitzpatrick-DeSalme, E.J., Ochipa, C., Coslett, H.B., & Mayer, N.H. (1995). Analysis of a disorder of everyday action. *Cognitive Neuropsychology, 12*, 863–892.

Schwartz, M.F., Saffran, E.M., Bloch, D.E., & Dell, G.S. (1994). Disordered speech production in aphasic and normal speakers. *Brain and Language, 47*, 52–88.

Semenza, C., Butterworth, B., Panzeri, M., & Ferreri, T. (1990). Word-formation: New evidence from aphasia. *Neuropsychologia, 28*, 499–502.

Semenza, C., Mondini, S., & Zettin, M. (1995). The anatomical basis of proper name processing. A critical review. *Neurocase, 1*, 183–188.

Semenza, C., & Zettin, M. (1988). Generating proper names: A case of selective inability. *Cognitive Neuropsychology, 5*, 711–721.

Sergent, J., Ohta, S., & MacDonald, B. (1992). Functional neuroanatomy of face and object processing. A positron emission tomography study. *Brain, 115*, 15–36.

Shapiro, K., & Caramazza, A. (2001a). Sometimes a noun is just a noun: Comments on Bird, Howard, and Franklin (2000). *Brain and Language, 76*, 202–212.

Shapiro, K., & Caramazza, A. (2001b). Language is more than its parts: A reply to Bird, Howard, and Franklin (2001). *Brain and Language, 78*, 397–401.

Shattuck-Hufnagel, S. (1979). Speech errors as evidence for a serial ordering mechanism in speech production. In W.E. Cooper & E.C.T. Walker (Eds.), *Sentence processing: Psycholinguistic studies presented to Merrill Garrett* (pp. 295–342). Hillsdale, NJ: Lawrence Erlbaum Associates Inc.

Silveri, M.C., & Di Betta, A.M. (1997). Noun–verb dissociation in brain-damaged patients: Further evidence. *Neurocase, 3*, 477–488.

Silveri, M-C., Gainotti, G., Perani, D., Cappelletti, J-Y., Carbone, G., & Fazie, F. (1997). Naming deficit for non-living items: Neuropsychological and PET study. *Neuropsychologia, 35*, 359–367.

Silveri, M-C., Perri, R., & Cappa, A. (2003). Grammatical class effects in brain-damaged patients: Functional locus of noun and verb deficit. *Brain and Language, 85*, 49–66.

Simons, J.S., & Graham, K.S. (2000). New learning in semantic dementia: Implications for cognitive and neuroanatomical models of long-term memory. *Revue de Neuropsychologie, 10*, 199–215.

Simons, J.S., Koutstaal, W., Prince, S., Wagner, A.D., & Schacter, D.L. (2003). Neural mechanisms of visual object priming: Evidence for perceptual and semantic distinctions in fusiform cortex. *NeuroImage, 19*, 613–626.

Small, S. (2004). A biological model of aphasia rehabilitation: A pharmacological perspective. *Aphasiology, 18*, 473–492.

Snodgrass, J.G., & Vanderwart, M. (1980). Standardized set of 260 pictures: Norms for name agreement, image agreement, familiarity and visual complexity. *Journal of Experimental Psychology, Human Learning and Memory, 6*, 174–215.

Snowden, J.S., Goulding, P.J., & Neary, D. (1989). Semantic dementia: A form of circumscribed cerebral atrophy. *Behavioural Neurology, 2*, 167–182.

Snowling, M.J. (2000). *Dyslexia. Second edition*. Oxford, UK: Blackwell.

Sommers, L.M., & Pierce, R.S. (1990). Naming and semantic judgements in dementia of Alzheimer's type. *Aphasiology, 4*, 573–586.

Sörös, P., Cornelissen, K., Laine, M., & Salmelin, R. (2003). Naming actions and objects: Cortical dynamics in healthy adults and in an anomic patient with a dissociation in action/object naming. *Neuroimage, 19*, 1787–1801.

Stemberger, J.P. (1985). An interactive model of language production. In A.W. Ellis (Ed.), *Progress in the psychology of language, vol. 1* (pp. 143–186). Hillsdale, NJ: Lawrence Erlbaum Associates Inc.

Stewart, L., Meyer, B-U., Frith, U., & Rothwell, U. (2001). Left posterior BA37 is involved in object recognition: A TMS study. *Neuropsychologia, 39*, 1–6.

Swinburn, K., Porter, G., & Howard, D. (2004). *The comprehensive aphasia test*. Hove, UK: Psychology Press.

Taub, E. (2002). CI therapy: A new rehabilitation technique for aphasia and motor disability after neurological injury. *Klinik & Forschung, 8*, 48–49.

Taub, E., Uswatte, G., & Pidikiti, R. (1999). Constraint-Induced Movement Therapy: A new family of techniques with broad application to physical rehabilitation—a clinical review. *Journal of Rehabilitation Research and Development, 36*, 237–251.

The Lund and Manchester Groups. (1994). Clinical and neuropathological criteria for frontotemporal dementia. *Journal of Neurology, Neurosurgery, and Psychiatry, 57*, 416–418.

Thompson-Schill, S.L. (2003). Neuroimaging studies of semantic memory: Inferring "how" from "where". *Neuropsychologia, 41*, 280–292.

Touradj, P., Manly, J.J., Jacobs, D.M., & Stern, Y. (2001). Neuropsychological test performance: A study of non-Hispanic White elderly. *Journal of Clinical and Experimental Neuropsychology, 23*, 643–649.

Tsukiura, T., Fujii, T., Fukatsu, R., Otsuki, T., Okuda, J., Umetsu, A. et al. (2002). Neural basis of the retrieval of people's names: Evidence from brain-damaged patients and fMRI. *Journal of Cognitive Neuroscience, 14*, 922–937.

Tyler, L.K., Bright, P., Fletcher, P., & Stamatakis, E.A. (2004). Neural processing of nouns and verbs: The role of inflectional morphology. *Neuropsychologia, 42*, 512–523.

Tyler, L.K., & Moss, H.E. (2001). Towards a distributed account of conceptual knowledge. *Trends in Cognitive Sciences, 5*, 244–252.

Tyler, L.K., Moss, H.E., Durrant-Peatfield, M.R., & Levy, J.P. (2000). Conceptual structure and the structure of concepts: A distributed account of category-specific deficits. *Brain and Language, 75*, 195–231.

Tyler, L.K., Russell, R., Fadili, J., & Moss, H.E. (2001). The neural representation of nouns and verbs. *Brain, 124*, 1619–1634.

Ullman, M.T., Corkin, S., Coppola, M., Hickok, G., Growdon, J.H., Koroshetz, W.J. et al. (1997). A neural dissociation within language: Evidence that the mental dictionary is part of declarative memory, and that grammatical rules are processed by the procedural system, *Journal of Cognitive Neuroscience, 9*, 266–276.

Ungerleider, L.G., & Haxby, J. (1994). "What" and "where" in the human brain. *Current Opinion in Neurobiology, 4*, 157–165.

Vallar, G., & Baddeley, A.D. (1984). Fractionation of working memory: Neuro-psychological evidence for a phonological short-term store. *Journal of Verbal Learning and Verbal Behavior, 23*, 151–161.

Van Mourick, M., & Van de Standt-Koenderman, W.M.E. (1992). Multicue. *Aphasiology, 6*, 179–183.

Valentine, T., Brennen, T. & Brédart, S., (1996). *The cognitive psychology of proper names*. London: Routledge.

Verstichtel, P., Cohen, L., & Crochet, G. (1996). Associated production and comprehension deficits for people's names following left temporal lesion. *Neurocase, 2*, 221–234.

Vousden, J.I., Brown, G.D.A., & Harley, T.A. (2000). Serial control of phonology in speech production: A hierarchical model. *Cognitive Psychology, 41*, 101–175.

Warburton, E., Wise, R.J., Price, C.J., Weiller, C., Hadar, U., Ramsay, S. et al. (1996). Noun and verb retrieval in normal subjects. Studies with PET. *Brain, 119*, 159–179.

Warrington, E.K. (1975). The selective impairment of semantic memory. *Quarterly Journal of Experimental Psychology, 27*, 635–657.

Warrington, E.K. (1981). Neuropsychological studies of verbal semantic systems. *Philosophical Transactions of the Royal Society of London, B295*, 411–423.

Warrington, E.K. (2002). The Graded Naming Test: A restandardisation. *Neuropsychological Rehabilitation, 7*, 143–146.

Warrington, E.K., & Cipolotti, L. (1996). Word comprehension. The distinction between refractory and storage impairments. *Brain, 119*, 611–625.

Warrington, E.K., & Shallice, T. (1979). Semantic access dyslexia. *Brain, 102*, 43–63.

Warrington, E.K., & Shallice, T. (1984). Category specific semantic impairments. *Brain, 107*, 829–854.

Weigl, E. (1961). The phenomenon of temporary de-blocking in aphasia. *Zeitschrift für Phonetik, Sprachwissenschaft und Kommunikationforschung, 14*, 337–364.

Welch, L.W., Doineau, D., Johnson, S., & King, D. (1996). Educational and gender normative data for the Boston Naming Test in a group of older adults. *Brain and Language, 53*, 260–266.

Wepman, J. (1953). A conceptual model for the processes involved in recovery from aphasia. *Journal of Speech and Hearing Disorders, 18*, 4–13.

Wernicke, C. (1874). *Der Aphasische Symptomenkomplex. Eine Psychologische Studie auf Anatomischer Basis*. Breslau: Cohn & Welgert.

Whatmough, C., Chertkow, H., Murtha, S., & Hanratty, K. (2002). Dissociable brain regions process object meaning and object structure during picture naming. *Neuropsychologia, 40*, 174–186.

Whiteside, S.P., & Varley, R.A. (1998). A reconceptualisation of apraxia of speech: A synthesis of evidence. *Cortex, 34*, 221–231.

Williams, S.E., & Canter, G.J. (1987). Action-naming performance in four syndromes of aphasia. *Brain and Language, 32*, 124–136.

Wilson, B.A., Baddeley, A.D., Evans, J., & Shiel, A. (1994). Errorless learning in the rehabilitation of memory impaired people. *Neuropsychological Rehabilitation, 4*, 307–326.

Woodworth, R.S. (1938). *Experimental psychology*. New York: Holt.

Worrall, L. (1995). The functional communication perspective. In C. Code & D. Müller (Eds.), *Treatment of aphasia: From theory to practice* (pp. 47–69). London: Whurr Publishers.

Worrall, L.E., Yiu, E.M.L., Hickson, L.M.H., & Barnett, H.M. (1995). Normative data for the Boston Naming Test in a group of older adults. *Aphasiology, 9*, 541–551.

Ylikoski, R., Ylikoski, A., Raininko, R., Keskivaara, P., Sulkava, R., Tilvis, R. et al. (2000). Cardiovascular diseases, health status, brain imaging findings and neuropsychological functioning in neurologically healthy elderly individuals. *Archives of Gerontology and Geriatrics, 30*, 115–130.

Zaidel, E. (1998). Language in the right hemisphere following callosal disconnection. In B. Stemmer & H. Whitaker (Eds.), *Handbook of neurolinguistics* (pp. 369–383). San Diego, CA: Academic Press.

Zingeser, L.B., & Berndt, R.S. (1990). Retrieval of nouns and verbs in agrammatism and anomia. *Brain and Language, 39*, 14–32.

# Author index

# Subject index